Functional C#

Uncover the secrets of functional programming using C# and change the way you approach your applications forever

Wisnu Anggoro

BIRMINGHAM - MUMBAI

Functional C#

First published: January 2017

Production reference: 1281216

Published by Packt Publishing Ltd.

Livery Place

35 Livery Street

Birmingham

B3 2PB, UK.

ISBN 978-1-78528-222-5

www.packtpub.com

Credits

Author

Wisnu Anggoro

Reviewer

Haridas Nair

Commissioning Editor

Kunal Parikh

Acquisition Editor

Denim Pinto

Content Development Editor

Priyanka Mehta

Technical Editors

Bhavin Savalia

Dhiraj Chandanshive

Copy Editor

Stuti Srivastava

Project Coordinator

Izzat Contractor

Proofreader

Safis Editing

Indexer

Rekha Nair

Production Coordinator

Shraddha Falebhai

About the Author

Wisnu Anggoro is a Microsoft Certified Professional in C# programming and an experienced C/C++ developer. He has also authored *Boost.Asio C++ Network Programming - Second Edition*, published by Packt. He has been programming since he was in junior high school (about 20 years ago) and started developing computer applications using the BASIC programming language in the MS-DOS environment. He has a solid experience of smart card programming as well as desktop and web application programming, such as designing, developing, and supporting live use applications for SIM Card Operating System Porting, personalization, PC/SC communication, and other smart card applications that require the use of C# and C/C++. He is currently a senior smart card software engineer at CIPTA, an Indonesian company that specializes in the innovation and technology of smart cards. You can write to him at `wisnu@anggoro.net`.

Acknowledgments

First and above all, I praise God, the almighty, for providing me with this opportunity and granting me the capability to proceed successfully. To my wife, dear Vivin, without whose support and encouragements I could not have finished this book. Thank you for reminding me of the deadline of each chapter, so I could always stay on the writing process schedule. To my beloved sons, the source of my joy: Olav, who makes my life worth living by giving me much happiness, and Oliver, who was born just after I submitted the draft of chapter 5. His first cry boosted my spirit to finish this book. And a thank you to my parents and family for their inspiration.

Also, I would like to express my gratitude to the following individuals who supported me in writing this book:

The team at Packt, especially Denim Pinto, my acquisition editor, who invited me to author this book; Priyanka Mehta, my content development editor, for her constant effort in encouraging me to supply the best content for this book; and to all reviewers who have given input and suggestions to make the content of this book much better.

My best mentor, teacher, and superior at CIPTA (`www.cipta.com`), Benediktus Dwi Desiyanto, who never let me stop learning new things and always encourages me to catch my dream. Hope this book can be the way to make all my dreams come true.

Chief Executive Officer of CIPTA, Steven Chandra, for providing me with a new Amazon Kindle. Since then, the number of books I have read has increased. The insight from the books I have read was helpful while I wrote this book.

Chief Human Capital Officer of CIPTA, Budi Setiawan, for appreciating my work in authoring my previous book and inviting me to join the C-MAG (CIPTA Magazine) press team. It helped me a lot in enhancing my writing skills.

All my friends and colleagues at CIPTA, especially Muhammad Abdurochman Sanjaya and Seno Budi Utomo, for the insight of C# programming in developing a smart card application. It helped me develop the application I presented in this book. And Andre Tampubolon, for the insight of functional programming in Haskell.

Dave Fancher, the author of *The Book of F#*, thank you for your amazing site, `https://davefancher.com/`, my one-stop place to learn functional programming. His website inspired my authoring of this book.

About the Reviewer

Haridas Nair works as a software architect within the Architecture Practice, providing both technical and solution architecture. He is responsibile for defining, documenting, and articulating functional and nonfunctional scope.

He manages various project teams varying in size and location in USA, UK, and offshore (India). The day-to-day duties range from assisting in technical presales activities, responding to RFPs, through to high-level and detailed design phases to actual implementation on enterprise-scale projects.

I would like to thank Praseed Pai for introducing me to this publisher. I would also like to thank the publisher for giving me this opportunity.

www.PacktPub.com

For support files and downloads related to your book, please visit www.PacktPub.com.

Did you know that Packt offers eBook versions of every book published, with PDF and ePub files available? You can upgrade to the eBook version at www.PacktPub.com and as a print book customer, you are entitled to a discount on the eBook copy. Get in touch with us at service@packtpub.com for more details.

At www.PacktPub.com, you can also read a collection of free technical articles, sign up for a range of free newsletters and receive exclusive discounts and offers on Packt books and eBooks.

https://www.packtpub.com/mapt

Get the most in-demand software skills with Mapt. Mapt gives you full access to all Packt books and video courses, as well as industry-leading tools to help you plan your personal development and advance your career.

Why subscribe?

- Fully searchable across every book published by Packt
- Copy and paste, print, and bookmark content
- On demand and accessible via a web browser

Customer Feedback

Thank you for purchasing this Packt book. We take our commitment to improving our content and products to meet your needs seriously--that's why your feedback is so valuable. Whatever your feelings about your purchase, please consider leaving a review on this book's Amazon page. Not only will this help us, more importantly it will also help others in the community to make an informed decision about the resources that they invest in to learn. You can also review for us on a regular basis by joining our reviewers' club. **If you're interested in joining, or would like to learn more about the benefits we offer, please contact us**: customerreviews@packtpub.com.

Table of Contents

Preface

Some of us may be used to developing an application using the object orientation programming technique and don't care about the functional programming technique. However, there are benefits to using functional programming. One of the benefits is that we will get a new perspective on our programming code since the function in functional programming is identical to a mathematical function. Because it's identical to a mathematical function, the function in functional programming contains no side-effects, which means that the function invocation will have no effect on other functions in the class. We will discuss more details about the benefits and other things related to functional programming in this book.

What this book covers

Chapter 1, *Tasting Functional Style in C#*, introduces the functional programming approach by discussing its concepts and the comparison between functional and imperative programming. We also try to refactor a simple imperative code into a functional approach.

Chapter 2, *Walkthrough Delegates*, covers the definition, syntax, and use of delegates. We also discuss the variance of delegates and the built-in delegate.

Chapter 3, *Expressing Anonymous Methods with Lambda Expressions*, walks us through the concept of delegates and uses it to create and use an anonymous method. After we dig through the anonymous method, we can transform it into a lambda expression and then apply it to functional programming.

Chapter 4, *Extending Object Functionality with Extension Methods*, elaborates the benefits of using the extension method in functional programming. Before that, we discuss the use of the extension method and also discuss how to get this new method in IntelliSense. Also, we try to invoke the extension method from other assemblies.

Chapter 5, *Querying Any Collection Easily with LINQ*, enumerates the LINQ operator provided by C# and compares the two LINQ syntaxes: Fluent Syntax and Query Expression Syntax. We also discuss deferred execution in the LINQ process.

Chapter 6, *Enhancing the Responsiveness of the Functional Program with Asynchronous Programming*, covers asynchronous programming for the functional approach. It will explain the Asynchronous Programming Model and the Task-based Asynchronous pattern.

Chapter 7, *Learning Recursion*, explains the advantages of recursion over the loop sequence. We also discuss direct and indirect recursion in this chapter.

Chapter 8, *Optimizing the Code Using Laziness and Caching Techniques*, covers the technique used to optimize the code in the functional approach. We talk about laziness thinking and the caching technique in order to optimize our code.

Chapter 9, *Working with Pattern*, covers the advantages of using patterns compared to conventional switch-case operations. We discuss pattern matching and monad in this chapter. We use the pattern matching feature, which is the new feature provided by C# 7.

Chapter 10, *Taking an Action in C# Functional Programming*, walks us through developing functional code based on given imperative code. We use our learning in the previous chapter to create an application using the functional approach.

Chapter 11, *Coding Best Practice and Testing the Functional Code*, explains the best practice in the functional approach, including the creation of an honest signature and dealing with the side-effects. We also separate the code into domain logic and mutable shell and then test it using unit testing.

What you need for this book

To walk through this book and successfully compile all the source code, we require a personal computer that runs Microsoft Windows 10 (or higher) with Visual Studio Community 2015 Update 3 installed for the running of code in chapters 1-8, 10, 11 and Visual Studio Community 2017 RC (Release Candidate) installed for the running of code in chapter 9. We also need the .NET Framework 4.6.2 unless you need to recode all the source code to run in your current version of .NET Framework. You also need .NET Core 1.0 if you want to compile all code in another platform since all code are compatible with .NET Core 1.0.

Who this book is for

This book is suitable for C# developers with basic prior knowledge of C# and with no functional programming experience at all.

Conventions

In this book, you will find a number of text styles that distinguish between different kinds of information. Here are some examples of these styles and an explanation of their meaning.

Code words in text, database table names, folder names, filenames, file extensions, pathnames, dummy URLs, user input, and Twitter handles are shown as follows: "We can include other contexts through the use of the `include` directive."

A block of code is set as follows:

```
namespace ActionFuncDelegates
{
  public partial class Program
  {
    static void Main(string[] args)
    {
      //ActionDelegateInvoke();
      FuncDelegateInvoke();
    }
  }
}
```

When we wish to draw your attention to a particular part of a code block, the relevant lines or items are set in bold:

```
Console.WriteLine("Prime Number from 0 - 49 are:");
foreach (int i in extractedData)
  Console.Write("{0} \t", i);
Console.WriteLine();
```

Any command-line input or output is written as follows:

```
C:\>dir | more
```

New terms and **important words** are shown in bold. Words that you see on the screen, for example, in menus or dialog boxes, appear in the text like this: "We have a **Body** property containing **{(a * b)}**, **NodeType** containing **Lambda**, **Type** containing the **Func** delegate with three templates."

Warnings or important notes appear in a box like this.

Tips and tricks appear like this.

Reader feedback

Feedback from our readers is always welcome. Let us know what you think about this book-what you liked or disliked. Reader feedback is important for us as it helps us develop titles that you will really get the most out of.

To send us general feedback, simply e-mail `feedback@packtpub.com`, and mention the book's title in the subject of your message.

If there is a topic that you have expertise in and you are interested in either writing or contributing to a book, see our author guide at `www.packtpub.com/authors`.

Customer support

Now that you are the proud owner of a Packt book, we have a number of things to help you to get the most from your purchase.

Downloading the example code

You can download the example code files for this book from your account at `http://www.packtpub.com`. If you purchased this book elsewhere, you can visit `http://www.packtpub.com/support` and register to have the files e-mailed directly to you.

You can download the code files by following these steps:

1. Log in or register to our website using your e-mail address and password.
2. Hover the mouse pointer on the **SUPPORT** tab at the top.
3. Click on **Code Downloads & Errata**.
4. Enter the name of the book in the **Search** box.
5. Select the book for which you're looking to download the code files.
6. Choose from the drop-down menu where you purchased this book from.
7. Click on **Code Download**.

Once the file is downloaded, please make sure that you unzip or extract the folder using the latest version of:

- WinRAR / 7-Zip for Windows
- Zipeg / iZip / UnRarX for Mac
- 7-Zip / PeaZip for Linux

The code bundle for the book is also hosted on GitHub at `https://github.com/PacktPubl ishing/Functional-CSharp`. We also have other code bundles from our rich catalog of books and videos available at `https://github.com/PacktPublishing/`. Check them out!

Errata

Although we have taken every care to ensure the accuracy of our content, mistakes do happen. If you find a mistake in one of our books-maybe a mistake in the text or the code-we would be grateful if you could report this to us. By doing so, you can save other readers from frustration and help us improve subsequent versions of this book. If you find any errata, please report them by visiting `http://www.packtpub.com/submit-errata`, selecting your book, clicking on the **Errata Submission Form** link, and entering the details of your errata. Once your errata are verified, your submission will be accepted and the errata will be uploaded to our website or added to any list of existing errata under the Errata section of that title.

To view the previously submitted errata, go to `https://www.packtpub.com/books/conten t/support`and enter the name of the book in the search field. The required information will appear under the **Errata** section.

Piracy

Piracy of copyrighted material on the Internet is an ongoing problem across all media. At Packt, we take the protection of our copyright and licenses very seriously. If you come across any illegal copies of our works in any form on the Internet, please provide us with the location address or website name immediately so that we can pursue a remedy.

Please contact us at `copyright@packtpub.com` with a link to the suspected pirated material.

We appreciate your help in protecting our authors and our ability to bring you valuable content.

Questions

If you have a problem with any aspect of this book, you can contact us at `questions@packtpub.com`, and we will do our best to address the problem.

1
Tasting Functional Style in C#

Functional programming is a style of constructing the elements and structure of computer program which treats computations like evaluations in mathematical functions. Although there are some specifically designed languages for creating functional programming, such as Haskell or Scala, we can also use C# to accomplish designing functional programming.

In the first chapter of this book, we are going to explore the functional programming by testing it. We will use the power of C# to construct some functional code. We will also deal with the features in C# that are mostly used in developing functional programs. By the end of this chapter, we will have an idea of what the functional approach in C# will be like. Here are the topics we will cover in this chapter:

- Introduction to functional programming concepts
- Comparison between the functional and imperative approach
- The concepts of functional programming
- Using the mathematical approach to understand functional programming
- Refactoring imperative code to functional code
- The advantages and disadvantages of functional programming

Introducing functional programming

In functional programming, we write functions without side effects the way we write in Mathematics. The variable in the code function represents the value of the function parameter, and it similar to the mathematical function. The idea is that a programmer defines the functions that contain the expression, definition, and the parameters that can be expressed by a variable in order to solve problems.

After a programmer builds the function and sends the function to the computer, it's the computer's turn to do its job. In general, the role of the computer is to evaluate the expression in the function and return the result. We can imagine that the computer acts like a calculator since it will analyze the expression from the function and yield the result to the user in a printed format. The calculator will evaluate a function which are composed of variables passed as parameters and expressions which form the body of the function. Variables are substituted by their values in the expression. We can give simple expression and compound expressions using algebraic operators. Since expressions without assignments never alter the value, sub expressions needs to be evaluated only once.

Suppose we have the expression `3 + 5` inside a function. The computer will definitely return `8` as the result right after it completely evaluates it. However, this is just a simple example of how the computer acts in evaluating an expression. In fact, a programmer can increase the ability of the computer by creating a complex definition and expression inside the function. Not only can the computer evaluate the simple expression, but it can also evaluate the complex calculation and expression.

Understanding definitions, scripts, and sessions

As we discussed earlier about a calculator that will analyze the expression from the function, let's imagine we have a calculator that has a console panel like a computer does. The difference between that and a conventional calculator is that we have to press *Enter* instead of = (equal to) in order to run the evaluation process of the expression. Here, we can type the expression and then press *Enter*. Now, imagine that we type the following expression:

```
3 x 9
```

Immediately after pressing *Enter*, the computer will print `27` in the console, and that's what we are expecting. The computer has done a great job of evaluating the expression we gave. Now, let's move to analyzing the following definitions. Imagine that we type them on our functional calculator:

```
square a = a * a
max a b  = a, if a >= b
         = b, if b > a
```

We have defined the two definitions, `square` and `max`. We can call the list of definitions script. By calling the `square` function followed by any number representing variable `a`, we will be given the square of that number. Also, in the `max` definition, we serve two numbers to represent variables `a` and `b`, and then the computer will evaluate this expression to find out the biggest number between the variables.

By defining these two definitions, we can use them as a function, which we can call session, as follows:

```
square (1 + 2)
```

The computer will definitely print 9 after evaluating the preceding function. The computer will also be able to evaluate the following function:

```
max 1 2
```

It will return 2 as the result based on the definition we defined earlier. This is also possible if we provide the following expression:

```
square (max 2 5)
```

Then, 25 will be displayed in our calculator console panel.

We can also modify a definition using the previous definition. Suppose we want to quadruple an integer number and take advantage of the definition of the square function; here is what we can send to our calculator:

```
quad q = square q * square q
quad 10
```

The first line of the preceding expression is a definition of the quad function. In the second line, we call that function, and we will be provided with 10000 as the result.

The script can define the variable value; for instance, take a look at the following:

```
radius = 20
```

So, we should expect the computer to be able to evaluate the following definition:

```
area = (22 / 7) * square (radius)
```

Using substitution and simplification to evaluate the expression

Using a mathematical method called **reduction**, we can evaluate expressions by substitution variables or expressions to simplify the expressions until no more substitution on reduction is possible. Let's take our preceding expression, square (1 + 2) , and look at the following reduction process:

```
square (1 + 2) -> square 3 (addition)
```

```
                -> 3 x 3      (square)
                -> 9          (multiply)
```

First, we have the symbol `->` to indicate the reduction. From the sequence, we can discover the reduction process-in other words, the evaluation process. In the first line, the computer will run the `1 + 2` expression and substitute it with `3` in order to reduce the expression. Then, it will reduce the expression in the second line by simplifying `square 3` to `3 x 3` expressions. Lastly, it will simplify `3 x 3` and substitute it with `9`, which is the result of that expression.

Actually, an expression can have more than one possibility in the reduction. The preceding reduction process is one of the possibilities of a reduction process. We can also create other possibilities, like the following:

```
square (1 + 2) -> (1 + 2) x (1 + 2) (square)
               -> 3 x (1 + 2)        (addition)
               -> 3 x 3              (addition)
               -> 9                  (multiply)
```

In the preceding sequence, firstly, we can see that the rule for a square is applied. The computer then substitutes `1 + 2` in line 2 and line 3. Lastly, it multiplies the number in the expression.

From the preceding two examples, we can conclude that the expression can be evaluated using simple substitution and simplification, the basic rule of mathematics. We can also see that the expression is a representation of the value, not the value itself. However, the expression will be in the normal form if it can't be reduced anymore.

Understanding the functions used for functional programming

Functional programming uses a technique of emphasizing functions and their application instead of commands and their execution. Most values in functional programming are function values. Let's take a look at the following mathematical notation:

```
f :: A -> B
```

From the preceding notation, we can say that function `f` is a relation of each element stated there, which is `A` and `B`. We call `A`, the source type, and `B`, the target type. In other words, the notation of `A -> B` states that `A` is an argument where we have to input the value, and `B` is a return value or the output of the function evaluation.

Consider that x denotes an element of A and x + 2 denotes an element of B, so we can create the mathematical notation as follows:

```
f(x) = x + 2
```

In mathematics, we use f(x) to denote a functional application. In functional programming, the function will be passed as an argument and will return the result after the evaluation of the expression.

We can construct many definitions for one and the same function. The following two definitions are similar and will triple the input passed as an argument:

```
triple y = y + y + y
triple' y = 3 * y
```

As we can see, triple and triple' have different expressions. However, they are the same functions, so we can say that triple = triple'. Although we have many definitions to express one function, we will find that there is only one definition that will prove to be the most efficient in the procedure of evaluation in the sense of the reducing the expression we discussed previously. Unfortunately, we cannot determine which one is the most efficient from our preceding two definitions since that depends on the characteristic of the evaluation mechanism.

Forming the definition

Now, let's go back to our discussion on definitions at the beginning of this chapter. We have the following definition in order to retrieve the value from the case analysis:

```
max a b  = a, if a >= b
         = b, if b > a
```

There are two expressions in this definition, distinguished by a Boolean-value expression. This distinguisher is called guards, and we use them to evaluate the value of True or False. The first line is one of the alternative result values for this function. It states that the return value will be a if the expression a >= b is True. In contrast, the function will return value b if the expression b >= a is True. Using these two cases, a >= b and b >= a, the max value depends on the value of a and b. The order of the cases doesn't matter. We can also define the max function using the special word otherwise. This word ensures that the otherwise case will be executed if no expression results in a True value. Here, we will refactor our max function using the word otherwise:

```
max a b  = a, if a >= b
         = b, otherwise
```

From the preceding function definition, we can see that if the first expression is `False`, the function will return `b` immediately without performing any evaluation. In other words, the otherwise case will always return `True` if all previous guards return `False`.

Another special word usually used in mathematical notations is `where`. This word is used to set the local definition for the expression of the function. Let's take a look at the following example:

```
f x y = (z + 2) * (z + 3)
        where z = x + y
```

In the preceding example, we have a function `f` with variable `z`, whose value is determined by `x` and `y`. There, we introduce a local `z` definition to the function. This local definition can also be used along with the case analysis we have discussed earlier. Here is an example of the conjunction local definition with the case analysis:

```
f x y = x + z, if x > 100
      = x - z, otherwise
        where z = triple(y + 3)
```

In the preceding function, there is a local `z` definition, which qualifies for both `x + z` and `x - z` expressions. As we discussed earlier, although the function has two equal to (=) signs, only one expression will return the value.

Currying

Currying is a simple technique of changing structure arguments by sequence. It will transform a n-ary function into n unary function. It is a technique which was created to circumvent limitations of Lambda functions which are unary functions. Let's go back to our max function again and get the following definition:

```
max a b  = a, if a >= b
         = b, if b > a
```

We can see that there is no bracket in the `max a b` function name. Also, there is no comma-separated `a` and `b` in the function name. We can add a bracket and a comma to the function definition, as follows:

```
max' (a,b)  = a, if a >= b
            = b, if b > a
```

At first glance, we find the two functions to be the same since they have the same expression. However, they are different because of their different types. The `max'` function has a single argument, which consists of a pair of numbers. The type of `max'` function can be written as follows:

```
max' :: (num, num) -> num
```

On the other hand, the `max` function has two arguments. The type of this function can be written as follows:

```
max :: num -> (num -> num)
```

The max function will take a number and then return a function from single number to many numbers. From the preceding max function, we pass the variable `a` to the `max` function, which returns a value. Then, that value is compared to variable `b` in order to find the maximum number.

Comparison between functional and imperative programming

The main difference between functional and imperative programming is that imperative programming produces side effects while functional programming doesn't. In imperative programming, the expressions are evaluated and its resulting value is assigned to variables. So, when we group series of expressions into a function, the resulting value depends upon the state of variables at that point in time. This is called side effects. Because of the continuous changes in state, the order of evaluation matters. In functional programming world, destructive assignment is forbidden and each time an assignment happens a new variable is induced.

Preparing the C# compiler

For the rest of the discussion in this chapter, we are going to create some code in C#. In order we have the same environment, let's define what we will use in configuration settings. We will use Visual Studio 2015 Community Edition and .NET Framework 4.6.2 in all of the source code we discuss in this book. We will also choose the console application project in order to ease the development of our code since it doesn't need many changes to the settings.

Here is the screenshot of the setting in creating Visual Studio projects we will use:

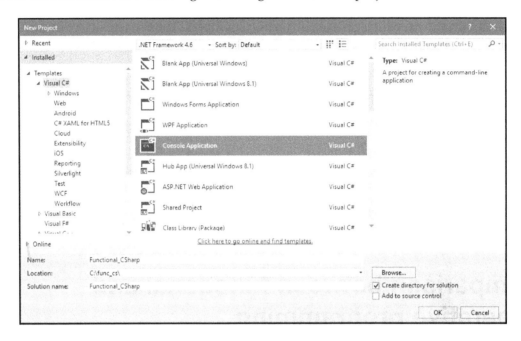

When we are discussing a source code that has a `csproj` filename-for instance, `FuncObject.csproj`-we can find it in one of solution files provided in the sample code. It will be in the `Program.cs` file. The following is a screenshot of the structure of the project in Visual Studio:

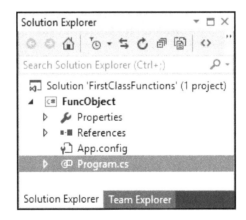

However, sometimes, we have more than one `.cs` file inside the project file. In this case, we can find the code we are discussing in one of the `.cs` files inside the project file. For instance, we have a project file named `FunctionalCode.csproj`. So, when we discuss any source code related to this project file, we can find it from the `.cs` files inside the project file. The structure of a project file consisting of more than one `.cs` files is as follows:

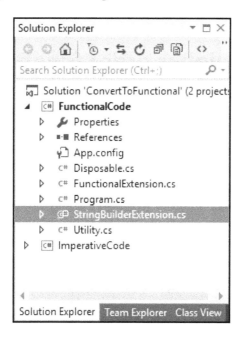

As we can see, inside the `FunctionalCode.csproj` file, not only do we have the `Program.cs` file, but also `Disposable.cs`, `FunctionalExtension.cs`, `StringBuilderExtension.cs`, and `Utility.cs`.

We will also find the `partial` keyword to the classes name in most of our code even though we write the classes in the same file. The purpose is to make the code snippet in this book easy to find in the sample code. By knowing the class name, it will be easier to find the source code in the file.

 We also need to install Visual Studio Community 2017 RC since we will use a new feature of C# 7 in `Chapter 9`, *Working with Pattern*.

Concepts of functional programming

We can also distinguish functional programming from imperative programming by the concepts. The core ideas of functional programming are encapsulated in the constructs such as first class functions, higher order functions, purity, recursion over loops, and partial functions. We will discuss the concepts in this topic.

First-class and higher-order functions

In imperative programming, the given data is more important and are passed through series of functions (with side effects). Functions are special constructs with their own semantics. In effect, functions do not have the same place as variables and constants. Since a function cannot be passed as a parameter or returned as a result, they are regarded as second class citizens of the programming world. In the functional programming world, we can pass a function as a parameter and return function as a result. They obey the same semantics as variables and their values. Thus, they are first class citizens. We can also create function of functions called second order function through composition. There is no limit imposed on the composability of functions and they are called higher order functions.

Fortunately, the C# language supports these two concepts since it has a feature called function object, which has types and values. To discuss more details about the function object, let's take a look at the following code:

```
class Program
{
  static void Main(string[] args)
  {
    Func<int, int> f = (x) => x + 2;
    int i = f(1);
    Console.WriteLine(i);

    f = (x) => 2 * x + 1;
    i = f(1);
    Console.WriteLine(i);
  }
}
```

We can find the code in `FuncObject.csproj`, and if we run it, it will display the following output on the console screen:

Why do we display it? Let's continue the discussion on function types and function values.

Hit *Ctrl + F5* instead of *F5* in order to run the code in debug mode but without the debugger. It's useful to stop the console from closing on the exit.

Function types

As with other objects in C#, function objects have a type as well. We can initialize the types in the function declaration. Here is the syntax to declare function objects:

```
Func<T1, T2, T3, T4, ..., T16, TResult>
```

Note that we have `T1` until `T16`, which are the types that correspond to input parameters, and `TResult` is a type that corresponds to the return type. If we need to convert our previous mathematical function, `f(x) = x + 2`, we can write it as follows:

```
Func<int, int> f = (x) => x + 2;
```

We now have a function `f`, which has one argument-typed integer and the integer return type as well. Here, we use a lambda expression to define a delegate to be assigned to the object named `f` with the `Func` type. Don't worry if you are not familiar with delegate and lambda expressions yet. We will discuss them further in our next chapters.

Function values

To assign a value to function variable, there are the following possibilities:

- A function variable can be assigned to an existing method inside a class by its name using a reference. We can use delegate as reference. Let's take a look at the following code snippet:

```
class Program
{
  delegate int DoubleAction(int inp);

  static void Main(string[] args)
  {
    DoubleAction da = Double;
    int doubledValue = da(2);
  }

  static int Double(int input)
  {
    return input * 2;
  }
}
```

- As we can see in the preceding code, we assign da variable to existing Double() method using delegate.

- A function variable can be assigned to an anonymous function using a lambda expression. Let's look at the following code snippet:

```
class Program
{
  static void Main(string[] args)
  {
    Func<int, int> da =
        input => input * 2;

    int doubledValue = da(2);
  }
}
```

- As we can see, the da variable is assigned using lambda expression and we can use the da variable like we use in previous code snippet.

Now we have a function variable and can assign a variable-integer-typed variable, for instance, to this function variable, as follows:

```
int i = f(1);
```

After executing the preceding code, the value of variable i will be 3 since we pass 1 as the argument, and it will return 1 + 2. We can also assign the function variable with another function, as follows:

```
f = (x) => 2 * x + 1;
i = f(1);
```

We assign a new function, 2 * x + 1, to variable f, so we will retrieve 3 if we run the preceding code.

Pure functions

In the functional programming, most of the functions do not have side effects. In other words, the function doesn't change any variables outside the function itself. Also, it is consistent, which means that it always returns the same value for the same input data. The following are example actions that will generate side effects in programming:

- Modifying a global variable or static variable since it will make a function interact with the outside world.
- Modifying the argument in a function. This usually happens if we pass a parameter as a reference.
- Raising an exception.
- Taking input and output outside-for instance, get a keystroke from the keyboard or write data to the screen.

 Although it does not satisfy the rule of a pure function, we will use many `Console.WriteLine()` methods in our program in order to ease our understanding in the code sample.

The following is the sample non-pure function that we can find in NonPureFunction1.csproj:

```
class Program
{
    private static string strValue = "First";

    public static void AddSpace(string str)
```

```
    {
      strValue += ' ' + str;
    }

    static void Main(string[] args)
    {
      AddSpace("Second");
      AddSpace("Third");
      Console.WriteLine(strValue);
    }
  }
```

If we run the preceding code, as expected, the following result will be displayed on the console:

In this code, we modify the strValue global variable inside the AddSpace function. Since it modifies the variable outside, it's not considered a pure function.

Let's take a look at another non-pure function example in NonPureFunction2.csproj:

```
class Program
{
  public static void AddSpace(StringBuilder sb, string str)
  {
    sb.Append(' ' + str);
  }

  static void Main(string[] args)
  {
    StringBuilder sb1 = new StringBuilder("First");
    AddSpace(sb1, "Second");
    AddSpace(sb1, "Third");
    Console.WriteLine(sb1);
  }
}
```

We see the AddSpace function again but this time with the addition of an argument-typed StringBuilder argument. In the function, we modify the sb argument with hyphen and str. Since we pass the sb variable by reference, it also modifies the sb1 variable in the Main function. Note that it will display the same output as NonPureFunction2.csproj.

To convert the preceding two examples of non-pure function code into pure function code, we can refactor the code to be the following. This code can be found at `PureFunction.csproj`:

```
class Program
{
  public static string AddSpace(string strSource, string str)
  {
    return (strSource + ' ' + str);
  }

  static void Main(string[] args)
  {
    string str1 = "First";
    string str2 = AddSpace(str1, "Second");
    string str3 = AddSpace(str2, "Third");
    Console.WriteLine(str3);
  }
}
```

Running `PureFunction.csproj`, we will get the same output compared to the two previous non-pure function code. However, in this pure function code, we have three variables in the `Main` function. This is because in functional programming, we cannot modify the variable we have initialized earlier. In the `AddSpace` function, instead of modifying the global variable or argument, it now returns a string value to satisfy the the functional rule.

The following are the advantages we will have if we implement the pure function in our code:

- Our code will be easy to be read and maintain because the function does not depend on external state and variables. It is also designed to perform specific tasks that increase maintainability.
- The design will be easier to be changed since it is easier to refactor.
- Testing and debugging will be easier since it's quite easy to isolate the pure function.

Recursive functions

In an imperative programming world, we have got destructive assignments to mutate the state if a variable. By using loops, one can change multiple variables to achieve the computational objective. In the functional programming world, since variables cannot be destructively assigned, we need a recursive function call to achieve the objective of looping.

Let's create a factorial function. In mathematical terms, the factorial of the nonnegative integer N is the multiplication of all positive integers less than or equal to N. This is usually denoted by N!. We can denote the factorial of 7 as follows:

```
7! = 7 x 6 x 5 x 4 x 3 x 2 x 1
   = 5040
```

If we look deeper at the preceding formula, we will discover that the pattern of the formula is as follows:

$$N! = N * (N-1) * (N-2) * (N-3) * (N-4) * (N-5) \dots$$

Now, let's take a look at the following factorial function in C#. It's an imperative approach and can be found in the `RecursiveImperative.csproj` file:

```
public partial class Program
{
  private static int GetFactorial(int intNumber)
  {
    if (intNumber == 0)
    {
      return 1;
    }

    return intNumber * GetFactorial(intNumber - 1);
  }
}
```

As we can see, we invoke the `GetFactorial()` function from the `GetFactorial()` function itself. This is what we call a recursive function. We can use this function by creating a `Main()` method containing the following code:

```
public partial class Program
{
  static void Main(string[] args)
  {
    Console.WriteLine(
      "Enter an integer number (Imperative approach)");
    int inputNumber = Convert.ToInt32(Console.ReadLine());
```

```
    int factorialNumber = GetFactorial(inputNumber);
    Console.WriteLine(
      "{0}! is {1}",
      inputNumber,
      factorialNumber);
  }
}
```

We invoke the GetFactorial() method and pass our desired number to the argument. The method will then multiply our number with what's returned by the GetFactorial() method, in which the argument has been subtracted by 1. The iteration will last until intNumber - 1 is equal to 0, which will return 1.

Now, let's compare the preceding recursive function in the imperative approach with one in the functional approach. We will use the power of the Aggregate operator in the LINQ feature to achieve this goal. We can find the code in the RecursiveFunctional.csproj file. The code will look like what is shown in the following:

```
class Program
{
  static void Main(string[] args)
  {
    Console.WriteLine(
      "Enter an integer number (Functional approach)");
    int inputNumber = Convert.ToInt32(Console.ReadLine());
    IEnumerable<int> ints = Enumerable.Range(1, inputNumber);
    int factorialNumber = ints.Aggregate((f, s) => f * s);
    Console.WriteLine(
      "{0}! is {1}",
      inputNumber,
      factorialNumber);
  }
}
```

We initialize the ints variable, which contains a value from 1 to our desired integer number in the preceding code, and then we iterate ints using the Aggregate operator. The output of RecursiveFunctional.csproj will be completely the same compared to the output of RecursiveImperative.csproj. However, we use the functional approach in the code in RecursiveFunctional.csproj.

Feeling functional in C#

This section will discuss about functional programming in C#. We will be discussing both the conceptual aspects of functional programming and write code in C#, as well. We will be kick-starting the discussion by discussing about currying, pipelining, and method chaining.

Using mathematical concept to understand functional approach

In functional programming, functions behave the way a mathematical function behaves by returning the same value for a given argument regardless of the context in which it is invoked. This is called **Referential Transparency**. To understand this in more detail, consider that we have the following mathematical function notation, and we want to turn it into functional programming in C#:

$$f(x) = 4x^2-14x-8$$

The functional programming in C# is as follows:

```
public partial class Program
{
  public static int f(int x)
  {
    return (4 * x * x - 14 * x - 8);
  }
}
```

From the preceding function, which we can find in the `FunctionF.csproj` file, if x is 5, we will obtain f of 5, which is 22. The notation will be as follows:

$$f(5) = 22$$

We can also invoke the f function in C#, as follows:

```
public partial class Program
{
  static void Main(string[] args)
  {
    int i = f(5);
    Console.WriteLine(i);
  }
}
```

Every time we run the function with 5 as the argument, which means that x is equal to 5, we always receive 22 as the return value.

Now, compare this with the imperative approach. Let's take a look at the following code, which will be stored in the ImperativeApproach.csproj file:

```
public partial class Program
{
  static int i = 0;

  static void increment()
  {
    i++;
  }

  static void set(int inpSet)
  {
    i = inpSet;
  }
}
```

We describe the following code in the Main() method:

```
public partial class Program
{
  static void Main(string[] args)
  {
    increment();
    Console.WriteLine("First increment(), i = {0}", i);

    set(6);
    increment();
    Console.WriteLine("Second increment(), i = {0}", i);

    set(2);
    increment();
    Console.WriteLine("Last increment(), i = {0}", i);

    return;
  }
}
```

If we run `ImperativeApproach.csproj`, the console screen should be like what is shown in the following screenshot:

In the preceding imperative approach code, we will get the different `i` output in every invocation of `increment` or `set` although we pass the identical argument. Here, we find the so-called side effect problem of the imperative approach. The `increment` or `set` functions are said to have a side effect since they modify the state of `i` and interact with the outside world.

That was about side effects, and now, we have the following code in C#:

```
public partial class Program
{
  public static string GetSign(int val)
  {
    string posOrNeg;

    if (val > 0)
      posOrNeg = "positive";
    else
      posOrNeg = "negative";

    return posOrNeg;
  }
}
```

The preceding code is statement style code, and we can find it in the `StatementStyle.csproj` file. It is an imperative programming technique that defines actions rather than producing results. We tell the computer what to do. We ask the computer to compare the value of the `value` variable with zero and then assign the `posOrNeg` variable to the associated value. We can try the preceding function by adding the following code to the project:

```
public partial class Program
{
  static void Main(string[] args)
  {
    Console.WriteLine(
```

```
        "Sign of -15 is {0}",
        GetSign(-15));
  }
}
```

The output in the console will be as follow:

And it agrees with our preceding discussion.

We can turn it into a functional approach by modifying it to expression style code. In C#, we can use the conditional operator to achieve this goal. The following is the code we have refactored from the `StatementStyle.csproj` code, and we can find it in the `ExpressionStyle.csproj` file:

```
public partial class Program
{
  public static string GetSign(int val)
  {
    return val > 0 ? "positive" : "negative";
  }
}
```

Now we have compact code that has the same behavior as our preceding many lines of code. However, as we discussed previously, the preceding code has no side-effect since it only returns the string value with no need to prepare the variable first. While in the statement style approach, we have to assign the `posOrNeg` variable twice. In other words, we can say that the functional approach will produce a side-effect-free function.

In contrast to imperative programming, in functional programming, we describe what we want as the result rather than specifying how to receive the result. Suppose we have a list of data and want to create a new list containing the *Nth* element from the source list. The imperative approach to achieve this is as follows:

```
public partial class Program
{
  static List<int> NthImperative(List<int> list, int n)
  {
    var newList = new List<int>();

    for (int i = 0; i < list.Count; i++)
    {
```

```
        if (i % n == 0) newList.Add(list[i]);
      }

    return newList;
  }
}
```

The preceding code can be found in the `NthElementImperative.csproj` file. As we can see, to retrieve the Nth element from the list in C#, we have to initialize the first element so that we define `i` as `0`. We then iterate through the list element and decide whether the current element is the Nth element. If so, we add `newList` the new data from the source list. Here, we find that the preceding source code is not a functional approach because the `newList` variable is assigned more than once when adding the new data. It also contains the loop process, which the functional approach doesn't have. However, we can turn the code into a functional approach as follows:

```
public partial class Program
{
  static List<int> NthFunctional(List<int> list, int n)
  {
    return list.Where((x, i) => i % n == 0).ToList();
  }
}
```

Again, we have compact code in the functional approach since we are using the power of the LINQ feature. If we want to try the preceding two functions, we can inset the following code to the `Main()` function:

```
public partial class Program
{
  static void Main(string[] args)
  {
    List<int> listing =
      new List<int>() {
        0, 1, 2, 3, 4, 5,
        6, 7, 8, 9, 10, 11,
        12, 13, 14, 15, 16 };

    var list3rd_imper = NthImperative(listing, 3);
    PrintIntList("Nth Imperative", list3rd_imper);

    var list3rd_funct = NthFunctional(listing, 3);
    PrintIntList("Nth Functional", list3rd_funct);
  }
}
```

For the `PrintIntList()` method, the implementation is as follows:

```
public partial class Program
{
  static void PrintIntList(
    string titleHeader,
    List<int> list)
  {
    Console.WriteLine(
      String.Format("{0}",
      titleHeader));

    foreach (int i in list)
    {
      Console.Write(String.Format("{0}\t", i));
    }

    Console.WriteLine("\n");
  }
}
```

Although we run the two functions with different approaches, we are still given the same output, as follows:

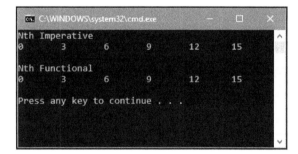

Applying tuple for functional C#

In .NET Framework 4, Tuples is introduced as a new set of generic classes to store a set of different typed elements. Tuples is immutable so it can be applied to functional programming. It is used to represent a data structure when we need the different data type in an object. Here is the available syntax to declare tuple objects:

```
public class Tuple <T1>
public class Tuple <T1, T2>
public class Tuple <T1, T2, T3>
```

```
public class Tuple <T1, T2, T3, T4>
public class Tuple <T1, T2, T3, T4, T5>
public class Tuple <T1, T2, T3, T4, T5, T6>
public class Tuple <T1, T2, T3, T4, T5, T6, T7>
public class Tuple <T1, T2, T3, T4, T5, T6, T7, T8>
```

As we can see in the preceding syntaxes, we can create a tuple with a maximum eight item type (T1, T2, and so on). `Tuple` has read-only properties that's why it's immutable. Let's look at the following code snippet we can find in `Tuple.csproj` project:

```
public partial class Program
{
  Tuple<string, int, int> geometry1 =
    new Tuple<string, int, int>(
        "Rectangle",
        2,
        3);
  Tuple<string, int, int> geometry2 =
  Tuple.Create(
        "Square",
        2,
        2);
}
```

To create Tuple, we have two different ways based on the preceding code. The former, we instantiate a new Tuple to a variable. The latter, we use `Tuple.Create()`. To consume the Tuple data, we can use its Item like the following code snippet:

```
public partial class Program
{
  private static void ConsumeTuple()
  {
    Console.WriteLine(
      "{0} has size {1} x {2}",
      geometry1.Item1,
      geometry1.Item2,
      geometry1.Item3);
    Console.WriteLine(
      "{0} has size {1} x {2}",
      geometry2.Item1,
      geometry2.Item2,
      geometry2.Item3);
  }
}
```

If we run `ConsumeTuple()` method above, we will get the following on the console:

```
C:\WINDOWS\system32\cmd.exe
Rectangle has size 2 x 3
Square has size 2 x 2
Press any key to continue . . .
```

We can also return a tuple data type like we do in the following code snippet:

```
public partial class Program
{
  private static Tuple<int, int> (
    string shape)
  { GetSize
    if (shape == "Rectangle")
    {
      return Tuple.Create(2, 3);
    }
    else if (shape == "Square")
    {
      return Tuple.Create(2, 2);
    }
    else
    {
      return Tuple.Create(0, 0);
    }
  }
}
```

As we can see, `GetSize()` method will return Tuple data type. We can add the following `ReturnTuple()` method:

```
public partial class Program
{
  private static void ReturnTuple()
  {
    var rect = GetSize("Rectangle");
    Console.WriteLine(
        "Rectangle has size {0} x {1}",
          rect.Item1,
          rect.Item2);
    var square = GetSize("Square");
    Console.WriteLine(
        "Square has size {0} x {1}",
          square.Item1,
```

```
                square.Item2);
        }
    }
```

And if we run `ReturnTuple()` method above, we will be displayed exactly same output as `ConsumeTuple()` method.

Fortunately, in C# 7, we can return Tuple data type without having to state the Tuple like the following code snippet:

```
public partial class Program
{
    (int, int) GetSizeInCS7(
            string shape)
    {
        if (shape == "Rectangle")
        {
            return (2, 3);
        }
        else if (shape == "Square")
        {
            return (2, 2);
        }
        else
        {
            return (0, 0);
        }
    }
}
```

And if we want to name all items in the Tuple, we can now do it in C# 7 by using the technique like the following code snippet:

```
public partial class Program
{
    private static (int x, int y) GetSizeNamedItem(
            string shape)
    {
        if (shape == "Rectangle")
        {
            return (2, 3);
        }
        else if (shape == "Square")
        {
            return (2, 2);
        }
        else
        {
```

```
        return (0, 0);
      }
    }
  }
```

And now it will be clearer when we access the Tuple items like the following code:

```
public partial class Program
{
  private static void ConsumeTupleByItemName()
  {
    var rect = GetSizeNamedItem("Rectangle");
    Console.WriteLine(
        "Rectangle has size {0} x {1}",
        rect.x,
        rect.y);
    var square = GetSizeNamedItem("Square");
    Console.WriteLine(
        "Square has size {0} x {1}",
        square.x,
        square.y);
  }
}
```

We no longer call the `Item1` and `Item2`, instead we call the x and y name.

In order to gain all new feature of Tuple in C# 7, we have to download `System.ValueTuple` NuGet package from `https://www.nuget.org/packages/System.ValueTuple`.

Currying in C#

We have theoretically discussed currying at the beginning of this chapter. We apply currying when we split a function that takes multiple arguments into a sequence of functions that occupy part of the argument. In other words, when we pass fewer arguments into a function, it will expect that we get back another function to complete the original function using the sequence of functions. Let's take a look at the following code from the `NonCurriedMethod.csproj` file:

```
public partial class Program
{
  public static int NonCurriedAdd(int a, int b) => a + b;
}
```

The preceding function will add the a and b arguments and then return the result. The usage of this function is commonly used in our daily programming; for instance, take a look at the following code snippet:

```
public partial class Program
{
   static void Main(string[] args)
   {
      int add = NonCurriedAdd(2, 3);
      Console.WriteLine(add);
   }
}
```

Now, let's move on to the curried method. The code will be found in the CurriedMethod.csproj file, and the function declaration will be as follows:

```
public partial class Program
{
   public static Func<int, int> CurriedAdd(int a) => b => a + b;
}
```

We use the Func<> delegate to create the CurriedAdd() method. We can invoke the preceding method in two ways, and the first is as follows:

```
public partial class Program
{
   public static void CurriedStyle1()
   {
      int add = CurriedAdd(2)(3);
      Console.WriteLine(add);
   }
}
```

In the preceding invocation of the CurriedAdd() method, we pass the argument with two brackets, which it might not be familiar with. In fact, we can also curry our CurriedAdd() method by passing one argument only. The code will be as follows:

```
public partial class Program
{
   public static void CurriedStyle2()
   {
      var addition = CurriedAdd(2);

      int x = addition(3);
      Console.WriteLine(x);
   }
}
```

From the preceding code, we supply one argument to the `CurriedAdd()` method in the following:

```
var addition = CurriedAdd(2);
```

Then, it waits for the other `addition` expression, which we provide in the following code:

```
int x = addition(3);
```

The result of the preceding code will be completely the same as the `NonCurried()` method.

Pipelining

Pipelining is a technique used to pass the output of one function as an input to the next function. The data in the operation will flow like the flow of water in a pipe. We usually find this technique in command-line interfaces. Let's take a look at the following command line:

```
C:\>dir | more
```

The preceding command line will pass the output of the `dir` command to the input of the `more` command. Now, let's take a look at the following C# code that we can find in the `NestedMethodCalls.csproj` file:

```
class Program
{
  static void Main(string[] args)
  {
    Console.WriteLine(
      Encoding.UTF8.GetString(
        new byte[] { 0x70, 0x69, 0x70, 0x65, 0x6C,
        0x69, 0x6E, 0x69, 0x6E, 0x67 }
      )
    );
  }
}
```

In the previous code, we used the nested method calls technique to write `pipelining` in console screen. If we want to refactor it to the pipelining approach, we can take a look at the following code that we can find in the `Pipelining.csproj` file:

```
class Program
{
  static void Main(string[] args)
  {
    var bytes = new byte[] {
      0x70, 0x69, 0x70, 0x65, 0x6C,
      0x69, 0x6E, 0x69, 0x6E, 0x67 };
    var stringFromBytes = Encoding.UTF8.GetString(bytes);
    Console.WriteLine(stringFromBytes);
  }
}
```

If run the preceding code, we will get exactly the same pipelining output, but this time, it will be in the pipelining style.

Method chaining

Method chaining is process of chaining multiple methods in one code line. The return from one method will be the input of the next method, and so on. Using method chaining, we don't need to declare many variables to store every method return. Instead, the return of the method will be passed to the next method argument. The following is the traditional method, which doesn't apply method chaining, and we can find the code at `TraditionalMethod.csproj`:

```
class Program
{
  static void Main(string[] args)
  {
    var sb = new StringBuilder("0123", 10);
    sb.Append(new char[] { '4', '5', '6' });
    sb.AppendFormat("{0}{1}{2}", 7, 8, 9);
    sb.Insert(0, "number: ");
    sb.Replace('n', 'N');
    var str = sb.ToString();
    Console.WriteLine(str);
  }
}
```

There are five methods of `StringBuilder` invoked inside the `Main` function and two variables: `sb` is used to initialize `StringBuilder` and `str` is used to store `StringBuilder` in the string format. Unfortunately, the five methods we invoked there modify the `sb` variable. We can refactor the code to apply method chaining in order to make it functional. The following is the functional code, and we can find it at `ChainingMethod.csproj`:

```
class Program
{
  static void Main(string[] args)
  {
    var str =
      new StringBuilder("0123", 10)
        .Append(new char[] { '4', '5', '6' })
        .AppendFormat("{0}{1}{2}", 7, 8, 9)
        .Insert(0, "number: ")
        .Replace('n', 'N')
        .ToString();
    Console.WriteLine(str);
  }
}
```

The same output will be displayed if we run both types of code. However, we now have functional code by chaining all the invoking methods.

Transforming imperative code to functional code

In this section, we will transform imperative code to functional code by leveraging method chaining. Suppose we want to create an HTML-ordered list containing the list of the planets in our solar system; the HTML will look as follows:

```
<ol id="thePlanets">
  <li>The Sun/li>
  <li value="0">Mercury</li>
  <li value="1">Venus</li>
  <li value="2">Earth</li>
  <li value="3">Mars</li>
  <li value="4">Jupiter</li>
  <li value="5">Saturn</li>
  <li value="6">Uranus</li>
  <li value="7">Neptune</li>
</ol>
```

The imperative code approach

We are going to list the name of planets, including the Sun. We will also mark the order of the planets with the value attribute in each `li` element. The preceding HTML code will be displayed in the console. We will create the list in `ImperativeCode.csproj`; here you go:

```
class Program
{
  static void Main(string[] args)
  {
    byte[] buffer;
    using (var stream = Utility.GeneratePlanetsStream())
    {
      buffer = new byte[stream.Length];
      stream.Read(buffer, 0, (int)stream.Length);
    }
    var options = Encoding.UTF8
      .GetString(buffer)
      .Split(new[] { Environment.NewLine, },
            StringSplitOptions.RemoveEmptyEntries)
      .Select((s, ix) => Tuple.Create(ix, s))
      .ToDictionary(k => k.Item1, v => v.Item2);
    var orderedList = Utility.GenerateOrderedList(
        options, "thePlanets", true);

    Console.WriteLine(orderedList);
  }
}
```

In the `Main()` method, we create a byte array, buffer, containing the planet stream we generate in other classes. The code snippet is as follows:

```
byte[] buffer;
using (var stream = Utility.GeneratePlanetsStream())
{
  buffer = new byte[stream.Length];
  stream.Read(buffer, 0, (int)stream.Length);
}
```

We can see that there is a class named `Utility`, containing the `GeneratePlanetStream()` method. This method is used to generate the list of planets in the solar system in a stream format. Let's take a look at the following code in order to find what is inside the method:

```
public static partial class Utility
{
  public static Stream GeneratePlanetsStream()
  {
    var planets =
    String.Join(
      Environment.NewLine,
      new[] {
        "Mercury", "Venus", "Earth",
        "Mars", "Jupiter", "Saturn",
        "Uranus", "Neptune"
    });

    var buffer = Encoding.UTF8.GetBytes(planets);
    var stream = new MemoryStream();
    stream.Write(buffer, 0, buffer.Length);
    stream.Position = 0L;

    return stream;
  }
}
```

Firstly, it creates a variable named `planets`, containing eight planets named separately on a new line. We get the bytes of the ASCII using the `GetBytes` method, and then it is converted into a stream. This stream will be returned to the caller function.

In the `main` function, we also have variable options, as follows:

```
var options = Encoding.UTF8
  .GetString(buffer)
  .Split(new[] { Environment.NewLine, },
    StringSplitOptions.RemoveEmptyEntries)
  .Select((s, ix) => Tuple.Create(ix, s))
  .ToDictionary(k => k.Item1, v => v.Item2);
```

This will create a dictionary-typed variable, which contains the name of the planet and its order in the solar system. We use LINQ here, but we will discuss it deeper in the next chapter.

Then, we invoke the `GenerateOrderedList()` method inside the `Utility` class. This method is used to generate an HTML-ordered list containing the order of the planets in the solar system. The code snippet is as follows:

```
var orderedList = Utility.GenerateOrderedList(
    options, "thePlanets", true);
```

If we take a look at the `GenerateOrderedList()` method, we will find the following code:

```
public static partial class Utility
{
  public static string GenerateOrderedList(
    IDictionary<int, string> options,
    string id,
    bool includeSun)
  {
    var html = new StringBuilder();
    html.AppendFormat("<ol id=\"{0}\">", id);
    html.AppendLine();

    if (includeSun)
    {
      html.AppendLine("\t<li>The Sun/li>");
    }

    foreach (var opt in options)
    {
      html.AppendFormat("\t<li value=\"{0}\">{1}</li>",
      opt.Key,
      opt.Value);
      html.AppendLine();
    }

    html.AppendLine("</ol>");

    return html.ToString();
  }
}
```

First, in this method, we create a `StringBuilder` function named `html` and add an opening `ol` tag, which means an *ordered list*. The code snippet is as follows:

```
var html = new StringBuilder();
    html.AppendFormat("<ol id=\"{0}\">", id);
    html.AppendLine();
```

We also have Boolean variable, `includeSun`, to define whether we need to include Sun in the list. We get the value of this variable from the argument of the method. After that, we iterate the content of the dictionary we get from argument. This dictionary is generated by LINQ in the `Main()` method. We list the content by adding the `li` tag. The `foreach` keyword is used to achieve this goal. Here is the code snippet:

```
foreach (var opt in options)
{
  html.AppendFormat("\t<li value="{0}">{1}</li>",
    opt.Key,
    opt.Value);
  html.AppendLine();
}
```

We can see that `AppendFormat` in the `StringBuilder` class is similar to `String.Format`, and we can pass `Key` and `Value` from dictionary. Do not forget to insert a new line for each `li` tag using the `AppendLine` method.

Lastly, we close the `ol` tag with the `</ol>` tag, which we define in the following snippet:

```
html.AppendLine("</ol>");
```

Then, we invoke the `ToString()` method to get a bunch of strings from `StringBuilder`. Now if we run the code, we will get the output on the console screen, as we discussed earlier.

The functional code approach

We have already developed imperative code in order to construct an HTML-ordered list of planet names, as discussed earlier. Now, from this imperative code, we are going to refactor it to functional code using method chaining. The functional code we build will be at `FunctionalCode.csproj`.

The GenerateOrderedList() method

We start with the `GenerateOrderedList()` method since we will modify its first three lines. It looks like the following in `ImperativeCode.csproj`:

```
var html = new StringBuilder();
  html.AppendFormat("<ol id="{0}">", id);
  html.AppendLine();
```

We can refactor the preceding code to this:

```
var html =
  new StringBuilder()
    .AppendFormat("<ol id="{0}">", id)
    .AppendLine();
```

The code becomes more natural now since it applies method chaining. However, we are still able to join the `AppendFormat()` method with the `AppendLine()` method in order to make it simple. To achieve this goal, we need help from method extension. We can create a method extension for `StringBuilder` as follows:

```
public static partial class StringBuilderExtension
{
  public static StringBuilder AppendFormattedLine(
    this StringBuilder @this,
    string format,
    params object[] args) =>
      @this.AppendFormat(format, args).AppendLine();
}
```

Now, because we have the `AppendFormattedLine()` method in the `StringBuilder` class, we can refactor our previous code snippet to the following:

```
var html =
  new StringBuilder()
    .AppendFormattedLine("<ol id="{0}">", id);
```

The code snippet becomes much simpler than earlier. We also have the invocation of `AppendFormat()` following `AppendLine()` inside the `foreach` loop, as follows:

```
foreach (var opt in options)
{
  html.AppendFormat("\t<li value="{0}">{1}</li>",
    opt.Key,
    opt.Value);
  html.AppendLine();
}
```

Therefore, we can also refactor the preceding code snippet using the `AppendFormattedLine()` function we added inside the `StringBuilder` class, as follows:

```
foreach (var opt in options)
{
  html.AppendFormattedLine(
    "\t<li value="{0}">{1}</li>",
    opt.Key,
```

```
      opt.Value);
  }
```

Next, we have `AppendLine()` inside the conditional keyword `if`. We also need to refactor it to apply method chaining using the extension method. We can create the extension method for `StringBuilder` named `AppendLineWhen()`. The use of this method is to compare the condition we provide, and then it should decide whether or not it needs to be written. The extension method will be as follows:

```
public static partial class StringBuilderExtension
{
  public static StringBuilder AppendLineWhen(
    this StringBuilder @this,
    Func<bool> predicate,
    string value) =>
        predicate()
          ? @this.AppendLine(value)
            : @this;
}
```

Since we now have the `AppendLineWhen()` method, we can chain it to the previous code snippet, as follows:

```
var html =
  new StringBuilder()
    .AppendFormattedLine("<ol id="{0}">", id)
    .AppendLineWhen(() => includeSun, "\t<li>The Sun/li>");
```

Thus, we are now confident about removing the following code from the `GenerateOrderedList()` method:

```
if (includeSun)
{
  html.AppendLine("\t<li>The Sun/li>");
}
```

We are also able to make the `AppendLineWhen()` method more general so that it not only accepts a string, but also takes a function as an argument. Let's modify the `AppendLineWhen()` method to the `AppendWhen()` method, as follows:

```
public static partial class StringBuilderExtension
{
  public static StringBuilder AppendWhen(
    this StringBuilder @this,
    Func<bool> predicate,
    Func<StringBuilder, StringBuilder> fn) =>
    predicate()
```

```
    ? fn(@this)
    : @this;
}
```

As we can see, the function now takes `Func<StringBuilder, StringBuilder> fn` as an argument to replace the string value. So, it now uses the function to decide the conditional with `fn(@this)`. We can refactor `var html` again with our new method, as follows:

```
var html =
  new StringBuilder()
  .AppendFormattedLine("<ol id="{0}">", id)
  .AppendWhen(
    () => includeSun,
    sb => sb.AppendLine("\t<li>The Sun/li>"));
```

We have chained two methods so far; they are `AppendFormattedLine()` and `AppendWhen()` methods. The remaining function we have is `foreach` loop that we need to chain to the `StringBuilder` object named `html`. For this purpose, we create an extension method to a `StringBuilder` named `AppendSequence()` again, as follows:

```
public static partial class StringBuilderExtension
{
  public static StringBuilder AppendSequence<T>(
    this StringBuilder @this,
    IEnumerable<T> sequence,
    Func<StringBuilder, T, StringBuilder> fn) =>
      sequence.Aggregate(@this, fn);
}
```

We use the `IEnumerable` interface to make this function iterate over the sequence. It also invokes the `Aggregate` method in `IEnumerable` as an accumulator that counts the increasing sequence.

Now, using `AppendSequence()`, we can refactor the `foreach` loop and chain the methods to `var html`, as follows:

```
var html =
  new StringBuilder()
  .AppendFormattedLine("<ol id="{0}">", id)
  .AppendWhen(
    () => includeSun,
    sb => sb.AppendLine("\t<li>The Sun/li>"))
  .AppendSequence(
    options,
    (sb, opt) =>
      sb.AppendFormattedLine(
      "\t<li value="{0}">{1}</li>",
```

```
      opt.Key,
      opt.Value));
```

The `AppendSequence()` method we add takes the options variable as the dictionary input and function of `sb` and `opt`. This method will iterate the dictionary content and then append the formatted string into `StringBuilder` `sb`. Now, the following `foreach` loop can be removed from the code:

```
foreach (var opt in options)
{
  html.AppendFormattedLine(
    "\t<li value="{0}">{1}</li>",
    opt.Key,
    opt.Value);
}
```

Next is the `html.AppendLine("</ol>")` function invocation we want to chain to the `var html` variable. This is quite simple because we just need to chain it without making many changes. Now let's take a look at a change in the `var html` assignment:

```
var html =
  new StringBuilder()
  .AppendFormattedLine("<ol id="{0}">", id)
  .AppendWhen(
    () => includeSun,
    sb => sb.AppendLine("\t<li>The Sun/li>"))
  .AppendSequence(
    options,
    (sb, opt) =>
      sb.AppendFormattedLine(
        "\t<li value="{0}">{1}</li>",
        opt.Key,
        opt.Value))
  .AppendLine("</ol>");
```

As we can see in the preceding code, we refactor the `AppendLine()` method, so it is now chained to the `StringBuilder` declaration.

In the `GenerateOrderedList()` method, we have the following line of code:

```
return html.ToString();
```

We can also refactor the line so that it will be chained to the `StringBuilder` declaration in `var html`. If we chain it, we will have the following `var html` initialization:

```
var html =
  new StringBuilder()
```

```
    .AppendFormattedLine("<ol id="{0}">", id)
    .AppendWhen(
      () => includeSun,
      sb => sb.AppendLine("\t<li>The Sun/li>"))
    .AppendSequence(
      options,
      (sb, opt) =>
        sb.AppendFormattedLine(
        "\t<li value="{0}">{1}</li>",
        opt.Key,
        opt.Value))
    .AppendLine("</ol>")
    .ToString();
```

Unfortunately, if we compile the code now, it will yield the *CS0161* error with the following explanation:

```
'Utility.GenerateOrderedList(IDictionary<int, string>, string, bool)': not
all code paths return a value
```

The error occurs because the method doesn't return any value when it's expected to return a string value. However, since it is functional programming, we can refactor this method in an expression member. The complete `GenerateOrderedList()` method will be as follows:

```
public static partial class Utility
{
  public static string GenerateOrderedList(
    IDictionary<int, string> options,
    string id,
    bool includeSun) =>
      new StringBuilder()
      .AppendFormattedLine("<ol id="{0}">", id)
      .AppendWhen(
        () => includeSun,
        sb => sb.AppendLine("\t<li>The Sun/li>"))
      .AppendSequence(
        options,
        (sb, opt) =>
          sb.AppendFormattedLine(
          "\t<li value="{0}">{1}</li>",
          opt.Key,
          opt.Value))
      .AppendLine("</ol>")
      .ToString();
}
```

We have removed the `return` keyword from the preceding code. We have also removed the `html` variable. We now have a function that has bodies as lambda-like expressions instead of statement blocks. This feature was announced in .NET Framework 4.6.

The Main() method

The `Main()` method in `FunctionalCode.csproj` is a typical method we usually face when programming in C#. The method flow is as follows: it reads data from the stream into the byte array and then converts those bytes into strings. After that, it performs a transformation to modify that string before passing it to the `GenerateOrderedList()` method.

If we look at the starting code lines, we get the following code snippet:

```
byte[] buffer;
using (var stream = Utility.GeneratePlanetsStream())
{
    buffer = new byte[stream.Length];
    stream.Read(buffer, 0, (int)stream.Length);
}
```

We need to refactor the preceding code to be able to be chained. For this purpose, we create a new class named `Disposable`, containing the `Using()` method. The `Using()` method inside the `Disposable` class is as follows:

```
public static class Disposable
{
  public static TResult Using<TDisposable, TResult>
  (
    Func<TDisposable> factory,
    Func<TDisposable, TResult> fn)
    where TDisposable : IDisposable
    {
      using (var disposable = factory())
      {
        return fn(disposable);
      }
    }
}
```

In the preceding `Using()` method, we take two arguments: `factory` and `fn`. The function to which the `IDisposable` interface applies is `factory`, and `fn` is the function that will be executed after declaring the `factory` function. Now we can refactor the starting lines in the `Main()` method as follows:

```
var buffer =
  Disposable
  .Using(
    Utility.GeneratePlanetsStream,
    stream =>
    {
      var buff = new byte[stream.Length];
      stream.Read(buff, 0, (int)stream.Length);
      return buff;
    });
```

Compared to imperative code, we have now refactored the code that reads the stream and stores it in a byte array with the help of the `Dispose.Using()` method. We ask the lambda stream function to return the buff content. Now, we have a buffer variable to be passed to the next phase, which is the `UTF8.GetString(buffer)` method. What we actually do in the `GetString(buffer)` method is transforming and then mapping the buffer to a string. In order to chain this method, we need to create the `Map` method extension. The method will look as follows:

```
public static partial class FunctionalExtensions
{
  public static TResult Map<TSource, TResult>(
    this TSource @this,
    Func<TSource, TResult> fn) =>
    fn(@this);
}
```

Since we need to make it a general method, we use a generic type in the arguments of the method. We also use a generic type in the returning value so that it won't return only the string value. Using the generic types, this `Map` extension method will be able to transform any static type value into another static type value. We need to use an expression body member for this method, so we use the lambda expression here. Now we can use this `Map` method for the `UTF8.GetString()` method. The `var buffer` initialization will be as follows:

```
var buffer =
  Disposable
  .Using(
    Utility.GeneratePlanetsStream,
    stream =>
```

```
  {
    var buff = new byte[stream.Length];
    stream.Read(buff, 0, (int)stream.Length);
    return buff;
  })
  .Map(Encoding.UTF8.GetString)
  .Split(new[] { Environment.NewLine, },
  StringSplitOptions.RemoveEmptyEntries)
.Select((s, ix) => Tuple.Create(ix, s))
.ToDictionary(k => k.Item1, v => v.Item2);
```

By applying the `Map` method like the preceding code snippet, we don't need the following code anymore:

```
var options =
  Encoding
  .UTF8
  .GetString(buffer)
  .Split(new[] { Environment.NewLine, },
    StringSplitOptions.RemoveEmptyEntries)
  .Select((s, ix) => Tuple.Create(ix, s))
  .ToDictionary(k => k.Item1, v => v.Item2);
```

However, the problem occurs since the next code needs variable options as arguments to the `GenerateOrderedList()` method, which we can see in following code snippet:

```
var orderedList = Utility.GenerateOrderedList(
  options, "thePlanets", true);
```

To solve this problem, we can use the `Map` methods as well to chain the `GenerateOrderedList()` method to the buffer variable initialization so that we can remove the `orderedList` variable. Now, the code will be look like what is shown in the following:

```
var buffer =
  Disposable
  .Using(
    Utility.GeneratePlanetsStream,
    stream =>
    {
      var buff = new byte[stream.Length];
      stream.Read(buff, 0, (int)stream.Length);
      return buff;
    })
  .Map(Encoding.UTF8.GetString)
  .Split(new[] { Environment.NewLine, },
    StringSplitOptions.RemoveEmptyEntries)
```

[49]

```
      .Select((s, ix) => Tuple.Create(ix, s))
      .ToDictionary(k => k.Item1, v => v.Item2)
      .Map(options => Utility.GenerateOrderedList(
        options, "thePlanets", true));
```

Since the last line of code is the `Console.WriteLine()` method, which takes the `orderedList` variable as an argument, we can modify the buffer variable to `orderedList`. The change will be as follows:

```
var orderedList =
  Disposable
  .Using(
    Utility.GeneratePlanetsStream,
    stream =>
    {
      var buff = new byte[stream.Length];
      stream.Read(buff, 0, (int)stream.Length);
      return buff;
    })
  .Map(Encoding.UTF8.GetString)
  .Split(new[] { Environment.NewLine, },
    StringSplitOptions.RemoveEmptyEntries)
  .Select((s, ix) => Tuple.Create(ix, s))
  .ToDictionary(k => k.Item1, v => v.Item2)
  .Map(options => Utility.GenerateOrderedList(
    options, "thePlanets", true));
```

The last line in the `GenerateOrderedList()` method is the `Console.WriteLine()` method. We will also chain this method to the `orderedList` variable. For this purpose, we need to extend a method called `Tee`, containing the pipelining technique we discussed earlier. Let's take a look at the following `Tee` method extension:

```
public static partial class FunctionalExtensions
{
  public static T Tee<T>(
    this T @this,
    Action<T> action)
  {
    action(@this);
    return @this;
  }
}
```

From the preceding code, we can see that the output of `Tee` will be passed to the input of the `Action` function. Then, we can chain the last line using `Tee`, as follows:

```
Disposable
  .Using(
    Utility.GeneratePlanetsStream,
    stream =>
    {
      var buff = new byte[stream.Length];
      stream.Read(buff, 0, (int)stream.Length);
      return buff;
    })
  .Map(Encoding.UTF8.GetString)
  .Split(new[] { Environment.NewLine, },
    StringSplitOptions.RemoveEmptyEntries)
  .Select((s, ix) => Tuple.Create(ix, s))
  .ToDictionary(k => k.Item1, v => v.Item2)
  .Map(options => Utility.GenerateOrderedList(
    options, "thePlanets", true))
  .Tee(Console.WriteLine);
```

`Tee` can return the HTML generated by the `GenerateOrderedList()` method so that we can remove the `orderedList` variable from the code.

We can also implement the `Tee` method to the lambda expression in the preceding code. We will refactor the following code snippet using `Tee`:

```
stream =>
{
  var buff = new byte[stream.Length];
  stream.Read(buff, 0, (int)stream.Length);
  return buff;
}
```

Let's understand what the preceding code snippet is actually doing. First, we initialize the byte array variable `buff` to store as many bytes as the length of the stream. It then populates this byte array using the `stream.Read` method before returning the byte array. We can also ask the `Tee` method to do this job. The code will be as follows:

```
Disposable
  .Using(
    Utility.GeneratePlanetsStream,
    stream => new byte[stream.Length]
  .Tee(b => stream.Read(
    b, 0, (int)stream.Length)))
  .Map(Encoding.UTF8.GetString)
  .Split(new[] { Environment.NewLine, },
```

```
    StringSplitOptions.RemoveEmptyEntries)
.Select((s, ix) => Tuple.Create(ix, s))
.ToDictionary(k => k.Item1, v => v.Item2)
.Map(options => Utility.GenerateOrderedList(
  options, "thePlanets", true))
.Tee(Console.WriteLine);
```

Now, we have a new `Main()` method, applying method chaining to approach functional programming.

The advantages and disadvantages of functional programming

So far, we have had to deal with functional programming by creating code using functional approach. Now, we can look at the advantages of the functional approach, such as the following:

- The order of execution doesn't matter since it is handled by the system to compute the value we have given rather than the one defined by programmer. In other words, the declarative of the expressions will become unique. Because functional programs have an approach toward mathematical concepts, the system will be designed with the notation as close as possible to the mathematical way of concept.

- Variables can be replaced by their value since the evaluation of expression can be done any time. The functional code is then more mathematically traceable because the program is allowed to be manipulated or transformed by substituting equals with equals. This feature is called referential transparency.

- Immutability makes the functional code free of side effects. A shared variable, which is an example of a side effect, is a serious obstacle for creating parallel code and result in non-deterministic execution. By removing the side effect, we can have a good coding approach.

- The power of lazy evaluation will make the program run faster because it only provides what we really required for the queries result. Suppose we have a large amount of data and want to filter it by a specific condition, such as showing only the data that contains the word Name. In imperative programming, we will have to evaluate each operation of all the data. The problem is that when the operation takes a long time, the program will need more time to run as well. Fortunately, the functional programming that applies LINQ will perform the filtering operation only when it is needed. That's why functional programming will save much of our time using lazy evaluation.

- We have a solution for complex problems using composability. It is a rule principle that manages a problem by dividing it, and it gives pieces of the problem to several functions. The concept is similar to a situation when we organize an event and ask different people to take up a particular responsibility. By doing this, we can ensure that everything will done properly by each person.

Beside the advantages of functional programming, there are several disadvantages as well. Here are some of them:

- Since there's no state and no update of variables is allowed, loss of performance will take place. The problem occurs when we deal with a large data structure and it needs to perform a duplication of any data even though it only changes a small part of the data.
- Compared to imperative programming, much garbage will be generated in functional programming due to the concept of immutability, which needs more variables to handle specific assignments. Because we cannot control the garbage collection, the performance will decrease as well.

Summary

So far, we have been acquainted with the functional approach by discussing the introduction of functional programming. We also have compared the functional approach to the mathematical concept when we create functional program. It's now clear that the functional approach uses the mathematical approach to compose a functional program.

There are three important points in constructing the function; they are definition, script, and session. The definition is the equation between particular expressions that describe the mathematical function. Script is a collection of definitions that are supplied by the programmer. Session is a situation where the program submits the expressions that can contain references to the function defined in the script to the computer for evaluation.

The comparison between functional and imperative programming also led us to the important point of distinguishing the two. It's now clear that in functional programming, the programmer focuses on the kind of desired information and the kind of required transformation, while in the imperative approach, the programmer focuses on the way of performing the task and tracking changes in the state.

We also explored several concepts of functional programming, such as first-class and higher-order functions, pure functions, and recursive functions. The first-class and higher-order functions concept treats the functions as values so that we can assign it to a variable and pass it to the argument of the function. The pure functions concept makes the function have no side-effect. Recursive functions help us iterate the function itself with the power of aggregate in LINQ. Also, functions in functional programming have several characteristics that we need to know, such as the following:

It always returns the same value every time it is given the same set of inputs.

It never references a variable defined outside the function.

It cannot change the value of the variable since it applies the immutable concept.

It doesn't contain any I/O, such as a fancy output or a keyboard stroke, since no side-effect occurrence is allowed.

When we test functional program in C#, we take the mathematical approach to find out how to compose a function in C# from a mathematical function. We learn how to curry the curried function to pass the second argument after we assign the first argument alone. Also, we now know how to make the program functional using pipelining and the method chaining technique.

After finishing with learning the techniques for creating functional programming, we translate the imperative approach code into the functional approach code. Here, we compose the imperative code from scratch and then refactor it into functional code.

Lastly, after we become more familiar with functional programming, we can grasp the advantages and disadvantages of functional programming itself. This will be the reason why we need to learn functional programming.

In the next chapter, we will talk about delegate data type to encapsulates a method that has particular parameters and return type. It is useful when we need create a cleaner and an easier function pointer.

2
Walkthrough Delegates

In the previous chapter, we applied delegates in the code we created. When we discussed the concept of functional programming, we applied one of the built-in delegates that C# has. In this chapter, we are going to delve into the delegates that will be used a lot in functional C# programming by discussing the following topics:

- The definition, syntax, and use of delegates
- Combining delegates into multicast delegates
- Using built-in delegates
- Understanding the variance in delegates

Introducing delegates

A delegate is a data type in C# that encapsulates a method that has particular parameters and return types (signatures). In other words, a delegate will define the parameters and the return type of a method. Delegates are similar to function pointers in C/C++ since both stores the reference to the method with a particular signature. Like a function pointer in C/C++, a delegate keeps a memory address of the method it refers to. The compiler will complain if it refers to a function with a different signature. However, because of the unmanaged nature of the C++ language, one can point functions to arbitrary locations (by casting).

Let's take a look at the following delegate syntax:

```
[AccessModifier] delegate ReturnType DelegateName([parameters]);
```

Here is the explanation for each element of the preceding delegate syntax:

- **AccessModifier**: This is the modifier that is used to set the accessibility of the delegate. It can be public, private, internal, or protected. However, we can omit it, and if we do that, the default modifier will be internal.
- **delegate**: This is the keyword we need in order to initialize a delegate.
- **ReturnType**: This is a returning data type of the method we assign to this delegate.
- **DelegateName**: This is the identity of the delegate.
- **parameters**: This is the list of parameters that the method we assign to this delegate takes.

By referring to the preceding syntax, we can initialize the delegate, for instance, `SingleStringDelegate`:

```
public delegate void SingleStringDelegate(string dataString);
```

Since we have the preceding delegate, we can assign a method possessing the same signature to the delegate. The method can be as follows:

```
private static void AssignData(string dataString)
{
  globalString = dataString;
}
```

Or, the method can be as follows:

```
private static void WriteToConsole(string dataText)
{
  Console.WriteLine(dataText);
}
```

Since both methods have an identical signature, we can assign them to `SingleStringDelegate` using the following syntax:

```
SingleStringDelegate delegate1 = AssignData;
```

The preceding syntax is used to assign the `AssignData()` method to a variable typed `SingleStringDelegate`, and for the `WriteToConsole()` method, we can use the following syntax:

```
SingleStringDelegate delegate2 = WriteToConsole;
```

It is common to name a delegate type ending with the word `Delegate`—for example, `SingleStringDelegate`—in order to be able to distinguish the delegate name and the method name. However, it is not mandatory and we can omit this.

Simple delegates

For further discussion on delegates, let's take a look at the following method, which we can find at `SimpleDelegates.csproj`:

```
public partial class Program
{
  static int Rectangle(int a, int b)
  {
    return a * b;
  }
}
```

The `Rectangle()` method in the preceding code can be assigned to the delegate variable given in the following code:

```
public partial class Program
{
  private delegate int AreaCalculatorDelegate(int x, int y);
}
```

The following method can also be assigned to the `AreaCalculatorDelegate` delegate because the signature of the method is what the delegate type expects:

```
public partial class Program
{
  static int Square(int x, int y)
  {
    return x * y;
  }
}
```

To assign a method to a delegate, we just need to create a variable of the delegate data type which has signature compatibility with the method to be assigned. The following is the `Main()` method, which will create the delegate variable and invoke the method:

```
public partial class Program
{
  static void Main(string[] args)
  {
```

```
        AreaCalculatorDelegate rect = Rectangle;
        AreaCalculatorDelegate sqr = Square;
        int i = rect(1, 2);
        int j = sqr(2, 3);
        Console.WriteLine("i = " + i);
        Console.WriteLine("j = " + j);
    }
}
```

From the preceding code, we create two variables named `rect` and `sqr` whose type is `AreaCalculatorDelegate`. Here is the code snippet:

```
    AreaCalculatorDelegate rect = Rectangle;
    AreaCalculatorDelegate sqr = Square;
```

Since we have assigned the `rect` and `sqr` variables to the `Rectangle()` and `Square()` methods, we can invoke these methods using the delegate variable. Let's take a look at the following code snippet:

```
    int i = rect(1, 2);
    int j = sqr(2, 3);
```

We assign variable `i` and `j` with the result of `rect()` and `sqr()`. Although both of them are variable names, they refer to the method address location. One invokes a method referred by these variables to execute the logic contained. We are effectively executing the two `Console.WriteLine()` methods to produce the following output:

It is now clear to the reader that why we display the output shown in the preceding screenshot. The `rect` and `sqr` variables now store the reference to `Rectangle()` and `Square()` methods respectively. We are effectively calling the `Rectangle()` method while invoking the `rect` delegate and `Square()` method, all the while invoking the `sqr` delegate.

Multicast delegates

We have just discussed a simple delegate where we assign a particular method to a delegate variable. We can call it a unicast delegate. However, the delegates can actually invoke multiple methods using one variable. For this purpose, we can call it a multicast delegate. In the case of multicast delegate, it is like a list of delegates stored inside an internal list. When we invoke a multicast delegate, the delegates in the list are synchronously called in the correct order. There are several ways to create a multicast delegate. The two we will discuss in detail are the `Delegate.Combine()` and `Delegate.Remove()` methods and the += and -= (increment and decrement) operators.

Using the Delegate.Combine() and Delegate.Remove() methods

Let's first examine the following code, creating a multicast delegate using the `Delegate.Combine()` method. Suppose we have a delegate named `CalculatorDelegate`, as follows, which we can find at `CombineDelegates.csproj`:

```
public partial class Program
{
  private delegate void CalculatorDelegate(int a, int b);
}
```

Then, we have the following four methods that have the same signature as the `CalculatorDelegate` signature:

```
public partial class Program
{
  private static void Add(int x, int y)
  {
    Console.WriteLine(
      "{0} + {1} = {2}",
      x,
      y,
      x + y);
  }
  private static void Subtract(int x, int y)
  {
    Console.WriteLine(
      "{0} - {1} = {2}",
      x,
      y,
      x - y);
  }
```

```
private static void Multiply(int x, int y)
{
  Console.WriteLine(
    "{0} * {1} = {2}",
    x,
    y,
    x * y);
}
private static void Division(int x, int y)
{
  Console.WriteLine(
    "{0} / {1} = {2}",
    x,
    y,
    x / y);
}
}
```

There are four methods, and they are `Add()`, `Subtract()`, `Multiply()`, and `Division()`. We are going to cast these methods in a single variable-typed delegate. Now, take a look at the following `CombineDelegate()` method to achieve this goal:

```
public partial class Program
{
  private static void CombineDelegate()
  {
    CalculatorDelegate calcMultiples =
      (CalculatorDelegate)Delegate.Combine(
      new CalculatorDelegate[] {
      Add,
      Subtract,
      Multiply,
      Division });
    Delegate[] calcList = calcMultiples.GetInvocationList();
    Console.WriteLine(
      "Total delegates in calcMultiples: {0}",
      calcList.Length);
    calcMultiples(6, 3);
  }
}
```

If we run this method, the following output will be displayed:

We have successfully invoked four methods by calling a single delegate. The delegate we called in the preceding code is in the following code snippet:

```
calcMultiples(6, 3);
```

Actually `calcMultiples` delegate has stored four delegates variables internally, corresponding to each of the method which we combined. Thanks to the `Delegate.Combine()` method, we can combine the delegates using the following syntax:

```
CalculatorDelegate calcMultiples =
  (CalculatorDelegate)Delegate.Combine(
    new CalculatorDelegate[] {
      Add,
      Subtract,
      Multiply,
      Division });
```

We can also create the array of delegates by calling `GetInvocationList()` from the delegate variable. By retrieving the delegate array, we can iterate over the array like we do for ordinary arrays. We can retrieve the `Length` property to count how many delegates are there in the invocation list.

In multicast delegates, we are able to combine as well remove delegates from the invocation list. Let's take a look at the following `RemoveDelegate()` method:

```
public partial class Program
{
  private static void RemoveDelegate()
  {
    CalculatorDelegate addDel = Add;
    CalculatorDelegate subDel = Subtract;
    CalculatorDelegate mulDel = Multiply;
    CalculatorDelegate divDel = Division;
    CalculatorDelegate calcDelegates1 =
      (CalculatorDelegate)Delegate.Combine(
      addDel,
      subDel);
    CalculatorDelegate calcDelegates2 =
```

```
        (CalculatorDelegate)Delegate.Combine(
        calcDelegates1,
        mulDel);
    CalculatorDelegate calcDelegates3 =
        (CalculatorDelegate)Delegate.Combine(
        calcDelegates2,
        divDel);
    Console.WriteLine(
        "Total delegates in calcDelegates3: {0}",
        calcDelegates3.GetInvocationList().Length);
    calcDelegates3(6, 3);
    CalculatorDelegate calcDelegates4 =
        (CalculatorDelegate)Delegate.Remove(
        calcDelegates3,
        mulDel);
    Console.WriteLine(
        "Total delegates in calcDelegates4: {0}",
        calcDelegates4.GetInvocationList().Length);
    calcDelegates4(6, 3);
    }
}
```

If we run the preceding method, the following output will be displayed in the console:

Similar to the `CombineDelegate()` method, we combine the four methods into a single variable-typed delegate in the `RemoveDelegate()` method. The `calcDelegates3` delegate is the delegate that keeps the four methods. Indeed, when we invoke `calcDelegates3`, it calls the four methods in a proper order. Next, in the `RemoveDelegate()` method, we invoke the `Delegate.Remove()` method in order to remove the selected delegate in the invocation list. Based on the preceding code, the syntax is as follows:

```
CalculatorDelegate calcDelegates4 =
    (CalculatorDelegate)Delegate.Remove(
    calcDelegates3,
    mulDel);
```

The preceding code snippet is used to remove the `mulDel` delegate variable from the invocation list. As we can see in the preceding figure displaying the output of the `RemoveDelegate()` invocation, the `Multiply()` method is no longer invoked right after it's removed from invocation list.

An invocation list associated with a delegate can contain duplicate entries. This means that we can add the same method to the invocation list more than once. Now let's try to insert the duplicate entries into the invocation list by adding the `DuplicateEntries()` method to the project, as follows:

```
public partial class Program
{
  private static void DuplicateEntries()
  {
    CalculatorDelegate addDel = Add;
    CalculatorDelegate subDel = Subtract;
    CalculatorDelegate mulDel = Multiply;
    CalculatorDelegate duplicateDelegates1 =
      (CalculatorDelegate)Delegate.Combine(
      addDel,
      subDel);
    CalculatorDelegate duplicateDelegates2 =
      (CalculatorDelegate)Delegate.Combine(
      duplicateDelegates1,
      mulDel);
    CalculatorDelegate duplicateDelegates3 =
      (CalculatorDelegate)Delegate.Combine(
      duplicateDelegates2,
      subDel);
    CalculatorDelegate duplicateDelegates4 =
      (CalculatorDelegate)Delegate.Combine(
      duplicateDelegates3,
      addDel);
    Console.WriteLine(
      "Total delegates in duplicateDelegates4: {0}",
      duplicateDelegates4.GetInvocationList().Length);
    duplicateDelegates4(6, 3);
  }
}
```

Now let's run the `DuplicateEntries()` method, and the console will show the following output:

By examining the preceding code, we can see that the `duplicateDelegates2` variable contains three invocation methods, which are `addDel`, `subDel`, and `mulDel`. Look at the following code snippet for more details:

```
CalculatorDelegate duplicateDelegates1 =
    (CalculatorDelegate)Delegate.Combine(
    addDel,
    subDel);
CalculatorDelegate duplicateDelegates2 =
    (CalculatorDelegate)Delegate.Combine(
    duplicateDelegates1,
    mulDel);
```

Again, we add `subDel` and `addDel` to the invocation list like we do in the following code snippet:

```
CalculatorDelegate duplicateDelegates3 =
    (CalculatorDelegate)Delegate.Combine(
    duplicateDelegates2,
    subDel);
CalculatorDelegate duplicateDelegates4 =
    (CalculatorDelegate)Delegate.Combine(
    duplicateDelegates3,
    addDel);
```

Now, the invocation list of `duplicateDelegates4` contains two duplicate methods. However, when we invoke the `DuplicateEntries()` method, `addDel` and `subDel` are invoked twice and the invocation order is just like the order in which we add the delegate to the invocation list.

The `Delegate.Combine()` and `Delegate.Remove()` static methods will return the `Delegate` data type instead of the instance of `Delegate` itself. As a result, casting the return of both methods to the expected instance delegate is required when using them.

Using += and -= operators

It's quite easy to create multicast delegates using += and -= operators since that will be like treating any data types in C#. We can also use the + and - operators to add and remove delegates in an invocation list. Here is the sample code we can find at `AddSubtractDelegates.csproj` in order to combine delegates and remove select delegates from the invocation list using the operator:

```
public partial class Program
{
  private static void AddSubtractDelegate()
  {
    CalculatorDelegate addDel = Add;
    CalculatorDelegate subDel = Subtract;
    CalculatorDelegate mulDel = Multiply;
    CalculatorDelegate divDel = Division;
    CalculatorDelegate multiDel = addDel + subDel;
    multiDel += mulDel;
    multiDel += divDel;
    Console.WriteLine(
      "Invoking multiDel delegate (four methods):");
    multiDel(8, 2);
    multiDel = multiDel - subDel;
    multiDel -= mulDel;
    Console.WriteLine(
      "Invoking multiDel delegate (after subtraction):");
    multiDel(8, 2);
  }
}
```

We also have the four methods that we use in the preceding project, `CombineDelegates.csproj`: `Add()`, `Subtract()`, `Multiply()`, and `Division()`. We will get the following output if we run the `AddSubtractDelegate()` method:

In the starting lines of the `AddSubtractDelegate()` method, we create four variables typed `CalculatorDelegate` for each of the four methods we have, just like we did in the previous project. We then create one more variable named `multiDel` in order to generate the multicast delegate. Here, we can see that we add the delegate to the multicast delegate variable using the operator only, in which we use the + and += operators. Let's take a look at the following code snippet:

```
CalculatorDelegate multiDel = addDel + subDel;
multiDel += mulDel;
multiDel += divDel;
Console.WriteLine(
  "Invoking multiDel delegate (four methods):");
multiDel(8, 2);
```

From the preceding code snippet, after combining all four delegates into the `multiDel` delegate, we call the `multiDel` delegate, and what we get based on the output console display is the program to invoke the four methods in a proper order. The four methods are `Add()`, `Subtract()`, `Multiply()`, and `Division()`.

To remove the delegate from the invocation list, we use the – and –= operators in the preceding code. Let's take a look at the following code snippet to examine what we have to do in order to remove the delegate:

```
multiDel = multiDel - subDel;
multiDel -= mulDel;
Console.WriteLine(
  "Invoking multiDel delegate (after subtraction):");
multiDel(8, 2);
```

Since we have removed the `subDel` and `mulDel` delegates from the invocation list, the program only calls two methods, the `Add()` and `Division()` methods, when we invoke the `mulDel` delegate. This proves that we have successfully removed the delegate from the invocation list using the – and –= operators.

> Using += and –= to assign a multicast delegate doesn't fit the functional programming approach since it breaks the immutability concept. However, we can still use the + and – operators to add a delegate to the invocation list and remove the delegate from the invocation list consecutively in a functional approach.

Built-in delegates

In C#, not only are we able to declare a delegate, but we are also able to use the built-in delegate from the C# standard library. This built-in delegate also applies to the generic data type, so let's discuss the generic delegate prior to discussing the built-in delegate.

Generic delegates

A delegate type can use a generic type as its parameter. Using the generic type, we can put off the specification of one or more types in parameters or return values until the delegate is initialized into a variable. In other words, we do not specify the data types of the delegate's parameters and return values when we define a delegate type. To discuss this in more detail, let's take a look at the following code, which we can find at `GenericDelegates.csproj`:

```
public partial class Program
{
  private delegate T FormulaDelegate<T>(T a, T b);
}
```

We have a delegate name, `FormulaDelegate`, using the generic data type. As we can see, there is a `T` symbol, which represents the data type we will define when declaring the variable typed `FormulaDelegate`. We continue by adding the following two methods that have completely different signatures:

```
public partial class Program
{
  private static int AddInt(int x, int y)
  {
    return x + y;
```

```
    }
    private static double AddDouble(double x, double y)
    {
      return x + y;
    }
  }
```

Now let's take a look at the following code in order to explain how we declare the variable-typed delegate and invoke the method from the delegate:

```
public partial class Program
{
  private static void GenericDelegateInvoke()
  {
    FormulaDelegate<int> intAddition = AddInt;
    FormulaDelegate<double> doubleAddition = AddDouble;
    Console.WriteLine("Invoking intAddition(2, 3)");
    Console.WriteLine(
      "Result = {0}",
      intAddition(2, 3));
    Console.WriteLine("Invoking doubleAddition(2.2, 3.5)");
    Console.WriteLine(
      "Result = {0}",
      doubleAddition(2.2, 3.5));
  }
}
```

The following result will be displayed in the console when we run the `GenericDelegateInvoke()` method:

From the preceding code, we can declare two methods that have different signature using only one delegate type. The `intAddition` delegate refers to the `AddInt()` method, which applies the `int` data type in its parameters and return value, while the `doubleAddition` delegate refers to the `AddDouble()` method, which applies the `double` data type in its parameters and return value. However, in order for the delegate to know the data type of the method it refers, we have to define the data type in angular brackets (<>) when we initialize the delegate. The following code snippet is the delegate initialization that uses the generic data type (symbolized by the angular brackets):

```
FormulaDelegate<int> intAddition = AddInt;
FormulaDelegate<double> doubleAddition = AddDouble;
```

Because we have defined the data type, the delegate can match the data type of the method it refers. That's why, from the output console, we can invoke the two methods that have different signatures.

We have successfully used a generic type for delegates, applying one generic template. The following code, which we can find at `MultiTemplateDelegates.csproj`, shows us that the delegate can also apply the multigeneric template in one delegate declaration:

```
public partial class Program
{
  private delegate void AdditionDelegate<T1, T2>(
    T1 value1, T2 value2);
}
```

The preceding code will create a new delegate named `AdditionDelegate`, which has two parameters with two different data types. `T1` and `T2` represent the data type that will be defined in the variable-typed delegate declaration. Now, let's create two methods that have different signatures, as follows:

```
public partial class Program
{
  private static void AddIntDouble(int x, double y)
  {
    Console.WriteLine(
      "int {0} + double {1} = {2}",
      x,
      y,
      x + y);
  }
  private static void AddFloatDouble(float x, double y)
  {
    Console.WriteLine(
      "float {0} + double {1} = {2}",
      x,
      y,
      x + y);
  }
}
```

To refer the `AdditionDelegate` delegate to the `AddIntDouble()` and `AddFloatDouble()` methods and invoke the delegate, we can create the `VoidDelegateInvoke()` method, as follows:

```
public partial class Program
{
  private static void VoidDelegateInvoke()
  {
    AdditionDelegate<int, double> intDoubleAdd =
      AddIntDouble;
    AdditionDelegate<float, double> floatDoubleAdd =
      AddFloatDouble;
    Console.WriteLine("Invoking intDoubleAdd delegate");
    intDoubleAdd(1, 2.5);
    Console.WriteLine("Invoking floatDoubleAdd delegate");
    floatDoubleAdd((float)1.2, 4.3);
  }
}
```

If we run the `VoidDelegateInvoke()` method, we will see the following output on our console:

From the preceding console output, it can be seen that we have successfully invoked the `intDoubleAdd` and `floatDoubleAdd` delegates although they have different method signatures. This is possible since we apply the `T1` and `T2` template in the `AdditionDelegate` delegate.

Let's try to create the multitemplate delegate again, but this time, we use the method that has a return value. The declaration of the delegate will be as follows:

```
public partial class Program
{
  private delegate TResult AddAndConvert<T1, T2, TResult>(
    T1 digit1, T2 digit2);
}
```

Then, we add the two methods `AddIntDoubleConvert()` and
`AddFloatDoubleConvert()` to our project:

```
public partial class Program
{
  private static float AddIntDoubleConvert(int x, double y)
  {
    float result = (float)(x + y);
    Console.WriteLine(
      "(int) {0} + (double) {1} = (float) {2}",
      x,
      y,
      result);
    return result;
  }
  private static int AddFloatDoubleConvert(float x, double y)
  {
    int result = (int)(x + y);
    Console.WriteLine(
      "(float) {0} + (double) {1} = (int) {2}",
      x,
      y,
      result);
    return result;
  }
}
```

In order to use the `AddAndConvert` delegate, we can create the
`ReturnValueDelegateInvoke()` method, as follows:

```
public partial class Program
{
  private static void ReturnValueDelegateInvoke()
  {
    AddAndConvert<int, double, float>
        intDoubleAddConvertToFloat = AddIntDoubleConvert;
    AddAndConvert<float, double, int>
        floatDoubleAddConvertToInt = AddFloatDoubleConvert;
    Console.WriteLine("Invoking intDoubleAddConvertToFloat delegate");
    float f = intDoubleAddConvertToFloat(5, 3.9);
    Console.WriteLine("Invoking floatDoubleAddConvertToInt delegate");
    int i = floatDoubleAddConvertToInt((float)4.3, 2.1);
  }
}
```

[71]

When we invoke the `ReturnValueDelegateInvoke()` method, we get the following output:

Again, we successfully invoke the two different signature methods using a multitemplate generic type.

The Action and Func delegates

Let's go back to the following delegate declaration we discussed earlier in the chapter:

```
public partial class Program
{
  private delegate void AdditionDelegate<T1, T2>(
    T1 value1, T2 value2);
}
```

C# has a built-in delegate that can take a maximum of 16 parameters and return void. It is called the `Action` delegate. In other words, the `Action` delegate will point to a method that return nothing and takes zero, one, or more input parameters. Due to the existence of the `Action` delegate, we no longer need to declare a delegate, and we can immediately assign any method to the delegate. We can modify the preceding `MultiTemplateDelegates.csproj` project and remove the `AdditionDelegate` delegate since we will now use the `Action` delegate. Then, the `ActionDelegateInvoke()` method in `MultiTemplateDelegates.csproj` will be modified to become `ActionDelegateInvoke()` with the following implementation:

```
public partial class Program
{
  private static void ActionDelegateInvoke()
  {
    Action<int, double> intDoubleAddAction =
      AddIntDouble;
    Action<float, double> floatDoubleAddAction =
      AddFloatDouble;
    Console.WriteLine(
      "Invoking intDoubleAddAction delegate");
    intDoubleAddAction(1, 2.5);
```

```
      Console.WriteLine(
        "Invoking floatDoubleAddAction delegate");
      floatDoubleAddAction((float)1.2, 4.3);
  }
}
```

We can find the preceding code in the `ActionFuncDelegates.csproj` project. As we can see, now we apply the `Action` delegate to replace the `AdditionDelegate` delegate in the `MultiTemplateDelegates.csproj` project, as follows:

```
Action<int, double> intDoubleAddAction =
  AddIntDouble;
Action<float, double> floatDoubleAddAction =
  AddFloatDouble;
```

C# has another built-in delegate that has a return value by taking a maximum of 16 parameters. They are `Func` delegates. Let's go back to the `MultiTemplateDelegates.csproj` project and find the following delegate:

```
public partial class Program
{
  private delegate TResult AddAndConvert<T1, T2, TResult>(
    T1 digit1, T2 digit2);
}
```

We can remove the preceding delegate since it matches the declaration of the `Func` delegate. So, we can modify the `ReturnValueDelegateInvoke()` method in the `MultiTemplateDelegates.csproj` project for it to become the `FuncDelegateInvoke()` method with the following implementation:

```
public partial class Program
{
  private static void FuncDelegateInvoke()
  {
    Func<int, double, float>
        intDoubleAddConvertToFloatFunc =
          AddIntDoubleConvert;
    Func<float, double, int>
        floatDoubleAddConvertToIntFunc =
          AddFloatDoubleConvert;
    Console.WriteLine(
      "Invoking intDoubleAddConvertToFloatFunc delegate");
    float f = intDoubleAddConvertToFloatFunc(5, 3.9);
    Console.WriteLine(
      "Invoking floatDoubleAddConvertToIntFunc delegate");
    int i = floatDoubleAddConvertToIntFunc((float)4.3, 2.1);
  }
```

```
        }
```

Now, we no longer need the `AddAndConvert` delegate anymore since we have applied the `Func` delegate, as follows:

```
Func<int, double, float>
   intDoubleAddConvertToFloatFunc = AddIntDoubleConvert;
Func<float, double, int>
   floatDoubleAddConvertToIntFunc = AddFloatDoubleConvert;
```

Using the `Action` and `Func` built-in delegates, the code becomes shorter and the definition of the delegate becomes easier and quicker.

Distinguishing variance in delegates

A generic delegate has the ability to be assigned by a method that has an unmatched signature to the delegate. We can call this variance in delegates. There are two variances in delegates, and they are covariance and contravariance. Covariance allows a method to have a return type that is more derived (subtype) than the return type that is defined in the delegate. On the other hand, contravariance allows a method to have parameter types that are less derived (supertype) than the parameter types that are defined in the delegate.

Covariance

The following is an example of covariance in delegates, which we can find in the `Covariance.csproj` project. First, we initialize the following delegate:

```
public partial class Program
{
   private delegate TextWriter CovarianceDelegate();
}
```

We now have a delegate returning the `TextWriter` data type. Then, we also create the `StreamWriterMethod()` method returning the `StreamWriter` object, which has the following implementation:

```
public partial class Program
{
   private static StreamWriter StreamWriterMethod()
   {
      DirectoryInfo[] arrDirs =
         new DirectoryInfo(@"C:\Windows")
      .GetDirectories(
```

```
      "s*",
       SearchOption.TopDirectoryOnly);

    StreamWriter sw = new StreamWriter(
    Console.OpenStandardOutput());

    foreach (DirectoryInfo dir in arrDirs)
    {
      sw.WriteLine(dir.Name);
    }

    return sw;
  }
}
```

We create the `StringWriterMethod()` method as well, returning the `StringWriter` object with the following implementation:

```
public partial class Program
{
  private static StringWriter StringWriterMethod()
  {
    StringWriter strWriter = new StringWriter();
    string[] arrString = new string[]{
      "Covariance",
      "example",
      "using",
      "StringWriter",
      "object"
    };
    foreach (string str in arrString)
    {
      strWriter.Write(str);
      strWriter.Write(' ');
    }
    return strWriter;
  }
}
```

Now, we have two methods returning different objects, `StreamWriter` and `StringWriter`. The return value data type of these methods is also different, with the `CovarianceDelegate` delegate returning the `TextWriter` object. However, since `StreamWriter` and `StringWriter` are derived from the `TextWriter` object, we can apply covariance in assigning these two methods to the `CovarianceDelegate` delegate.

Here is the `CovarianceStreamWriterInvoke()` method implementation, which assigns the `StreamWriterMethod()` method to the `CovarianceDelegate` delegate:

```
public partial class Program
{
  private static void CovarianceStreamWriterInvoke()
  {
    CovarianceDelegate covDelegate;
    Console.WriteLine(
      "Invoking CovarianceStreamWriterInvoke method:");
      covDelegate = StreamWriterMethod;
    StreamWriter sw = (StreamWriter)covDelegate();
    sw.AutoFlush = true;
    Console.SetOut(sw);
  }
}
```

In the `StreamWriterMethod()` method, we create `StreamWriter`, writing content to the console using the following code:

```
StreamWriter sw = new StreamWriter(
  Console.OpenStandardOutput());
```

Then, in the `CovarianceStreamWriterInvoke()` method, we call this code in order to write the content to the console:

```
sw.AutoFlush = true;
Console.SetOut(sw);
```

If we run the `CovarianceStreamWriterInvoke()` method, the following output will be displayed in the console:

From the preceding output console, we serve the list of directories we have inside the Visual Studio 2015 installation path. Indeed, you might have a different list if you installed a different version of Visual Studio.

Now, we are going to utilize the `StringWriterMethod()` method to create a `CovarianceDelegate` delegate. We create the `CovarianceStringWriterInvoke()` method, which has the following implementation:

```
public partial class Program
{
  private static void CovarianceStringWriterInvoke()
  {
    CovarianceDelegate covDelegate;
    Console.WriteLine(
      "Invoking CovarianceStringWriterInvoke method:");
    covDelegate = StringWriterMethod;
    StringWriter strW = (StringWriter)covDelegate();
    Console.WriteLine(strW.ToString());
  }
}
```

We have generated `StringWriter` in the `StringWriterMethod()` method using the following code:

```
StringWriter strWriter = new StringWriter();
string[] arrString = new string[]{
  // Array of string
};
foreach (string str in arrString)
{
  strWriter.Write(str);
  strWriter.Write(' ');
}
```

Then, we call the following code to write the string to the console:

```
Console.WriteLine(strW.ToString());
```

If we run the `CovarianceStringWriterInvoke()` method, the string we have defined in the `arrString` string array in the `StringWriterMethod()` method will be displayed, as follows:

```
C:\WINDOWS\system32\cmd.exe                                    —   □   ×
Invoking CovarianceStringWriterInvoke method:
Covariance example using StringWriter object
Press any key to continue . . .
```

Now, from our discussion on covariance, we have proved the covariance in delegates. The `CovarianceDelegate` delegate returning `TextWriter` can be assigned to the method returning `StreamWriter` and `StringWriter`. The following code snippet is taken from several preceding codes to conclude the covariance in delegates:

```
private delegate TextWriter CovarianceDelegate();
CovarianceDelegate covDelegate;
covDelegate = StreamWriterMethod;
covDelegate = StringWriterMethod;
```

Contravariance

Now, let's continue our discussion on variance in delegates by discussing contravariance. The following is the `ContravarianceDelegate` delegate declaration, which we can find in the `Contravariance.csproj` project:

```
public partial class Program
{
  private delegate void ContravarianceDelegate(StreamWriter sw);
}
```

The preceding delegate is going to be assigned to the following method, which has the `TextWriter` data type parameter, as follows:

```
public partial class Program
{
  private static void TextWriterMethod(TextWriter tw)
  {
    string[] arrString = new string[]{
      "Contravariance",
      "example",
      "using",
      "TextWriter",
      "object"
```

```
      };
      tw = new StreamWriter(Console.OpenStandardOutput());
      foreach (string str in arrString)
      {
        tw.Write(str);
        tw.Write(' ');
      }
      tw.WriteLine();
      Console.SetOut(tw);
      tw.Flush();
    }
}
```

The assignment will be as follows:

```
public partial class Program
{
  private static void ContravarianceTextWriterInvoke()
  {
    ContravarianceDelegate contravDelegate = TextWriterMethod;
    TextWriter tw = null;
    Console.WriteLine(
      "Invoking ContravarianceTextWriterInvoke method:");
    contravDelegate((StreamWriter)tw);
  }
}
```

If we run the `ContravarianceTextWriterInvoke()` method, the console will display the following output:

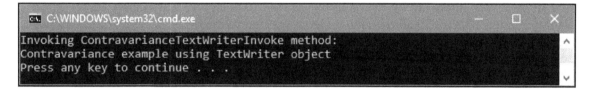

From the preceding output, we have successfully assigned a method, taking the `TextWriter` parameter to the delegate taking the `StreamWriter` parameter. This happens because `StreamWriter` is derived from `TextWriter`. Let's take a look at the following code snippet:

```
private delegate void ContravarianceDelegate(StreamWriter sw);
private static void TextWriterMethod(TextWriter tw)
{
  // Implementation
}
```

```
ContravarianceDelegate contravDelegate = TextWriterMethod;
TextWriter tw = null;
contravDelegate((StreamWriter)tw);
```

The preceding code snippet is taken from the code we discussed in contravariance. Here, we can see that `contravDelegate`, a variable typed `ContravarianceDelegate`, can be assigned to the `TextWriterMethod()` method even though they both have different signatures. This is because `StreamWriter` is derived from the `TextWriter` object. Since the `TextWriterMethod()` method can work with a `TextWriter` data type, it will surely be able to work with a `StreamWriter` data type as well.

Summary

A delegate is useful in order to encapsulate a method. It is like any data type in C# in which a variable can be initialized to have the delegate data type. Since it similar to data types, increment and decrement operations can be applied to the delegate, making it possible to create a multicast delegate from several delegates. However, one thing to remember, since the `Delegate.Combine()` and `Delegate.Remove()` methods return the `Delegate` data type, is that we have to cast the return of both methods to the expected instance delegate when using them. Compared to the += and -= operators use, however, since they are implemented at the language level in the compiler and the delegate type is known, there's no need to cast the result of the increment and decrement delegate operation.

C# also has built-in delegates, `Action` and `Func`, which make the code shorter, and the definition of the delegate becomes easier and quicker. As a result, the code gets simpler to be analyzed. Also, there are two variances in the use of delegates; covariance and contravariance, which will allow us to assign a method to the delegate. Covariance allows a method to have a return type that is more derived than the return type that is defined in the delegate, while contravariance allows a method to have the parameter types that are less derived than the parameter types that are defined in the delegate.

We now have a better understanding about delegates. Let's move on to the next chapter, where we are going to leverage the power of delegates to express anonymous methods using the lambda expression.

3

Expressing Anonymous Methods with Lambda Expressions

We covered delegates in the previous chapter, as it was a pre-requisite for understanding anonymous methods and lambda expressions, the subject of the current chapter. By using an anonymous method, we can create a delegate instance with no need to have a separate method. By using the lambda expression, we can create a shorthand syntax for the anonymous method. In this chapter, we are going to dig up the anonymous methods as well as Lambda expressions. The topics in this chapter are as follows:

- Applying delegate to create and use anonymous methods
- Transformation of anonymous methods to lambda expressions
- Understanding expression trees and its relation to lambda
- Subscribing for events using lambda expressions
- Elaborating the benefit of lambda expressions in the use of functional programming

Getting to know anonymous methods

In the previous chapter, we already discussed how to declare a delegate using named methods. When using named methods, we've have to create a method first, give it a name, and then associate it with the delegate. To refresh our memory, a simple delegate declaration associated with a named method is provided as follows:

```
delegate void DelDelegate(int x);
```

```
void DoSomething(int i) { /* Implementation */ }
DelDelegate d = DoSomething;
```

From the preceding code, we simply create a delegate data type named `DelDelegate`, and we also create a method named `DoSomething`. After we have a named method, we can associate the delegate with the method. Fortunately, anonymous methods were announced in C# 2.0 to ease the use of delegates. They provide us with a shortcut to create a simple and short method that will be used once. The syntax to declare an anonymous method is as follows:

```
delegate([parameters]) { implementation }
```

The explanation for each element of the anonymous method syntax is as follows:

- **Delegate**: The keyword we need in order to initialize a delegate.
- **Parameters**: The list of parameters that the method we assign to this delegate takes.
- **Implementation**: The code that will be executed by the method. It can apply a return statement if the method needs to return a value.

From the preceding syntax, we can see that an anonymous method is a method that doesn't have a name. We just need to define the arguments and the implementation of the method.

Creating anonymous methods

For further discussion, let's create a simple anonymous method, which we can find in the `SimpleAnonymousMethods.csproj` project, as follows:

```
public partial class Program
{
  static Func<string, string> displayMessageDelegate =
    delegate (string str)
  {
    return String.Format("Message: {0}", str);
  };
}
```

We now have an anonymous method we assign to the delegate `displayMessageDelegate` delegate. We create the `displayMessageDelegate` delegate using the `Func` built-in delegate, which takes only one string argument and a return string value as well. If we need to run the anonymous method, we can invoke the delegate as follows:

```
public partial class Program
{
  static void Main(string[] args)
  {
    Console.WriteLine(
      displayMessageDelegate(
        "A simple anonymous method sample."));
  }
}
```

After running the preceding code, we will get the following output on the console:

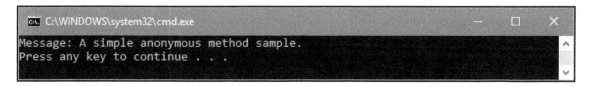

As we can see in the output console window, we have successfully invoked the anonymous method by calling the delegate name. Now, let's go back to the previous chapter to use some code from there and refactor it to an anonymous method. We are going to refactor the code of `SimpleDelegates.csproj`, which we've discussed in the previous chapter. The following is the declaration of anonymous methods, and it can be found in the `SimpleDelegatesRefactor.csproj` project:

```
public partial class Program
{
  private static Func<int, int, int> AreaRectangleDelegate =
    delegate (int a, int b)
  {
    return a * b;
  };

  private static Func<int, int, int> AreaSquareDelegate =
    delegate (int x, int y)
  {
    return x * y;
  };
}
```

We have two anonymous methods in our preceding code. We also use the `Func` delegate, the built-in delegate we discussed in the previous chapter. To invoke the methods, we can invoke the delegate name as follows:

```
public partial class Program
{
```

```
static void Main(string[] args)
{
  int i = AreaRectangleDelegate(1, 2);
  int j = AreaSquareDelegate(2, 3);
  Console.WriteLine("i = " + i);
  Console.WriteLine("j = " + j);
}
}
```

If we run the project, we will get an output like this:

Compared to the code in the `SimpleDelegates.csproj` project, our code in the preceding `SimpleDelegatesRefactor.csproj` project becomes simpler and shorter since we don't need to declare the delegate. The delegate is declared simultaneously with the creation of an anonymous method, such as the following code snippet:

```
private static Func<int, int, int> AreaRectangleDelegate =
  delegate (int a, int b)
{
  return a * b;
};
```

Here is the code we used in our previous chapter, named `SimpleDelegates.csproj`:

```
public partial class Program
{
  private delegate int AreaCalculatorDelegate(int x, int y);
  static int Square(int x, int y)
  {
    return x * y;
  }
}
```

Using anonymous delegation , we have simplified our code compared to the code produced in the previous chapter.

Using an anonymous method as an argument

We have now executed an anonymous method. However, the anonymous method can also be passed to a method as a parameter. Let's look at the following code, which we can find in the AnonymousMethodAsArgument.csproj project:

```
public partial class Program
{
  private static bool IsMultipleOfSeven(int i)
  {
    return i % 7 == 0;
  }
}
```

First, we have a method named FindMultipleOfSeven in this project. The method will be passed to the argument of the following method:

```
public partial class Program
{
  private static int FindMultipleOfSeven(List<int> numList)
  {
    return numList.Find(IsMultipleOfSeven);
  }
}
```

Then, we call the FindMultipleOfSeven() method from the following method:

```
public partial class Program
{
  private static void PrintResult()
  {
    Console.WriteLine(
      "The Multiple of 7 from the number list is {0}",
      FindMultipleOfSeven(numbers));
  }
}
```

We can also define the following List variable to be passed to the FindMultipleOfSeven() method argument:

```
public partial class Program
{
  static List<int> numbers = new List<int>()
  {
    54, 24, 91, 70, 72, 44, 61, 93,
    73, 3, 56, 5, 38, 60, 29, 32,
    86, 44, 34, 25, 22, 44, 66, 7,
```

```
    9, 59, 70, 47, 55, 95, 6, 42
  };
}
```

If we invoke the `PrintResult()` method, we will get the following output:

```
C:\WINDOWS\system32\cmd.exe                              —   □   X
The Multiple of 7 from the number list is 91
Press any key to continue . . .
```

The goal of the preceding program is to find a number that is multiplied by seven from the number list. And since `91` is the first number that meet this criteria, the `FindMultipleOfSeven()` method returns that number.

Inside the `FindMultipleOfSeven()` method, we can find the `Find()` method passing the `IsMultipleOfSeven()` method as an argument, as shown in the following code snippet:

```
return numList.Find(IsMultipleOfSeven);
```

We can, if we want, replace this method with the anonymous method, as follows:

```
public partial class Program
{
  private static int FindMultipleOfSevenLambda(
    List<int> numList)
  {
    return numList.Find(
      delegate(int i)
      {
        return i % 7 == 0;
      }
    );
  }
}
```

We now have the `FindMultipleOfSevenLambda()` method, which invokes the `Find()` method and passes the anonymous method to the method argument. Since we have passed the anonymous method, we don't need the `FindMultipleOfSeven()` method any longer. We can invoke the `FindMultipleOfSevenLambda()` method using the `PrintResultLambda()` method, as follows:

```
public partial class Program
{
  private static void PrintResultLambda()
```

```
    {
      Console.WriteLine(
        "({0}) The Multiple of 7 from the number list is {1}",
        "Lambda",
        FindMultipleOfSevenLambda(numbers));
    }
  }
```

We will get the following output we after we have executed the `PrintResultLambda()` method:

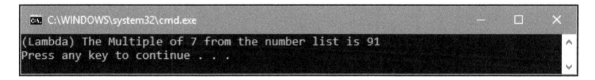

As we can see from the output window, we still retrieve `91` as a result of a number multiplication of `7`. However, we have successfully passed the anonymous method as the method argument.

Writing anonymous methods – some guidelines

When writing anonymous methods, here are some things that we should keep in mind:

- An anonymous method has no return type in its declaration. Consider the following code snippet:

```
delegate (int a, int b)
{
  return a * b;
};
```

  In the preceding delegate declaration, we don't find the return type, although we find the `return` keyword in the method implementation. This is because the compiler infers the return type based on the delegate signature.

- We have to match the declaration of the delegate's signature with the method's argument. This will be similar to assigning a named method to a delegate. Let's take a look at the following code snippet:

```
private static Func<int, int, int> AreaRectangleDelegate =
  delegate (int a, int b)
```

```
{
  return a * b;
};
```

 In the preceding code snippet, we declare a delegate that takes two int arguments and returns an int value. Refer to the delegate signature; we use the same signature when declaring the anonymous method.

- We are not allowed to declare variables whose names conflict with the variables of the anonymous method that is declared. Take a look at the following code snippet:

```
public partial class Program
{
  private static void Conflict()
  {
    for (int i = 0; i < numbers.Count; i++)
    {
      Action<int> actDelegate = delegate(int i)
      {
        Console.WriteLine("{0}", i);
      };
      actDelegate(i);
    }
  }
}
```

 We will never be able to compile the preceding code since we declare the variable i twice both in Conflict() method and in actDelegate delegate.

Advantages of the anonymous methods

Here are some advantages of using anonymous methods:

- Since we do not attach a name to a method, they are a good solution if we want to invoke the method only once.
- We can write the code in place rather than writing the logic in other parts of a code.
- We don't need to declare the return type of the anonymous method since it will be inferred from the signature of the delegate that is assigned to the anonymous method.

- We can access local variables of the outer method from the anonymous method. Outer variables are captured inside the anonymous method.
- We do not need to create a named method for snippets of logic that are invoked once.

Lambda expressions

We now have an idea that anonymous methods can help us create a simple and short method. However, in C# 3.0, lambda expressions were announced in order to complement anonymous methods in providing a shorthand notation to create anonymous methods. In fact, lambda expressions become the preferred way when writing new code.

Now, let's examine the simplest lambda expression syntax, as follows:

```
([parameters]) => expression;
```

In the lambda expression syntax, we only find two elements, which are `parameters` and `expression`. Like any method, a lambda expression has an argument symbolized by parameters. The implementation of the lambda expression is symbolized by the expression. We can also omit the parenthesis of parameters if only one parameter is required.

Let's create a simple lambda expression, which we can find in the `SimpleLambdaExpression.csproj` project, as follows:

```
public partial class Program
{
  static Func<string, string> displayMessageDelegate =
    str => String.Format(Message: {0}", str);
}
```

In the preceding code, we declare the `displayMessageDelegate` delegate and assign it to the `Func` delegate using a lambda expression. Similar to the method in the `SimpleDelegates.csproj` project, in order to invoke the delegate, we use the following code:

```
public partial class Program
{
  static void Main(string[] args)
  {
    Console.WriteLine(
      displayMessageDelegate(
      "A simple lambda expression sample."));
  }
```

```
    }
```

We call the `displayMessageDelegate` delegate like a method name. The output will be sent to the console, as follows:

Now, let's compare the method declaration between an anonymous method in `SimpleAnonymousMethods.csproj` and a lambda expression in the `SimpleLambdaExpression.csproj` project:

```
static Func<string, string> displayMessageDelegate =
  delegate (string str)
{
  return String.Format("Message: {0}", str);
};
```

The preceding code snippet is an anonymous method declaration that is shorter and simpler than a named method declaration.

```
static Func<string, string> displayMessageDelegate =
  str => String.Format("Message: {0}", str);
```

The preceding code snippet is a lambda expression declaration that is shorter and simpler than an anonymous method. The lambda expressions are brief compared to anonymous methods.

Transforming an anonymous method to a lambda expression

Now, let's discuss the transformation of an anonymous method to a lambda expression. We have the following anonymous method:

```
delegate (string str)
{
  return String.Format("Message: {0}", str);
};
```

And we want to transform it to a lambda expression, as follows:

```
str => String.Format("Message: {0}", str);
```

First, we take out the `delegate` keyword since we don't need it anymore; so, the code will be as follows:

```
(string str)
{
  return String.Format("Message: {0}", str);
};
```

Then, we supersede the curly braces with a => lambda operator in order to make it the inline lambda expression:

```
(string str) => return String.Format("Message: {0}", str);
```

We can also remove the `return` keyword since it is only a single line code that returns a value. The code will be as follows:

```
(string str) => String.Format("Message: {0}", str);
```

Since the preceding syntax is now an expression instead of a complete statement, the semicolon can be removed from the preceding code and the code will be as follows:

```
(string str) => String.Format("Message: {0}", str);
```

The preceding expression is a valid lambda expression. However, we can simplify the code more in order to take advantage of the lambda expression. The code will be as follows:

```
(str) => String.Format("Message: {0}", str);
```

Since we have taken out `string` data type, we can now take out the parenthesis as well:

```
str => String.Format("Message: {0}", str);
```

The preceding syntax is our final lambda expression. As we can see, now, our code becomes more readable because of its simplicity.

 The parenthesis in the parameters list of lambda expressions can be omitted if it contains only one argument.

Using lambda expressions, we can actually create delegates and expression tree types in anonymous methods. Now, let's find out the difference between these two types in the upcoming topics.

Creating a delegate type using lambda expresions

We discussed lambda expressions in a delegate type when we created code in the `SimpleLambdaExpression.csproj` project. Now, let's create another project name in order to discuss this by referring to the following code:

```
public partial class Program
{
  private static Func<int, int, int> AreaRectangleDelegate =
    (a, b) => a * b;
  private static Func<int, int, int> AreaSquareDelegate =
    (x, y) => x * y;
}
```

Again, we refactor the `SimpleDelegatesRefactor.csproj` project and replace the anonymous method with a lambda expression. As we can see, the lambda expression is assigned to a variable typed delegate. Here, we create a lambda expression in a delegate type. We can use the `Main()` method we had used in the `SimpleDelegatesRefactor.csproj` project to invoke `AreaRectangleDelegate` and `AreaSquareDelegate`. The result of the two projects will be completely the same.

Expression trees and lambda expressions

Besides creating a delegate, we can create expression trees, which are data structures which represents the expression elements (expr, term, factor) as a tree. By traversing the tree, one can interpret the expression trees or we can mutate a node in the tree for transforming the code. In compiler parlance, expressions trees are called **abstract syntax trees** (**AST**).

Now, let's take a look at the following code snippet in order to assign a lambda expression to the delegate that we discussed earlier:

```
Func<int, int, int> AreaRectangleDelegate =
  (a, b) => a * b;
```

As we can see, there are three sections in the preceding statement. They are as follows:

- **A variable typed delegate declaration**: `Func<int, int, int> AreaRectangleDelegate`
- **An equal operator**: `=`
- **A lambda expression**: `(a, b) => a * b`

We are going to translate the preceding code statement into data. To achieve this goal, we need to create an instance of the `Expression<T>` type, and `T` is delegate type. The `Expression<T>` type is defined in the `System.Linq.Expressions` namespace. After using this namespace in the project, we can translate our preceding code into an expression tree, as follows:

```
public partial class Program
{
  static void Main(string[] args)
  {
    Expression<Func<int, int, int>> expression =
      (a, b) => a * b;
  }
}
```

We have converted our preceding delegate lambda expression into the expression tree declared to be of type `Expression<T>`. The variable expression in the preceding code is not executable code but a data structure called an expression tree. There are four essentials properties in the `Expression<T>` class that we will discuss in detail. They are as follows:

- **Body**: This contains the body of the expression
- **Parameters**: This contain the parameters of the lambda expression
- **NodeType**: This contains the `ExpressionType` type of node in the tree
- **Type**: This contains the static type of the expression

Now, let's add a breakpoint in the expression variable and run the debugging process by pressing F5 in the `LambdaExpressionInExpressionTree.csproj` project. After executing the expression declaration line, we can take a peek at the variable window in the Visual Studio IDE, and we will get the following screenshot:

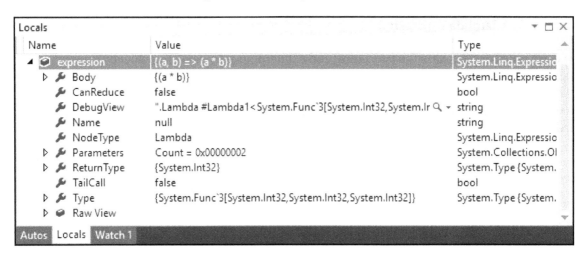

From the preceding screenshot, we have a `Body` property containing `{(a * b)}`, `NodeType` containing Lambda, `Type` containing the `Func` delegate with three templates, and are two parameters. If we expand the `Body` information in the variable window, we will get a result similar to what is shown in the following screenshot:

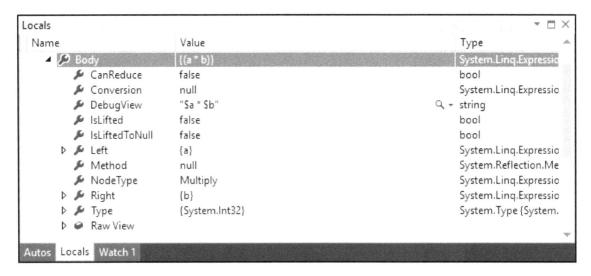

From the preceding screenshot, we can see that we have the `Left` property containing `{a}` and the `Right` property containing `{b}`. Using these properties, we can also explore the body of expression tree programmatically. The following code is the `exploreBody()` method, which will explore the properties of `Body`:

```
public partial class Program
{
  private static void exploreBody(
    Expression<Func<int, int, int>> expr)
  {
    BinaryExpression body =
      (BinaryExpression)expr.Body;
    ParameterExpression left =
      (ParameterExpression)body.Left;
    ParameterExpression right =
      (ParameterExpression)body.Right;
    Console.WriteLine(expr.Body);
    Console.WriteLine(
      "\tThe left part of the expression: {0}\n" +
      "\tThe NodeType: {1}\n" +
      "\tThe right part: {2}\n" +
      "\tThe Type: {3}\n",
      left.Name,
      body.NodeType,
      right.Name,
      body.Type);
  }
}
```

If we run the preceding `exploreBody()` method, we will get the following output:

In the preceding code, we access the Body properties of `Expression<T>` programmatically. We need to create a `BinaryExpression` data type in order to get the `Body` content, and `ParameterExpression` in order to get the `Left` and `Right` properties content. The code snippet for the `BinaryExpression` and `ParameterExpression` data is as follows:

```
BinaryExpression body =
  (BinaryExpression)expr.Body;
ParameterExpression left =
  (ParameterExpression)body.Left;
ParameterExpression right =
  (ParameterExpression)body.Right;
```

We have successfully created a data structure from the code in the expression tree. We can, if we want, convert this data back into code by compiling the expression. The expression we have is as follows:

```
Expression<Func<int, int, int>> expression =
  (a, b) => a * b;
```

So, we can compile the expression and run the code in the expression using the following `compilingExpr()` method:

```
public partial class Program
{
  private static void compilingExpr(
    Expression<Func<int, int, int>> expr)
  {
    int a = 2;
    int b = 3;
    int compResult = expr.Compile()(a, b);
    Console.WriteLine(
      "The result of expression {0}"+
      " with a = {1} and b = {2} is {3}",
      expr.Body,
      a,
      b,
      compResult);
  }
}
```

If we run the `compilingExpr()` method, the following output will be displayed on the console window:

```
C:\WINDOWS\system32\cmd.exe
The result of expression (a * b) with a = 2 and b = 3 is 6
Press any key to continue . . .
```

As we can see, we have compiled the expression using the `Compile()` method in the expression class, as follows:

```
int compResult = expr.Compile()(a, b);
```

The `expr.Compile()` method produces a delegate of type `Func<int, int, int>` in accordance with the type of the expression. We give the `Compile()` method the arguments a and b based on its signature, then it returns the `int` value.

Subscribing for events using lambda expressions

In C#, an object or a class can be used to inform other objects or classes when something happens, which is known as an event. There are two kinds of classes in the event, they are publishers and subscribers. The publisher is a class or object that sends (or raises) the event, while the subscriber is a class or object that receives (or handles) the event. Fortunately, lambda expressions can also be used to handle events. Let's take a look at the following code to discuss events further:

```
public class EventClassWithoutEvent
{
  public Action OnChange { get; set; }
  public void Raise()
  {
    if (OnChange != null)
    {
      OnChange();
    }
  }
}
```

The preceding code can be found in the `EventsInLambda.csproj` project. As we can see, a class named `EventClassWithoutEvent` has been created in the project. The class has a property named `OnChange`. This property's role is to store the action that subscribes the class and will be run when the `Raise()` method is invoked. Now, let's consume the `Raise()` method using the following code:

```
public partial class Program
{
  private static void CreateAndRaiseEvent()
  {
    EventClassWithoutEvent ev = new EventClassWithoutEvent();
    ev.OnChange += () =>
      Console.WriteLine("1st: Event raised");
    ev.OnChange += () =>
      Console.WriteLine("2nd: Event raised");
    ev.OnChange += () =>
      Console.WriteLine("3rd: Event raised");
    ev.OnChange += () =>
      Console.WriteLine("4th: Event raised");
    ev.OnChange += () =>
      Console.WriteLine("5th: Event raised");
    ev.Raise();
  }
}
```

If we run the preceding `CreateAndRaiseEvent()` method, we will retrieve the following output on the console:

From the code, we can see that when we invoke the `CreateAndRaiseEvent()` method, the code instances an `EventClassWithoutEvent` class. It then subscribes to the event with five different methods inside the lambda expression and then raises the event by invoking the `Raise()` method. The following code snippet will explain this further:

```
EventClassWithoutEvent ev = new EventClassWithoutEvent();
ev.OnChange += () =>
  Console.WriteLine("1st: Event raised");
ev.Raise();
```

From the preceding code snippet, we can see that the lambda expression can be used to subscribe to the event since it uses a delegate to store the subscribed method. However, there is still a weakness in the preceding code. Take a look at the last `OnChange` assignment from this code:

```
ev.OnChange += () =>
   Console.WriteLine("5th: Event raised");
```

Now, suppose that we change it to this:

```
ev.OnChange = () =>
   Console.WriteLine("5th: Event raised");
```

Then, we will remove all four previous subscribers. Another weakness is that `EventClassWithoutEvent` raises the event but nothing can stop the users of the class from raising this event. By invoking `OnChange()`, all users of the class can raise the event to all subscribers.

Using the event keyword

The use of the `event` keyword can solve our preceding problem since it will enforce the users of the class to subscribe something only using either the += or −= operator. Let's take a look at the following code to explain this further:

```
public class EventClassWithEvent
{
  public event Action OnChange = () => { };
  public void Raise()
  {
    OnChange();
  }
}
```

From the preceding code, we can see that we are no longer using a public property but a public field in the `EventClassWithEvent` class. Using the `event` keyword, the compiler will secure our field from unwanted access. The event keyword will also protect the subscription list since it cannot be assigned to any lambda expression using the = operator but has to be used with the += or −= operator. Now, let's take a look at the following code to prove this:

```
public partial class Program
{
  private static void CreateAndRaiseEvent2()
  {
```

```
      EventClassWithEvent ev = new EventClassWithEvent();
      ev.OnChange += () =>
        Console.WriteLine("1st: Event raised");
      ev.OnChange += () =>
        Console.WriteLine("2nd: Event raised");
      ev.OnChange += () =>
        Console.WriteLine("3rd: Event raised");
      ev.OnChange += () =>
        Console.WriteLine("4th: Event raised");
      ev.OnChange = () =>
        Console.WriteLine("5th: Event raised");
      ev.Raise();
    }
  }
```

We now have a method named CreateAndRaiseEvent2(), which is exactly same as the CreateAndRaiseEvent() method except that the last OnChange assignment used the = operator instead of the += operator. However, since we have applied the event keyword to the OnChange field, the code cannot be compiled and the CS0070 error code will occur, as shown in the following screenshot:

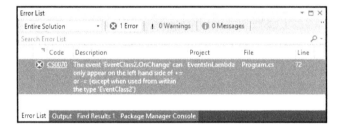

There is no risk anymore since the event keyword has restricted the use of the = operator. The event keyword also prevents the outside user of the class from raising the event. Only the part of the class that defines the event can raise the event. Let's take a look at the difference between the EventClassWithoutEvent and EventClassWithEvent class:

```
  public partial class Program
  {
    private static void CreateAndRaiseEvent3()
    {
      EventClassWithoutEvent ev = new EventClassWithoutEvent();
      ev.OnChange += () =>
        Console.WriteLine("1st: Event raised");
      ev.OnChange += () =>
        Console.WriteLine("2nd: Event raised");
      ev.OnChange += () =>
        Console.WriteLine("3rd: Event raised");
```

```
      ev.OnChange();
      ev.OnChange += () =>
        Console.WriteLine("4th: Event raised");
      ev.OnChange += () =>
        Console.WriteLine("5th: Event raised");
      ev.Raise();
    }
  }
```

The reference of the preceding `CreateAndRaiseEvent3()` method is
`CreateAndRaiseEvent()`, but we insert `ev.OnChange();` in between the third event and
fourth event. If we run the method, it will run successfully, and we will see the following
output on the console:

As we can see from the output, `OnChange()` in the `EventClassWithoutEvent` class can
raise the event. Compared to the `EventClassWithEvent` class, if we insert `OnChange()`
between any subscribing event, the compiler will create a compile error, as shown in the
following code:

```
public partial class Program
{
  private static void CreateAndRaiseEvent4()
  {
    EventClassWithEvent ev = new EventClassWithEvent();
    ev.OnChange += () =>
      Console.WriteLine("1st: Event raised");
    ev.OnChange += () =>
      Console.WriteLine("2nd: Event raised");
    ev.OnChange += () =>
      Console.WriteLine("3rd: Event raised");
    ev.OnChange();
    ev.OnChange += () =>
      Console.WriteLine("4th: Event raised");
    ev.OnChange += () =>
      Console.WriteLine("5th: Event raised");
```

```
        ev.Raise();
    }
}
```

If we compile the preceding code, we will get the CS0070 error code again, since we insert ev.OnChange(); in between the third event and the fourth event.

Using EventHandler or EventHandler<T>

Actually, C# has a class named EventHandler or EventHandler<T> that we can use to initialize an event instead of using an Action class. An EventHandler class takes a sender object and event arguments. The sender is the object that raises the event. Using EventHandler<T>, we can define the type of event arguments. Let's take a look at the following code, which we can find in the EventWithEventHandler.csproj project:

```
public class MyArgs : EventArgs
{
  public int Value { get; set; }
  public MyArgs(int value)
  {
    Value = value;
  }
}
public class EventClassWithEventHandler
{
  public event EventHandler<MyArgs> OnChange =
    (sender, e) => { };
  public void Raise()
  {
    OnChange(this, new MyArgs(100));
  }
}
```

We have two classes, named MyArgs and EventClassWithEventHandler. The EventClassWithEventHandler class uses EventHandler<MyArgs>, which defines the event argument's type. We need to pass an instance of MyArgs when raising the event. Subscribers of the event can access the arguments and use them. Now, let's take a look at the following CreateAndRaiseEvent() method code:

```
public partial class Program
{
  private static void CreateAndRaiseEvent()
  {
    EventClassWithEventHandler ev =
      new EventClassWithEventHandler();
```

```
    ev.OnChange += (sender, e)
      => Console.WriteLine(
         "Event raised with args: {0}", e.Value);
    ev.Raise();
  }
 }
```

If we run the preceding code, we will get the following output on the console:

From the preceding code, we can see that the lambda expression plays its role to subscribe to an event, as follows:

```
ev.OnChange += (sender, e)
  => Console.WriteLine(
     "Event raised with args: {0}", e.Value);
```

The advantages of using lambda expression in functional programming

Lambda expressions are not only a powerful way to provide a shorthand notation for anonymous methods, but they are also used in functional programming. In this section, we will go through the advantages of using the lambda expression in the context of functional programming.

First-class functions

In Chapter 1, *Tasting Functional Style in C#*, we discussed the idea of first-class functions when we were discussing functional programming. If functions are fire class Functions, functions obey value semantics. They can be passed as a parameter, returned from a function, and so on. If we go back to the earlier topic about lambda expressions, we have a project named SimpleLambdaExpression.csproj, which has the following simple lambda expression:

```
public partial class Program
{
  static Func<string, string> displayMessageDelegate =
```

```
      str => String.Format(Message: {0}", str);
   }
```

Then, we can add the following `firstClassConcept()` method to the project in order to demonstrate the first-class function using a lambda expression:

```
public partial class Program
{
  static private void firstClassConcept()
  {
    string str = displayMessageDelegate(
      "Assign displayMessageDelegate() to variable");
      Console.WriteLine(str);
  }
}
```

As we can see, we have successfully assigned the `displayMessageDelegate()` method to the variable named `str`, as follows:

```
string str = displayMessageDelegate(
  "Assign displayMessageDelegate() to variable");
```

If we run the code, we will get the following output on the console:

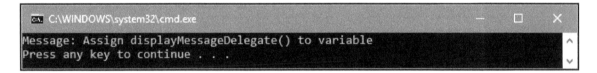

We can also pass the lambda expression as the argument of the other function. Using `displayMessageDelegate`, let's take a look at the following code:

```
public partial class Program
{
  static private void firstClassConcept2(
    Func<string, string> funct,
    string message)
  {
    Console.WriteLine(funct(message));
  }
}
```

We have a method named `firstClassConcept2`, which takes `Func` and string parameters. We can run the method as follows:

```
public partial class Program
{
```

```
static void Main(string[] args)
{
  firstClassConcept2(
    displayMessageDelegate,
    "Pass lambda expression to argument");
}
}
```

As we can see, we pass `displayMessageDelegate`, which is a lambda expression, to the `firstClassConcept2()` method. If we run the project, we will have the following output on the console window:

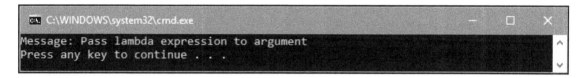

Since we have successfully assigned a function to a variable and passed a function to another function parameter, we can say that the lambda expression is a power tool to create first-class functions in functional programming.

Closure

Closure is a function that is able to be assigned to a variable (a first-class function) with free variables, which are bound in the lexical environment. A free variable is a variable that is not a parameter; or it is a local variable. In a closure, any variable that is not bound will be captured from the lexical environment where the closure is defined. To avoid getting confused about this term, let's take a look at the following code, which we can find in the `Closure.csproj` project:

```
public partial class Program
{
  private static Func<int, int> GetFunction()
  {
    int localVar = 1;
    Func<int, int> returnFunc = scopeVar =>
    {
      localVar *= 2;
      return scopeVar + localVar;
    };
    return returnFunc;
  }
}
```

From the preceding code, we can see that we've got a local variable named `localVar`, and it will be multiplied by 2 when the `GetFunction()` method is invoked. The `localVar` variable is bound inside the lambda expression when `returnValue` is returned. By analyzing the preceding code without running it, we might guess that `GetFunction()` will return `returnFunc`, which will always return the same value every time it's passed to the same argument. This is because `localVar` will always be *1* every time `GetFunction()` is invoked, since it's a local variable. As we learned in programming, the local variables are created on the stack and they will go away when the method has finished execution. Now, let's invoke the `GetFunction()` method to prove our guess using the following code:

```
public partial class Program
{
  static void Main(string[] args)
  {
    Func<int, int> incrementFunc = GetFunction();
    for (int i = 0; i < 10; i++)
    {
      Console.WriteLine(
        "Invoking {0}: incrementFunc(1) = {1}",
        i,
        incrementFunc(1));
    }
  }
}
```

We are going to invoke the `incrementFunc()` method, which is the return value of the `GetFunction()` method ten times, but we always pass 1 as the argument. From our previous guessing, we can say that the `incrementFunc(1)` method will always return 3 for all ten invocations. Now, let's run the project, and we will see the following output on the console:

According to the preceding output, we made a wrong guess. The `localVar` variable lives along with the `GetFunction()` method. It stores its value after being multiplied by 2 each time the method is called. We have successfully bound a free variable in the lexical environment and this is what we call closure.

Summary

In this chapter, we discovered that an anonymous method is a method that doesn't have a name. We just need to define the arguments and the implementation of the method. It's a shorthand notation from delegates. Then, we looked at lambda expressions, the powerful tool in functional programming, which can provide a shorthand notation from an anonymous method.

The lambda expression can also be used to form an expression tree that will be useful when we need to express our code in regular C#, deconstruct it, inspect it, and interpret it. The expression tree is like an explanation of the code. If we have a `<Func<int, int, int>>` expression, it explains how it will provide an `int` return if we give the code two integers.

Subscribing an event is also done by a lambda expression. There are two kinds of classes in the event, they are publisher and subscribers, and we can subscribe to the event using a lambda expression. It doesn't matter whether we use the `event` keyword or the `EventHandler` keyword, the lambda is always used to subscribe to the event.

The first-class function concept is also fulfilled by lambda expressions since by using it, we can assign the function into a variable or pass the function as an argument of other functions. Using lambda expressions, we can also apply a closure concept, which makes a local variable live along within the function.

For now, it's enough to discuss lambda expressions. However, we will discuss lambda expressions again in more more detail when we talk about LINQ in Chapter 5, *Querying Any Collections Easily with LINQ*. And, in the next chapter, we are going to talk about the extension method that can be used to extend method abilities.

4
Extending Object Functionality with Extension Methods

As we have already mentioned in the previous chapter, we are going to discuss extension methods in greater detail in this chapter. It will be helpful when we talk about LINQ, the essential technique of functional programming in C#, in the next chapter. The following are the topics we will cover in this chapter:

- Practicing the use of extension methods and getting this new method in IntelliSense
- Invoking extension methods from other assemblies
- Creating new methods for an interface, collection, enumeration, and other objects
- The advantages of extension methods in relation to functional programming
- The limitations of extension methods

Getting closer to extension methods

An extension method is a capability that can extend the ability of an existing class or type without making any modification to the existing class or type. This means that an extension method enables us to add methods to the existing class or type without having to either create a new derived type or recompile.

Extension methods were introduced in C# 3.0 and can be applied to our own types or existing types in .NET. The extension method will be used a lot in functional programming since it suits the method chaining concept, which we have already used in Chapter 1, *Tasting Functional Style in C#*, when refactoring code in a functional style.

Creating an extension method

Extension methods have to be declared in a static, nongeneric, and non-nested class. They are a static method inside a static class. To create an extension method, first we have to create a `public static` class since the extension methods have to be included in the `static` class. After the `public static` class is successfully created, we define a method inside the class and add the `this` keyword to the first method argument to indicate that it is an `extension` method. The first argument in the method that has the `this` keyword has to refer to a specific instance of the class we want to extend. In order to make the explanation clearer, let's take a look at the following code, creating a extension method that we can find in the `Palindrome.csproj` project:

```
public static class ExtensionMethods
{
  public static bool IsPalindrome(this string str)
  {
    char[] array = str.ToCharArray();
    Array.Reverse(array);
    string backwards = new string(array);
    return str == backwards;
  }
}
```

Now let's dissect the preceding code to understand how the extension method is created. First, we have to successfully create the `public static` class, as shown in the following code snippet:

```
public static class ExtensionMethods
{
  ...
}
```

Then, we create a `static` method inside the class, as shown in the following code snippet:

```
public static bool IsPalindrome(this string str)
{
  ...
}
```

As we can see in the preceding method, we add the `this` keyword in the first argument of the method. This indicates that the method is an `extension` method. Also, the type of the first argument, which is string, indicates that the type we want to extend is the `string` data type. Now, by defining the `IsPalindrome()` extension method for the `string` type, all instances of string have the `IsPalindrome()` method. Let's take a look at the following code to prove this:

```
public class Program
{
  static void Main(string[] args)
  {
    string[] strArray = {
      "room",
      "level",
      "channel",
      "heat",
      "burn",
      "madam",
      "machine",
      "jump",
      "radar",
      "brain"
    };
    foreach (string s instrArray)
    {
      Console.WriteLine("{0} = {1}", s, s.IsPalindrome());
    }
  }
}
```

The preceding `Main()` function will examine all members of the `strArray` array, whether or not it is palindrome. We can call the `IsPalindrome()` method from the `s` variable in which it's a `string` type variable. The code snippet when the `IsPalindrome()` method is invoked from an instance of the string type is as follows:

```
foreach (string s instrArray)
{
  Console.WriteLine("{0} = {1}", s, s.IsPalindrome());
}
```

If we run the `Palindrome.csproj` project, we can get the following output on the console:

Since the palindrome is a word or another sequence of characters that will be the same whether we read backward or forward, only `level`, `madam`, and `radar` will return `true` if we invoke the `IsPalindrome()` method to them. Our extension method has been successfully created and run.

Extension methods in the code IntelliSense

When we create an extension method for instance, to a type there will be no apparent difference compared to the existing methods in a class or type. This is because we will do the same thing when invoking extension methods or methods that are actually defined in a type. However, we can inspect the code IntelliSense to understand whether or not the method inside the type is an extension method since the extension method will be displayed in the IntelliSense. The following screenshot is the method list for the string instance when the `IsPalindrome()` extension method has not been defined yet:

And the following screenshot is the method list for the string instance when the `IsPalindrome()` extension method has been defined:

We can see from the preceding two images that the extension will be listed in the code IntelliSense of Visual Studio. However, we can now find the distinction between extension methods and methods that are actually defined in a type that is the icon. There is an arrow pointing down at the icon of extension methods although we cannot find it in the method that is actually defined in a type. This is because the icon is different but the way we invoke the method is totally the same.

Calling extension methods in the other assemblies

We have successfully created the `IsPalindrome()` extension method in the previous section. It's quite easy to call the extension method since it's defined inside the same namespace as the caller method. In other words, the `IsPalindrome()` extension method and the `Main()` method are in the same namespace. We don't need to add a reference to any module since the method is there along with the caller. However, in common practice, we can create extension methods in the other assemblies, which we usually call class library. The use of the library will ease the use of the extension method since it can be reused, so we can use the extension method in many projects.

Referencing a namespace

We are going to create an extension method in the `Class Library` and call it in another project. Let's create a new `Class Library` project named `ReferencingNamespaceLib.csproj` and insert the following code into the `ExtensionMethodsClass.cs` file:

```
using System;
namespaceReferencingNamespaceLib
{
  public static class ExtensionMethodsClass
  {
    public static byte[] ConvertToHex(this string str)
    {
      int i = 0;
      byte[] HexArray = new byte[str.Length];
      foreach (char ch in str)
      {
        HexArray[i++] = Convert.ToByte(ch);
      }
      returnHexArray;
    }
  }
}
```

From the preceding code, we can see that we create the `ConvertToHex()` extension method inside the `ExtensionMethodsClass` class in the `ReferencingNamespaceLib` namespace. The use of the `ConvertToHex()` extension method is to convert each character in the string to ASCII code and store it in the byte array. Now let's take a look at the following code, which will call the extension method, which we can find in the `ReferencingNamespace.csproj` project:

```
using System;
using ReferencingNamespaceLib;
namespace ReferencingNamespace
{
  class Program
  {
    static void Main(string[] args)
    {
      int i = 0;
      string strData = "Functional in C#";
      byte[] byteData = strData.ConvertToHex();
      foreach (char c in strData)
      {
        Console.WriteLine("{0} = 0x{1:X2} ({2})",
```

```
            c.ToString(),
            byteData[i],
            byteData[i++]);
        }
      }
    }
  }
```

From the preceding code, we can see that we call the `ConvertToHex()` extension method from the instance of string, which is `strData`, as follows:

```
string strData = "Functional in C#";
byte[] byteData = strData.ConvertToHex();
```

However, in order to invoke the `ConvertToHex()` method from the string instance, we have to refer to the `ReferencingNamespaceLib` assembly and also import the namespace of the reference assembly. To import the assembly, we have to use `using` along with `ReferencingNamespaceLib` as shown in the following code snippet:

```
usingReferencingNamespaceLib;
```

If we run the `ReferencingNamespace.csproj` project, we will get the following output on the console:

As we can see, each character in C# sentences is converted into ASCII code invoked the extension method we created for the string type by referencing a namespace in both hexadecimal and decimal formats. This also proves that we have successfully in another assembly.

Piggybacking a namespace

We can, if we want, piggyback on the namespace where the string type lives, which is the System namespace, so that we don't need to import a custom namespace to use the extension method. Piggybacking a namespace is also good for our standard programming approach. Let's refactor our previous `ReferencingNamespaceLib.csproj` code using the following code, which we can find in the `PiggybackingNamespaceLib.csproj` project:

```
namespace System
{
  public static class ExtensionMethodsClass
  {
    public static byte[] ConvertToHex(this string str)
    {
      int i = 0;
      byte[] HexArray = new byte[str.Length];
      foreach (char ch in str)
      {
        HexArray[i++] = Convert.ToByte(ch);
      }
      return HexArray;
    }
  }
}
```

If we observe the class name, the `ConvertToHex()` method signature, or the implementation of the method, we will find that there's no difference between the `ReferencingNamespaceLib.csproj` and `PiggybackingNamespaceLib.csproj` projects. However, if we look at the namespace name, we will find that now it's System instead of `PiggybackingNamespaceLib`. The reason we use the System namespace is to create an extension method in the selected namespace. Since we want to extend the ability of the string type that lives in the System namespace, we have to extend the System namespace as well. We do not need to import the System namespace using a using keyword since the `ConvertToHex()` method lives in the System namespace. Now, let's take a look at the following code in order to invoke the `ConvertToHex()` method inside the System namespace, which we can find in the `PiggybackingNamespace.csproj` project:

```
using System;
namespace PiggybackingNamespace
{
  class Program
  {
    static void Main(string[] args)
    {
      int i = 0;
```

```
        string strData = "Piggybacking";
        byte[] byteData = strData.ConvertToHex();
        foreach (char c in strData)
        {
            Console.WriteLine("{0} = 0x{1:X2} ({2})",
            c.ToString(),
            byteData[i],
            byteData[i++]);
        }
    }
  }
}
```

We refactor the preceding code from the ReferencingNamespace.csproj project, and again, we don't find any differences between the PiggybackingNamespace.csproj and ReferencingNamespace.csproj projects except that there is no import to the custom namespace in the PiggybackingNamespace.csproj project, which the ReferencingNamespace.csproj project has:

```
using ReferencingNamespaceLib;
```

We don't need to import the custom namespace since we create the extension method in the System namespace. However, we still need to refer to the assembly where the extension method is defined. We can expect an output like what is shown in the following screenshot:

We have successfully invoked the ConvertToHex() extension method and found it useful for getting the ASCII code from the string data type.

Leveraging the interface, collection, and object

Not only can classes and types apply an extension method, but interfaces, collections, and any other objects can be functionally extended using an extension method as well. We are going to discuss this in the upcoming sections.

Extending the interface

We can extend the method in an interface in the same way we extend the method in a class or type. We still need the `public static` class and the `public static` method. By extending the interface abilities, we can use the extension method just after we create it without the need to create the implementation inside the class that we inherit from the interface, since the implementation is done when we declare the extension method. Let's take a look at the following `DataItem` class, which we can find in the `ExtendingInterface.csproj` project:

```
namespace ExtendingInterface
{
  public class DataItem
  {
    public string Name { get; set; }
    public string Gender { get; set; }
  }
}
```

We also have the following `IDataSource` interface:

```
namespace ExtendingInterface
{
  public interface IDataSource
  {
    IEnumerable<DataItem> GetItems();
  }
}
```

As we can see, the `IDataSource` interface has only one signature of the method, which is named `GetItems()`, returning `IEnumerable<DataItem>`. Now, we can create a class to inherit the `IDataSource` interface, which we give a name, `ClubMember`; it has the implementation of the `GetItems()` method, as follows:

```
public partial class ClubMember : IDataSource
{
```

```
    public IEnumerable<DataItem> GetItems()
    {
      foreach (var item in DataItemList)
      {
        yield return item;
      }
    }
}
```

From the preceding class, the GetItems() method will yield all the data in the
DataItemList, whose content will be as follows:

```
public partial class ClubMember : IDataSource
{
  List<DataItem> DataItemList = new List<DataItem>()
  {
    newDataItem{
      Name ="Dorian Villarreal",
      Gender ="Male"},
    newDataItem{
      Name ="Olivia Bradley",
      Gender ="Female"},
    newDataItem{
      Name ="Jocelyn Garrison",
      Gender ="Female"},
    newDataItem{
      Name ="Connor Hopkins",
      Gender ="Male"},
    newDataItem{
      Name ="Rose Moore",
      Gender ="Female"},
    newDataItem{
      Name ="Conner Avery",
      Gender ="Male"},
    newDataItem{
      Name ="Lexie Irwin",
      Gender ="Female"},
    newDataItem{
      Name ="Bobby Armstrong",
      Gender ="Male"},
    newDataItem{
      Name ="Stanley Wilson",
      Gender ="Male"},
    newDataItem{
      Name ="Chloe Steele",
      Gender ="Female"}
  };
}
```

There are ten `DataItem` classes in the `DataItemList`. We can display all the items in the `DataItemList` with the help of the `GetItems()` method, as follows:

```
public class Program
{
static void Main(string[] args)
  {
    ClubMember cm = new ClubMember();
    foreach (var item in cm.GetItems())
    {
      Console.WriteLine(
        "Name: {0}\tGender: {1}",
          item.Name,
            item.Gender);
    }
  }
}
```

As we can can see in the preceding code, since we have inherited the `ClubMember` class to the `IDataSource` interface and have implemented the `GetItems()` method, the instance of `ClubMember`, which is `cm`, can invoke the `GetItems()` method. The output will be like what is shown in the following screenshot when we run the project:

Now, if we want to add the method to the interface without having to modify it, we can create a method extension to the interface. Consider that we are going to add the `GetItemsByGender()` method to the `IDataSource` interface; we can create the extension method as follows:

```
namespaceExtendingInterface
{
  public static class IDataSourceExtension
  {
    public static IEnumerable<DataItem>
```

```
      GetItemsByGender(thisIDataSourcesrc,string gender)
    {
      foreach (DataItem item in src.GetItems())
      {
        if (item.Gender == gender)
          yield return item;
      }
    }
  }
}
```

By creating the preceding extension method, the instance of the `ClubMember` class now has a method named `GetItemsByGender()`. We can use this extension method in the same way as we use the method class, as follows:

```
public class Program
{
  static void Main(string[] args)
  {
    ClubMember cm = new ClubMember();
    foreach (var item in cm.GetItemsByGender("Female"))
    {
      Console.WriteLine(
        "Name: {0}\tGender: {1}",
        item.Name,
        item.Gender);
    }
  }
}
```

The `GetItemsByGender()` method will return the `IEnumerable` interface of the selected gender of `DataItemList`. Since we only need to get all female members in the list, the output will be as follows:

We can now extend the method in the interface, and there's no need to implement the method in the inherited class since it has been done in the extension method definition.

Extending the collection

In our previous discussion, we discovered that we apply the `IEnumerable` interface in order to collect all the data we need. We can also extend the `IEnumerable` interface, which is a collection type, so that we can add a method in an instance of a collection type.

The following is the code in the `ExtendingCollection.csproj` project and we still use `DataItem.cs` and `IDataSource.cs`, which we use in the `ExtendingInterface.csproj` project. Let's take a look at the following code:

```
public static partial class IDataSourceCollectionExtension
{
  public static IEnumerable<DataItem>
    GetAllItemsByGender_IEnum(this IEnumerable src, string gender)
  {
    var items = new List<DataItem>();
    foreach (var s in src)
    {
      var refDataSource = s as IDataSource;
      if (refDataSource != null)
      {
        items.AddRange(refDataSource.GetItemsByGender(gender));
      }
    }
    return items;
  }
}
```

The preceding code is the extension method for the `IEnumerable` type. To prevent the occurrence of an error, we have to cast the type of all sources' items using the following code snippet:

```
var refDataSource = s as IDataSource;
```

We can also extend the `IEnumerable<T>` type, as follows:

```
public static partial class IDataSourceCollectionExtension
{
  public static IEnumerable<DataItem>
  GetAllItemsByGender_IEnumTemplate
    (this IEnumerable<IDataSource> src, string gender)
  {
    return src.SelectMany(x => x.GetItemsByGender(gender));
  }
}
```

Using the preceding method, we can extend the IEnumerable<T> type to have a method named GetAllItemsByGender_IEnumTemplate(), which is used to get the items by a specific gender.

Now, we are ready to invoke these two extension methods. However, before we call them, let's create the following two classes, named ClubMember1 and ClubMember2:

```
public class ClubMember1 : IDataSource
{
  public IEnumerable<DataItem> GetItems()
  {
    return new List<DataItem>
    {
      newDataItem{
        Name ="Dorian Villarreal",
        Gender ="Male"},
      newDataItem{
        Name ="Olivia Bradley",
        Gender ="Female"},
      newDataItem{
        Name ="Jocelyn Garrison",
        Gender ="Female"},
      newDataItem{
        Name ="Connor Hopkins",
        Gender ="Male"},
      newDataItem{
        Name ="Rose Moore",
        Gender ="Female"}
    };
  }
}
public class ClubMember2 : IDataSource
{
  public IEnumerable<DataItem> GetItems()
  {
    return new List<DataItem>
    {
      newDataItem{
        Name ="Conner Avery",
        Gender ="Male"},
      newDataItem{
        Name ="Lexie Irwin",
        Gender ="Female"},
      newDataItem{
        Name ="Bobby Armstrong",
        Gender ="Male"},
      newDataItem{
```

```
          Name ="Stanley Wilson",
          Gender ="Male"},
        newDataItem{
          Name ="Chloe Steele",
          Gender ="Female"}
      };
    }
  }
```

Now, we are going to invoke the `GetAllItemsByGender_IEnum()` and `GetAllItemsByGender_IEnumTemplate()` extension methods. The code will be as follows:

```
public class Program
{
  static void Main(string[] args)
  {
    var sources = new IDataSource[]
    {
      new ClubMember1(),
      new ClubMember2()
    };
    var items = sources.GetAllItemsByGender_IEnum("Female");
    Console.WriteLine("Invoking GetAllItemsByGender_IEnum()");
    foreach (var item in items)
    {
      Console.WriteLine(
        "Name: {0}\tGender: {1}",
        item.Name,
        item.Gender);
    }
  }
}
```

From the preceding code, first we create a `sources` variable containing the array of `IDataSource`. We get the data for `sources` from the `ClubMember1` and `ClubMember2` classes. Since the source is a collection of `IDataSource`, the `GetAllItemsByGender_IEnum()` method can be applied to it. If we run the preceding `Main()` method, the following output will be displayed on the console:

We have successfully invoked the `GetAllItemsByGender_IEnum()` extension method. Now, let's try to invoke the `GetAllItemsByGender_IEnumTemplate` extension method using the following code:

```
public class Program
{
  static void Main(string[] args)
  {
    var sources = new List<IDataSource>
    {
      new ClubMember1(),
      new ClubMember2()
    };
    var items =
      sources.GetAllItemsByGender_IEnumTemplate("Female");
    Console.WriteLine(
      "Invoking GetAllItemsByGender_IEnumTemplate()");
    foreach (var item in items)
    {
      Console.WriteLine("Name: {0}\tGender: {1}",
        item.Name, item.Gender);
    }
  }
}
```

We declare the `sources` variable in the yet-to-be-displayed code, in the same way as we declared it in the previous `Main()` method. Also, we can apply the `GetAllItemsByGender_IEnumTemplate()` extension method to the source variable. The output will be as follows if we run the preceding code:

By comparing the two images of the output, we can see that there's no difference between them, although they extend the different collection types.

Extending an object

Not only can we extend an interface and a collection, we can actually extend an object as well, which means that we can extend everything. To discuss this, let's take a look at the following code, which we can find in the `ExtendingObject.csproj` project:

```
public static class ObjectExtension
{
  public static void WriteToConsole(this object o,    stringobjectName)
  {
    Console.WriteLine(
      String.Format(
        "{0}: {1}\n",
        objectName,
        o.ToString()));
  }
}
```

We have a method extension named `WriteToConsole()`, which can be applied to all objects in C# since it extends the `Object` class. To use it, we can apply it to various objects, as shown in the following code:

```
public class Program
{
  static void Main(string[] args)
  {
    var obj1 = UInt64.MaxValue;
    obj1.WriteToConsole(nameof(obj1));
    var obj2 = new DateTime(2016, 1, 1);
    obj2.WriteToConsole(nameof(obj2));
    var obj3 = new DataItem
    {
      Name = "Marcos Raymond",
      Gender = "Male"
    };
    obj3.WriteToConsole(nameof(obj3));
    IEnumerable<IDataSource> obj4 =new List<IDataSource>
    {
      new ClubMember1(),
      new ClubMember2()
    };
    obj4.WriteToConsole(nameof(obj4));
  }
}
```

Before we dissect the preceding code, let's run this `Main()` method, and we will get the following output on the console:

```
C:\WINDOWS\system32\cmd.exe

obj1: 18446744073709551615

obj2: 1/1/2016 00:00:00

obj3: ExtendingObject.DataItem

obj4: System.Collections.Generic.List`1[ExtendingObject.IDataSource]

Press any key to continue . . .
```

From the preceding code, we can see that all objects that are `UInt64`, `DateTime`, `DataItem`, and `IEnumerable<IDataSource>` can invoke the `WriteToConsole()` extension method that we declare use the `this` object as an argument.

 Creating an extension method in the object type causes all types in the framework to be able to access the method. We have to ensure that the implementation of the method can be applied to the different types supported by the framework.

Advantages of using extension methods in functional programming

Method chaining in functional programming relies on extension methods. As we have already discussed in Chapter 1, *Tasting Functional Style in C#*, method chaining will make our code easier to read since it can decrease the lines of code. For the sake of code readability in the extension method, let's take a look at the following code, which we can find in the `CodeReadability.csproj` project:

```
using System.Linq;
namespace CodeReadability
{
  public static class HelperMethods
  {
    public static string TrimAllSpace(string str)
    {
      string retValue = "";
      foreach (char c in str)
      {
        retValue +=!char.IsWhiteSpace(c) ?c.ToString() :"";
      }
      return retValue;
```

```
    }
    public static string Capitalize(string str)
    {
      string retValue = "";
      string[] allWords = str.Split(' ');
      foreach (string s inallWords)
      {
        retValue += s.First()
        .ToString()
        .ToUpper()
        + s.Substring(1)
        + " ";
      }
      return retValue.Trim();
    }
  }
}
```

The preceding code is the `static` method inside the `static` class. It is not an extension method since we don't use the `this` keyword in the method argument. We can find it in the `HelperMethods.cs` file. The use of the `TrimAllSpace()` method is to remove all white space characters from the string, while the use of the `Capitalize()` method is to make the first letter of a string uppercase in the sentence. We also have exactly same methods as `HelperMethods`, which we can find in the `ExtensionMethods.cs` file. Let's look at the following code, in which we declare `TrimAllSpace()` and `Capitalize()` as the extension methods:

```
using System.Linq;
namespace CodeReadability
{
  public static class ExtensionMethods
  {
    public static string TrimAllSpace(this string str)
    {
      string retValue = "";
      foreach (char c in str)
      {
        retValue +=!char.IsWhiteSpace(c) ?c.ToString() :"";
      }
      return retValue;
    }
    public static string Capitalize(string str)
    {
      string retValue = "";
      string[] allWords = str.Split(' ');
      foreach (string s inallWords)
      {
```

```
            retValue += s.First()
               .ToString()
               .ToUpper()
               + s.Substring(1)
               + " ";
        }
        return retValue.Trim();
    }
  }
}
```

Now, we will create code that will trim all the whitespace in the given string and then capitalize each string in the sentence. The following is the code implemented in the HelperMethods class:

```
static void Main(string[] args)
{
  string sntc = "";
  foreach (string str in sentences)
  {
    string strTemp = str;
    strTemp = HelperMethods.TrimAllSpace(strTemp);
    strTemp = HelperMethods.Capitalize(strTemp);
    sntc += strTemp + " ";
  }
  Console.WriteLine(sntc.Trim());
}
```

We also declare a string array named sentences, as follows:

```
static string[] sentences = new string[]
{
  " h o w ",
  " t o ",
  " a p p l y ",
  " e x t e n s i o n ",
  " m e t h o d s ",
  " i n ",
  " c s h a r p ",
  " p r o g r a m m i n g "
};
```

The preceding code will give the following output:

We can, if we want, simplify the preceding `Main()` method, which uses `HelperMethods`, using extension methods we have already created, as follows:

```
static void Main(string[] args)
{
  string sntc = "";
  foreach (string str in sentences)
  {
    sntc += str.TrimAllSpace().Capitalize() + " ";
  }
  Console.WriteLine(sntc.Trim());
}
```

If we run the preceding `Main()` method, we will get eactly the same output on the console. However, we have refactored the following code snippet:

```
string strTemp = str;
strTemp = HelperMethods.TrimAllSpace(strTemp);
strTemp = HelperMethods.Capitalize(strTemp);
sntc += strTemp + " ";
```

Using the extension method, we just need this one-line code to replace the the four lines of code:

```
sntc += str.TrimAllSpace().Capitalize() + " ";
```

The point is that we have reduced the line of code so it now becomes simpler and more readable and the flow of the process is clearer.

Limitations of the extension method

Although the extension method is a powerful tool to achieve our functional programming, this technique still has some limitations. Here, we elaborate on the limitations the extension methods face so that we can avoid their use.

Extending a static class

As we discuss extension methods further, we know that an extension method is a static method that has public accessibility inside the static class that has public accessibility as well. The extension method will appear in the type or class we target. However, not all classes can be extended using the extension method. The existing static class will not be able to be extended. For example, the `Math` class has been provided by .NET. Even though the class has provided a mathematical functionality we usually use, it might be that, sometimes, we need to add another functionality to the `Math` class.

However, since the `Math` class is a static class, it's nearly impossible to extend this class by adding a single method to it. Suppose we want to add the `Square()` method to find the result of multiplying a number by itself. Here is the code, which we can find in the `ExtendingStaticClass.csproj` project, if we try to add the extension method to the `Math` class:

```
public static class StaticClassExtensionMethod
{
  public static int Square(this Math m, inti)
  {
    return i * i;
  }
}
```

When we compile the preceding code, there will be an error similar to what is shown in the following screenshot:

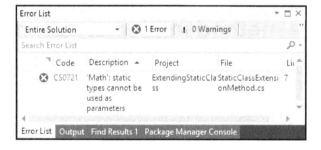

The error message says that the `Math` static method cannot be used as a parameter of the `Square()` extension method. What we can do to overcome this limitation is now extend the types instead of the `Math` class. We can extend the `int` types by adding the `Square()` method instead of extending the `Math` class. Here's the code to extend the `int` class:

```
public static class StaticClassExtensionMethod
{
  public static int Square(this inti)
  {
    return i * i;
  }
}
```

As we can see, we extend the `int` types so that if we want to invoke the `Square()` method, we can invoke it using the following code:

```
public class Program
{
  static void Main(string[] args)
  {
    int i = 60;
    Console.WriteLine(i.Square());
  }
}
```

However, using this technique, we also need to extend the other types, such as `float` and `double`, to accommodate the `Square()` functionality in various data types.

Modifying the method implementation in the existing class or type

Although the extension method can be applied to the existing classes and types, we cannot modify the implementation of the existing method the class or type has. We can try it using the following code, which we can find in the `ModifyingExistingMethod.csproj` project:

```
namespace ModifyingExistingMethod
{
  public static class ExtensionMethods
  {
    public static string ToString(this string str)
    {
      return "ToString() extension method";
    }
  }
```

```
}
```

In the preceding code, we try to replace the existing `ToString()` method, which the string type has, with a `ToString()` extension method such as the one in the preceding code. Fortunately, the code will be able to be compiled successfully. Now, let's add the following code to the `Main()` method in the project:

```
namespace ModifyingExistingMethod
{
  public class Program
  {
    static void Main(string[] args)
    {
      stringstr = "This is string";
      Console.WriteLine(str.ToString());
    }
  }
}
```

However, if we run the project, the `ToString()` extension method will never be executed. We will get the output from the existing `ToString()` method instead.

Summary

Extension methods give us an easy way to add a new method to an existing class or type without having to modify the original class or type. Besides, we don't need to recompile the code since just after we create the extension method it will be recognized by the code in the project. An extension method has to be declared as a static method inside a static class. As there is no apparent difference compared to the existing methods in a class or type, the method will also appear in the IntelliSense.

Extension methods can also be declared in another assembly, and we have to refer to the namespace of the static class defined the method stored in the other assemblies. However, we can use the piggyback namespace technique, which uses the existing namespace so that we don't need to refer to any other namespace anymore. Not only can we extend the class and type functionality, but we can also extend the interface, collection, and any objects in the framework.

Like other C# technologies, extension methods also have their advantages and limitations. One of the advantages related to functional programming is that the extension method will make our code apply method chaining so that it can apply the functional approach. However, we cannot extend a static and we cannot modify the method implementation in an existing class or type, which is a limitation of the extension method.

In the next chapter, we will dig into LINQ techniques since we already have enough understanding of delegates, lambda expressions, and extension methods. We will also discuss the convenient way to code a functional program provided by LINQ.

5
Querying Any Collection Easily with LINQ

After having a discussion on delegates, lambda expressions, and extension methods, we are now ready to continue our discussion about LINQ. In this chapter, we will delve into LINQ, which is essential in composing functional code. Here, we will discuss the following topics:

- Introducing LINQ Queries
- Understanding deferred execution in LINQ
- Comparing LINQ fluent syntax and LINQ query expression syntax
- Enumerating LINQ operator

Getting started with LINQ

Language Integrated Query (**LINQ**), which was introduced in C# 3.0, is a language feature of .NET Framework that enables us to query data in collections easily implementing the `IEnumerable<T>` interface, such as `ArrayList<T>`, `List<T>`, an XML document, and a database. It becomes easier to query any data in a collection since, using LINQ, we do not need to learn a different syntax for a different source of data. For instance, we don't need to learn SQL if we use LINQ when the data source is a database. Also, using LINQ, we don't have to learn XQuery when we deal with an XML document. Fortunately, LINQ has eased our use of a common syntax for all the sources of data.

There are two basic data units in LINQ; they are sequences, which include any object that implements `IEnumerable<T>`, and elements, which include the items in the sequence. Suppose we have the following `int` array named `intArray`:

```
int[] intArray =
{
   0,  1,  2,  3,  4,  5,  6,  7,  8,  9,
  10, 11, 12, 13, 14, 15, 16, 17, 18, 19,
  20, 21, 22, 23, 24, 25, 26, 27, 28, 29,
  30, 31, 32, 33, 34, 35, 36, 37, 38, 39,
  40, 41, 42, 43, 44, 45, 46, 47, 48, 49
};
```

From the preceding collection, we can say that `intArray` is a sequence, and the contents of the array, which include the numbers from 0 to 49, are the elements.

A sequence can be transformed using a method called a query operator. The query operator accepts an input sequence and then produce the transformed sequence. The query will transform the sequence when it is enumerated. The query consists of at least an input sequence and an operator. Let's take a look at the following code, which we can find in the `SequencesAndElements.csproj` project, which will look for the prime number from our preceding collection, `intArray`:

```
public partial class Program
{
  public static void ExtractArray()
  {
    IEnumerable<int> extractedData =
      System.Linq.Enumerable.Where
      (intArray, i => i.IsPrime());
    Console.WriteLine
      ("Prime Number from 0 - 49 are:");
    foreach (int i in extractedData)
      Console.Write("{0} \t", i);
    Console.WriteLine();
  }
}
```

The `IsPrime()` extension method will have the following implementation:

```
public static class ExtensionMethods
{
  public static bool IsPrime(this int i)
  {
    if ((i % 2) == 0)
    {
      return i == 2;
```

```
    }
    int sqrt = (int)Math.Sqrt(i);
    for (int t = 3; t <= sqrt; t = t + 2)
    {
      if (i % t == 0)
      {
        return false;
      }
    }
    return i != 1;
  }
}
```

From our preceding code, we can see that we use the `Where` operator, which can be found in the `System.Linq.Enumerable` class, to transform the `intArray` sequence into the `extractedData` sequence, as shown in the following code snippet:

```
IEnumerable<int> extractedData =
  System.Linq.Enumerable.Where
    (intArray, i => i.IsPrime());
```

The `extractedData` collection will now contain the prime numbers obtained from the `intArray` collection. If we run the project, we will get the following output on the console:

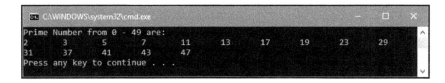

We can actually modify our preceding code snippet in a simpler way since all query operators are extension methods and can be used directly in the collection. The modification of the preceding code snippet is as follows:

```
IEnumerable<int> extractedData =
  intArray.Where(i => i.IsPrime());
```

By modifying the invocation of the `Where` operator, we will get the complete implementation, as follows:

```
public partial class Program
{
  public static void ExtractArrayWithMethodSyntax()
  {
    IEnumerable<int> extractedData =
      intArray.Where(i => i.IsPrime());
```

```
      Console.WriteLine("Prime Number from 0 - 49 are:");
      foreach (int i in extractedData)
        Console.Write("{0} \t", i);
      Console.WriteLine();
  }
}
```

If we run the preceding `ExtractArrayWithMethodSyntax()` method, we will get the exact same output with the `ExtractArray()` method.

Deferring LINQ execution

LINQ implements a deferred execution concept when we query the data from a collection. This means that the query will not be executed in the constructor time but in the enumeration process instead. For example, we use the `Where` operator to query data from a collection. Actually, the query is not executed until we enumerate it. We can use the `foreach` operation to call the `MoveNext` command in order to enumerate the query. To discuss deferred execution in further detail, let's take a look at the following code, which we can find in the `DeferredExecution.csproj` project:

```
public partial class Program
{
  public static void DeferredExecution()
  {
    List memberList = new List()
    {
      new Member
      {
        ID = 1,
        Name = "Eddie Morgan",
        Gender = "Male",
        MemberSince = new DateTime(2016, 2, 10)
      },
      new Member
      {
        ID = 2,
        Name = "Millie Duncan",
        Gender = "Female",
        MemberSince = new DateTime(2015, 4, 3)
      },
      new Member
      {
        ID = 3,
        Name = "Thiago Hubbard",
        Gender = "Male",
```

```
          MemberSince = new DateTime(2014, 1, 8)
      },
      new Member
      {
        ID = 4,
        Name = "Emilia Shaw",
        Gender = "Female",
        MemberSince = new DateTime(2015, 11, 15)
      }
    };
    IEnumerable<Member> memberQuery =
      from m in memberList
      where m.MemberSince.Year > 2014
      orderby m.Name
      select m;
      memberList.Add(new Member
      {
        ID = 5,
        Name = "Chloe Day",
        Gender = "Female",
        MemberSince = new DateTime(2016, 5, 28)
      });
    foreach (Member m in memberQuery)
    {
      Console.WriteLine(m.Name);
    }
  }
}
```

As you can see in the implementation of the preceding `DeferredExecution()` method, we construct a `List<Member>` member list named `memberList`, which contains four instances of every member who has joined to the club. The `Member` class itself is as follows:

```
public class Member
{
  public int ID { get; set; }
  public string Name { get; set; }
  public string Gender { get; set; }
  public DateTime MemberSince { get; set; }
}
```

After constructing `memberList`, we query the data from `memberList`, which includes the all members who joined after 2014. Here, we can confirm that only three of four members satisfy the requirements. They are Eddie Morgan, Millie Duncan, and Emilia Shaw in ascending order, of course, since we use the `orderby m.Name` phrase in the query.

After we have the query, we add a new member to `memberList` and then run the `foreach` operation in order to enumerate the query. What will happen next is that, because most of the query operators implement deferred execution, which will be executed only in the enumeration process, we will have four members after enumerating the query since the last member we add to `memberList` satisfies the query requirement. To make this clear, let's take a look at the following output we get on the console after invoking the `DeferredExecution()` method:

As you can see, `Chloe Day`, who is the last member to have joined the club, is included in the query result as well. This is where the deferred execution plays its role.

Almost all query operators provide deferred execution but not the operators that:

- Return a scalar value or a single element, such as `Count` and `First`.
- Convert the result of a query, such as `ToList`, `ToArray`, `ToDictionary`, and `ToLookup`. They are also called conversion operators.

The `Count()` and `First()` method will be executed immediately since they return a single object, so it's almost impossible to provide deferred execution as well as conversion operators. Using the conversion operator, we can obtain a cached copy of the query results and can avoid repeating the process due to the reevaluate operation in deferred execution. Now, let's take a look at the following code, which we can find in the `NonDeferredExecution.csproj` project, to demonstrate the nondeferred execution process:

```
public partial class Program
{
  private static void NonDeferred()
  {
    List<int> intList = new List<int>
    {
      0, 1, 2, 3, 4, 5, 6, 7, 8, 9
    };
    IEnumerable<int> queryInt = intList.Select(i => i * 2);
    int queryIntCount = queryInt.Count();
    List<int> queryIntCached = queryInt.ToList();
```

```
      int queryIntCachedCount = queryIntCached.Count();
      intList.Clear();
      Console.WriteLine(
        String.Format(
          "Enumerate queryInt.Count {0}.", queryIntCount));
      foreach (int i in queryInt)
      {
        Console.WriteLine(i);
      }
      Console.WriteLine(String.Format(
        "Enumerate queryIntCached.Count {0}.",
        queryIntCachedCount));
      foreach (int i in queryIntCached)
      {
        Console.WriteLine(i);
      }
    }
  }
```

First, in the preceding code, we have a List<int> integer list named intList, which contains numbers from 0 to 9. We then create a query named queryInt in order to select all members of intList and multiply them by 2. We also count the total of the query data using the Count() method. Since queryInt is not executed yet, we create a new query named queryIntCached, which converts queryInt to List<int> using the ToList() conversion operator. We also count the total of the data in that query. We have two queries now, queryInt and queryIntCached. We then clear intList and enumerate the two queries. The following is the result of them being displayed on the console:

As you can see in the preceding console, the enumeration of `queryInt` results in no item. This is clear since we have removed all `intList` items, so `queryInt` will find no item in `intList`. However, `queryInt` is counted as ten items since we have run the `Count()` method before we clear `intList`, and the method is immediately executed right after we construct it. In contrast to `queryInt`, we have ten items' data when we enumerate `queryIntCached`. This is because we have invoked the `ToList()` conversion operator and it is immediately executed as well.

 There is one more type of deferred execution. It happens when we chain the `OrderBy` method after a `Select` method, for instance. The `Select` method will only retrieve one element at the time that it has to produce an element, while the `OrderBy` method has to consume the entire input sequence before it returns the first element. So, when we chain an `OrderBy` method after the `Select` method, the execution will be deferred until we retrieve the first element, and then the `OrderBy` method will ask `Select` for all the elements.

Choosing between fluent syntax and query expression syntax

From our preceding discussion, we found two types of querying syntaxes so far. Let's discuss this further by distinguishing these two syntaxes.

```
IEnumerable<int> queryInt =
    intList.Select(i => i * 2);
int queryIntCount = queryInt.Count();
```

The preceding code snippet is the fluent syntax type. We invoke the `Select` and `Count` operators by invoking their extension method in the `Enumerable` class. Using the fluent syntax, we can also chain the method so it will approach functional programming as follows:

```
IEnumerable<int> queryInt =
    intList
        .Select(i => i * 2);
        .Count();
```

Another syntax type we can use in querying data in LINQ is query expression syntax. We applied this syntax type when we discussed deferred execution in the previous topic. The code snippet of the query expression syntax is as follows:

```
IEnumerable<Member> memberQuery =
  from m in memberList
  where m.MemberSince.Year > 2014
  orderby m.Name
  select m;
```

In fact, the fluent syntax and the query expression syntax will do the same thing. The difference between them is only the syntax. Each keyword in the query expression syntax has its own extension method in the `Enumerable` class. To prove this, we can refactor the preceding code snippet to the following fluent syntax type:

```
IEnumerable<Member> memberQuery =
  memberList
  .Where(m => m.MemberSince.Year > 2014)
  .OrderBy(m => m.Name)
  .Select(m => m);
```

Indeed, we will get the exact same output for these two types of syntaxes. However, the fluent syntax is closer to the functional approach than the query expression syntax.

Understanding the LINQ fluent syntax

Basically, the LINQ fluent syntax is the extension methods found in the `Enumerable` class. The method will extend any variable implementing the `IEnumerable<T>` interface. The fluent syntax takes a lambda expression as the parameter to represent the logic that will be performed in the sequence enumeration. As we discussed earlier, the fluent syntax implemented the method chain so that it can be used in the functional approach. In the beginning of this chapter, we had also discussed the extension method from which the query operator can be invoked directly using the static method from its class, which is the `Enumerable` class. However, by invoking the method directly from its class, we cannot implement the method chain we usually use in the functional approach. Let's take at the following code, which we can find in the `FluentSyntax.csproj` project, to demonstrate the advantages of the fluent syntax by invoking the extension method instead of the conventional `static` method:

```
public partial class Program
{
  private static void UsingExtensionMethod()
  {
```

```
        IEnumerable<string> query = names
          .Where(n => n.Length > 4)
          .OrderBy(n => n[0])
          .Select(n => n.ToUpper());
        foreach (string s in query)
        {
          Console.WriteLine(s);
        }
      }
    }
```

The names collection we used in the preceding code is as follows:

```
    public partial class Program
    {
      static List<string> names = new List<string>
      {
        "Howard", "Pat",
        "Jaclyn", "Kathryn",
        "Ben", "Aaron",
        "Stacey", "Levi",
        "Patrick", "Tara",
        "Joe", "Ruby",
        "Bruce", "Cathy",
        "Jimmy", "Kim",
        "Kelsey", "Becky",
        "Scott", "Dick"
      };
    }
```

As you can see, we use three query operators when we query the data from a collection in the preceding code. They are the `Where`, `OrderBy`, and `Select` operators. Let's take a look at the following code snippet to make this clear:

```
    IEnumerable<string> query =
      names
      .Where(n => n.Length > 4)
      .OrderBy(n => n[0])
      .Select(n => n.ToUpper());
```

Based on the preceding query, we will get the string collection in which each string contains more than four characters. The collection will be sorted in an ascending order by its first letter, and the string will be in uppercase characters. Here's what we get on the console if we run the `UsingExtensionMethod()` method as shown in the following screenshot:

Now, let's refactor the preceding query to use the conventional static method. But before we go through it, here are the signatures of the three methods we have used in the preceding query:

```
public static IEnumerable<TSource> Where<TSource>(
   this IEnumerable<TSource> source,
   Func<TSource, bool> predicate
)

public static IEnumerable<TSource> OrderBy<TSource, TKey>(
   this IEnumerable<TSource> source,
   Func<TSource, TKey> keySelector
)

public static IEnumerable<TResult> Select<TSource, TResult>(
   this IEnumerable<TSource> source,
   Func<TSource, TResult> selector
)
```

As you can see, all three methods take `IEnumerable<TSource>` as the first parameter and also return `IEnumerable<TResult>`. We can use this similarity so that the return from the first method can be fed to the argument of the second method, the return from the second method can be fed to the argument of the third method, and so on.

In the `Where()` method, we use the second parameter, predicate, to filter the sequence based on it. It's a `Func<TSource, bool>` delegate, so we can use a lambda expression here. The `Func<TSource, TKey>` delegate can also be found in the second parameter of the `OrderBy()` method, which is used as the key to sort the element of the sequence in an ascending order. It can be fed by anonymous method. The last is the `Select()` method, in which we use its second parameter, `selector`, to project each element in the sequence in the new form. The anonymous method can also be used as the argument.

Based on the signature of the methods we used in the previous `UsingExtensionMethod()` method, we can refactor the query as follows:

```
IEnumerable<string> query = Enumerable.Select(
  Enumerable.OrderBy(Enumerable.Where(names, n => n.Length > 4),
  n => n[0]), n => n.ToUpper());
```

Here is the complete `UsingStaticMethod()` method, which is the refactoring code when we use a conventional static method instead of the extension method:

```
public partial class Program
{
  private static void UsingStaticMethod()
  {
    IEnumerable<string> query =
     Enumerable.Select(
       Enumerable.OrderBy(
         Enumerable.Where(
           names, n => n.Length > 4),
           n => n[0]), n => n.ToUpper());
    foreach (string s in query)
    {
      Console.WriteLine(s);
    }
  }
}
```

By running the `UsingStaticMethod()` method, we will get the exact output on the console compared to the `UsingExtensionMethod()` method.

Understanding the LINQ query expression syntax

A LINQ query expression syntax is a shorthand syntax that we can use to perform LINQ queries. In a query expression syntax, .NET framework provides the keywords for each query operator but not all operators. By using the query syntax, we can invoke the operator like we query the data using SQL in the database. Our code will be more readable and will require less coding when we use the query expression syntax.

In the fluent syntax discussion, we created a query to extract the string from the string list that contains more than four characters, sorted in an ascending order by its first letter and converted to uppercase characters. We can do this using the query expression syntax, as shown in the following code, which we can find in the `QueryExpressionSyntax.csproj` project:

```
public partial class Program
{
  private static void InvokingQueryExpression()
  {
    IEnumerable<string> query =
      from n in names
      where n.Length > 4
      orderby n[0]
      select n.ToUpper();
    foreach (string s in query)
    {
      Console.WriteLine(s);
    }
  }
}
```

As you can see, we have refactored the previous code, which uses the fluent syntax for the query expression syntax. Indeed, if we run the `InvokingQueryExpression()` method, the exact same output will be displayed will be displayed compared to the `UsingExtensionMethod()` method.

Unfortunately, there are several LINQ operators that have no keyword in the query expression syntax, such as the `distinct` operator since it doesn't take a lambda expression. In this case, we have to use the fluent syntax, at least in part if we still want to use it. The following are the operators that have a keyword in the query expression syntax:

- `Where`
- `Select`
- `SelectMany`
- `OrderBy`

- ThenBy
- OrderByDescending
- ThenByDescending
- GroupBy
- Join
- GroupJoin

Actually, the compiler converts the query expression syntax into fluent syntax in the compiling process. Although the query expression syntax is sometimes easier to read, we cannot perform all the operations using it; instead, we have to use the fluent syntax, for instance, count operators as we discussed in *Deferring LINQ execution* topic. What we write in the query expression syntax can also be written in the fluent syntax. Therefore, the fluent syntax is the best approach when we code using LINQ, especially in the functional approach.

Enumerating standard query operators

There are more than 50 query operators in the Enumerable class included in the System.Linq namespace. They are also known as standard query operators. Based on the function of the operators, we can divide them into several operations. Here, we are going to discuss all the query operators in LINQ provided by .NET Framework.

Filtering

Filtering is an operation that will evaluate the element of data so that only the element satisfying the condition will be selected. There are six filtering operators; they are Where, Take, Skip, TakeWhile, SkipWhile, and Distinct. As we know, we have already discussed the Where operator in our previous sample code, both in the fluent syntax and the query expression syntax, and have an idea that it will return a subset of elements satisfying a condition given by a predicate. Since we are clear enough about the Where operator, we can skip it and continue with the remaining five filtering operators.

The Take operator returns the first n elements and dumps the rest. In contrast, the Skip operator ignores the first n elements and returns the rest. Let's take a look at the following code from the FilteringOperation.csproj project:

```
public partial class Program
```

```
{
  public static void SimplyTakeAndSkipOperator()
  {
    IEnumerable<int> queryTake =
      intList.Take(10);
    Console.WriteLine("Take operator");
    foreach (int i in queryTake)
    {
      Console.Write(String.Format("{0}\t", i));
    }
    Console.WriteLine();
    IEnumerable<int> querySkip = intList.Skip(10);
    Console.WriteLine("Skip operator");
    foreach (int i in querySkip)
    {
      Console.Write(String.Format("{0}\t", i));
    }
    Console.WriteLine();
  }
}
```

We have two queries in the preceding code, `queryTake`, which applies the `Take` operator, and `querySkip`, which applies the `Skip` operator. They both consume `intList`, which is actually a list of integers containing the following data:

```
public partial class Program
{
static List<int> intList = new List<int>
  {
    0,  1,  2,  3,  4,
    5,  6,  7,  8,  9,
    10, 11, 12, 13, 14,
    15, 16, 17, 18, 19
  };
}
```

If we run the preceding `SimplyTakeAndSkipOperator()` method, we will get the following output:

The preceding `Take` and `Skip` operator sample is simple code, since it deals with a collection containing only twenty elements. In fact, the `Take` and `Skip` operators are useful when we work with a huge collection, or maybe a database, to ease user access to the data. Suppose we have a million elements of the integer collection and we are looking for the element that is multiplied by two and seven. Without using the `Take` and `Skip` operators, we will have a ton of results, and if we show them on the console, they will clutter the console display. Let's take a look at the following code to prove this:

```
public partial class Program
{
  public static void NoTakeSkipOperator()
  {
    IEnumerable<int> intCollection =
      Enumerable.Range(1, 1000000);
    IEnumerable<int> hugeQuery =
       intCollection
      .Where(h => h % 2 == 0 && h % 7 == 0);
    foreach (int x in hugeQuery)
    {
      Console.WriteLine(x);
    }
  }
}
```

As you can see here, we have `hugeQuery` containing huge data. If we run the method, it needs about ten seconds to complete the iteration of all elements. We can also add the `Count` operator if we want to retrieve the actual elements `hugeQuery` contains, which is *71428* elements.

Now, we can modify the code by adding the `Take` and `Skip` operators around the `foreach` loop, as shown in the following code:

```
public partial class Program
{
  public static void TakeAndSkipOperator()
  {
    IEnumerable<int> intCollection =
      Enumerable.Range(1, 1000000);
    IEnumerable<int> hugeQuery =
      intCollection
        .Where(h => h % 2 == 0 && h % 7 == 0);
    int pageSize = 10;
    for (int i = 0; i < hugeQuery.Count()/ pageSize; i++)
    {
      IEnumerable<int> paginationQuery =hugeQuery
        .Skip(i * pageSize)
```

```
        .Take(pageSize);
      foreach (int x in paginationQuery)
      {
        Console.WriteLine(x);
      }
      Console.WriteLine(
        "Press Enter to continue, " +
          "other key will stop process!");
      if (Console.ReadKey().Key != ConsoleKey.Enter)
        break;
    }
  }
}
```

In the preceding `TakeAndSkipOperator()` method, we add a couple of line of code in the highlighted lines. Now, although we have a lot of data, the output will be displayed conveniently when we run the method, as follows:

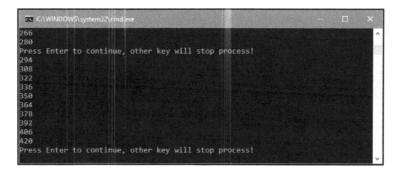

As you can see, the entire result is not presented on the console, only ten integers each time. Users can press Enter key if they want to continue to read the rest of data. This is what we usually call pagination. The `Take` and `Skip` operators have done a good job to achieve it.

Besides discussing `Take` and `Skip` operators, we are going to discuss `TakeWhile` and `SkipWhile` operators in filtering operators. In `TakeWhile` operator, the input collection will be enumerated and each element will be sent to the query until the predicate is `false`. In contrast, the input collection will be enumerated, and when the predicate is `true`, the element will be sent to the query. Now, let's take a look at the following code to demonstrate the `TakeWhile` and `SkipWhile` operators:

```
public partial class Program
{
  public static void TakeWhileAndSkipWhileOperators()
  {
    int[] intArray = { 10, 4, 27, 53, 2, 96, 48 };
```

```
    IEnumerable<int> queryTakeWhile =
        intArray.TakeWhile(n => n < 50);
    Console.WriteLine("TakeWhile operator");
    foreach (int i in queryTakeWhile)
    {
      Console.Write(String.Format("{0}\t", i));
    }
    Console.WriteLine();
    IEnumerable<int> querySkipWhile =
        intArray.SkipWhile(n => n < 50);
    Console.WriteLine("SkipWhile operator");
    foreach (int i in querySkipWhile)
    {
      Console.Write(String.Format("{0}\t", i));
    }
    Console.WriteLine();
  }
}
```

When we run the preceding method, we will get the following output on the console:

Since we have `n < 50` in the predicate, in `TakeWhile`, the enumeration will emit the elements until it reaches 53, and in `SkipWhile`, the element start to be emitted when the enumeration reaches 53.

We also have the `Distinct` operator in this filtering operation. The `Distinct` operator will return the input sequence without any duplicate elements. Suppose we have the following code:

```
public partial class Program
{
  public static void DistinctOperator()
  {
    string words = "TheQuickBrownFoxJumpsOverTheLazyDog";
      IEnumerable <char> queryDistinct = words.Distinct();
    string distinctWords = "";
    foreach (char c in queryDistinct)
    {
      distinctWords += c.ToString();
    }
```

```
            Console.WriteLine(distinctWords);
      }
   }
```

In the preceding code, we have a string and we intend to remove all duplicate letters in that string. We use the `Distinct` operator to get the query and then enumerate it. The result will be as follows:

As you can see, there are some letters that have disappeared due to the use of the `Distinct` operator. There are no duplicate letters that appear in this case.

Projection

Projection is an operation that transforms an object into a new form. There are two projection operators; they are `Select` and `SelectMany`. Using the `Select` operator, we can transform each input element based on the given lambda expression, whereas using the `SelectMany` operator, we can transform each input element and then and flatten the resulting sequences into one sequence by concatenating them.

We had applied the `Select` operator when we discussed deferring LINQ execution. The following is the code snippet that uses the `Select` operator that we extract from the sample in Deferring LINQ execution topic:

```
IEnumerable<Member> memberQuery =
   from m in memberList
   where m.MemberSince.Year > 2014
   orderby m.Name
   select m;
```

As you can see, we use the `Select` operator, which is the `Select` keyword in this case since we use the query expression syntax, to select all the resulting elements filtered by the `Where` keyword. As we know from the `Select` operator, the object can be transformed into another form, and we can transform that element typed `Member` class object into the element typed `RecentMember` class object using the following code:

```
IEnumerable<RecentMember> memberQuery =
   from m in memberList
   where m.MemberSince.Year > 2014
```

```
   orderby m.Name
   select new RecentMember{
     FirstName = m.Name.GetFirstName(),
     LastName = m.Name.GetLastName(),
     Gender = m.Gender,
     MemberSince = m.MemberSince,
     Status = "Valid"
   };
```

Using the preceding code, we assume that there is a class named `RecentMember`, as follows:

```
public class RecentMember
{
  public string FirstName { get; set; }
  public string LastName { get; set; }
  public string Gender { get; set; }
  public DateTime MemberSince { get; set; }
  public string Status { get; set; }
}
```

From the preceding code snippet, we can see that we transform each input element using the `Select` operator. We can insert the code snippet into the following complete source:

```
public partial class Program
{
  public static void SelectOperator()
  {
    List<Member> memberList = new List<Member>()
    {
      new Member
      {
        ID = 1,
        Name = "Eddie Morgan",
        Gender = "Male",
        MemberSince = new DateTime(2016, 2, 10)
      },
      new Member
      {
        ID = 2,
        Name = "Millie Duncan",
        Gender = "Female",
        MemberSince = new DateTime(2015, 4, 3)
      },
      new Member
      {
        ID = 3,
        Name = "Thiago Hubbard",
```

```
      Gender = "Male",
      MemberSince = new DateTime(2014, 1, 8)
    },
    new Member
    {
      ID = 4,
      Name = "Emilia Shaw",
      Gender = "Female",
      MemberSince = new DateTime(2015, 11, 15)
    }
  };
  IEnumerable<RecentMember> memberQuery =
    from m in memberList
    where m.MemberSince.Year > 2014
    orderby m.Name
    select new RecentMember{
      FirstName = m.Name.GetFirstName(),
      LastName = m.Name.GetLastName(),
      Gender = m.Gender,
      MemberSince = m.MemberSince,
      Status = "Valid"
    };
  foreach (RecentMember rm in memberQuery)
  {
    Console.WriteLine(
      "First Name  : " + rm.FirstName);
    Console.WriteLine(
      "Last Name   : " + rm.LastName);
    Console.WriteLine(
      "Gender      : " + rm.Gender);
    Console.WriteLine
      ("Member Since: " + rm.MemberSince.ToString("dd/MM/yyyy"));
    Console.WriteLine(
      "Status      : " + rm.Status);
    Console.WriteLine();
  }
  }
}
```

Since we have enumerated the query using the `foreach` iterator and have written the element to the console using the `Console.WriteLine()` method, after running the preceding `SelectOperator()` method, we will get the following output on the console:

From the preceding console screenshot, we can see that we have successfully transformed the `Member` type input elements into the `RecentMember` type output elements. We can also use the fluent syntax to produce the exact same result, as shown in the following code snippet:

```
IEnumerable<RecentMember> memberQuery =
   memberList
   .Where(m => m.MemberSince.Year > 2014)
   .OrderBy(m => m.Name)
   .Select(m => new RecentMember
{
   FirstName = m.Name.GetFirstName(),
   LastName = m.Name.GetLastName(),
   Gender = m.Gender,
   MemberSince = m.MemberSince,
   Status = "Valid"
});
```

Now, let's move on to the `SelectMany` operator. Using this operator, we can select more than one sequence and then flatten the result into one sequence. Suppose we have two collections and we are going to select all of them; we can achieve the goal using the following code:

```
public partial class Program
{
   public static void SelectManyOperator()
   {
```

```
List<string> numberTypes = new List<string>()
{
  "Multiplied by 2",
  "Multiplied by 3"
};
List<int> numbers = new List<int>()
{
  6, 12, 18, 24
};
IEnumerable<NumberType> query =
    numbers.SelectMany(
      num => numberTypes,
      (n, t) =>new NumberType
      {
        TheNumber = n,
        TheType = t
      });
foreach (NumberType nt in query)
{
  Console.WriteLine(String.Format(
    "Number: {0,2} - Types: {1}",
      nt.TheNumber,
        nt.TheType));
}
}
}
```

As you can see, we have two collections named `numberTypes` and `numbers` and want to take any possible combination from their elements. The result is in a new form typed `NumberType` with the following definition:

```
public class NumberType
{
  public int TheNumber { get; set; }
  public string TheType { get; set; }
}
```

If we run the preceding `SelectManyOperator()` method, the following output will be displayed on the console:

```
C:\WINDOWS\system32\cmd.exe
Number:   6 - Types: Multiplied by 2
Number:   6 - Types: Multiplied by 3
Number:  12 - Types: Multiplied by 2
Number:  12 - Types: Multiplied by 3
Number:  18 - Types: Multiplied by 2
Number:  18 - Types: Multiplied by 3
Number:  24 - Types: Multiplied by 2
Number:  24 - Types: Multiplied by 3
Press any key to continue . . .
```

In this code, we actually iterate the two collections to construct the combination of two collections since the implementation of the `SelectMany` operator is as follows:

```
public static IEnumerable<TResult> SelectMany<TSource, TResult>(
  this IEnumerable<TSource> source,
  Func<TSource, IEnumerable<TResult>> selector)
{
  foreach (TSource element in source)
  foreach (TResult subElement in selector (element))
  yield return subElement;
}
```

We can also apply the query expression syntax to replace the preceding fluent syntax using the following code snippet:

```
IEnumerable<NumberType> query =
  from n in numbers
  from t in numberTypes
  select new NumberType
{
  TheNumber = n,
  TheType = t
};
```

The output from the query expression syntax will be exactly the same as the fluent syntax.

The `from` keyword has two different meanings in the query expression syntax. When we use the keyword at the start of the syntax, it will introduce the original range variable and the input sequence. When we use the keyword anywhere other than at the beginning, it will be translated into the `SelectMany` operator.

Joining

Joining is an operation that meshes different source sequences with no direct object model relationship into a single output sequence. Nevertheless, the elements in each source have to share a value that can be compared for equality. There are two joining operators in LINQ; they are `Join` and `GroupJoin`.

The `Join` operator uses a lookup technique to match elements from two sequences and then returns a flat result set. To explain this further, let's take a look at the following code, which we can find in the `Joining.csproj` project:

```
public partial class Program
{
  public static void JoinOperator()
  {
    Course hci = new Course{
      Title = "Human Computer Interaction",
      CreditHours = 3};
    Course iis = new Course{
      Title = "Information in Society",
      CreditHours = 2};
    Course modr = new Course{
      Title = "Management of Digital Records",
      CreditHours = 3};
    Course micd = new Course{
      Title = "Moving Image Collection Development",
      CreditHours = 2};
    Student carol = new Student{
      Name = "Carol Burks",
      CourseTaken = modr};
    Student river = new Student{
      Name = "River Downs",
      CourseTaken = micd};
    Student raylee = new Student{
      Name = "Raylee Price",
      CourseTaken = hci};
    Student jordan = new Student{
      Name = "Jordan Owen",
      CourseTaken = modr};
    Student denny = new Student{
      Name = "Denny Edwards",
      CourseTaken = hci};
    Student hayden = new Student{
      Name = "Hayden Winters",
      CourseTaken = iis};
    List<Course> courses = new List<Course>{
      hci, iis, modr, micd};
```

```
      List<Student> students = new List<Student>{
        carol, river, raylee, jordan, denny, hayden};
    var query = courses.Join(
      students,
      course => course,
      student => student.CourseTaken,
      (course, student) =>
        new {StudentName = student.Name,
          CourseTaken = course.Title });
    foreach (var item in query)
    {
      Console.WriteLine(
        "{0} - {1}",
        item.StudentName,
        item.CourseTaken);
    }
  }
}
```

The preceding code consumes `Student` and `Course` classes with the following implementation:

```
public class Student
{
  public string Name { get; set; }
  public Course CourseTaken { get; set; }
}
public class Course
{
  public string Title { get; set; }
  public int CreditHours { get; set; }
}
```

If we run the preceding `JoinOperator()` method, we will get the following output on the console:

From the preceding code, we can see that we have two sequences, which are `courses` and `students`. We can join these two sequences using the `Join` operator and then we create an anonymous type as the result. We can also use the query expression syntax to join these two sequences. The following is the code snippet we have to replace in our previous query creation:

```
var query =
from c in courses
join s in students on c.Title equals s.CourseTaken.Title
select new {
  StudentName = s.Name,
  CourseTaken = c.Title };
```

If we run the `JoinOperator()` method again, we will get the exact same output on the console.

The `GroupJoin` operator uses the same technique that the `Join` operator uses, but it returns a hierarchical result set. Let's take a look at the following code that explains the `GroupJoin` operator:

```
public partial class Program
{
  public static void GroupJoinOperator()
  {
    Course hci = new Course{
      Title = "Human Computer Interaction",
      CreditHours = 3};

    Course iis = new Course{
      Title = "Information in Society",
      CreditHours = 2};

    Course modr = new Course{
      Title = "Management of Digital Records",
      CreditHours = 3};

    Course micd = new Course{
      Title = "Moving Image Collection Development",
      CreditHours = 2};

    Student carol = new Student{
      Name = "Carol Burks",
      CourseTaken = modr};

    Student river = new Student{
      Name = "River Downs",
      CourseTaken = micd};
```

```
Student raylee = new Student{
  Name = "Raylee Price",
  CourseTaken = hci};

Student jordan = new Student{
  Name = "Jordan Owen",
  CourseTaken = modr};

Student denny = new Student{
  Name = "Denny Edwards",
  CourseTaken = hci};

Student hayden = new Student{
  Name = "Hayden Winters",
  CourseTaken = iis};

List<Course> courses = new List<Course>{
  hci, iis, modr, micd};

List<Student> students = new List<Student>{
  carol, river, raylee, jordan, denny, hayden};

var query = courses.GroupJoin(
  students,
  course => course,
  student => student.CourseTaken,
  (course, studentCollection) =>
  new{
    CourseTaken = course.Title,
    Students =
    studentCollection
    .Select(student => student.Name)
  });

  foreach (var item in query)
  {
    Console.WriteLine("{0}:", item.CourseTaken);
    foreach (string stdnt in item.Students)
    {
      Console.WriteLine("  {0}", stdnt);
    }
  }
}
}
```

The preceding code is similar to the Join operator code that we discussed earlier. The difference is in the way we create the query. In the `GroupJoin` operator, we join the two sequences into another sequence with a key. Let's invoke the preceding `GroupJoinOperator()` method, and we will get the following output on the console:

As you can see in the output, we group all the students who take a particular course. We then enumerate the query to get the result.

Ordering

Ordering is an operation that will sort the return sequence from the input sequence using the default comparer. For instance, if we have a sequence in the string type, the default comparer will perform an alphabetical sort from A to Z. Let's take a look at the following code, which we can find in the `Ordering.csproj` project:

```
public partial class Program
{
  public static void OrderByOperator()
  {
    IEnumerable<string> query =
      nameList.OrderBy(n => n);

    foreach (string s in query)
    {
      Console.WriteLine(s);
    }
  }
}
```

For the sequence that we have to feed to the query, the code is as follows:

```
public partial class Program
{
  static List<string> nameList = new List<string>()
```

```
  {
    "Blair", "Lane", "Jessie", "Aiden",
    "Reggie", "Tanner", "Maddox", "Kerry"
  };
}
```

If we run the preceding `OrderByOperator()` method, we will get the following output on the console:

As you can see, we execute the ordering operation using the default comparer, so the sequence is sorted alphabetically. We can also use the query expression syntax to replace the following code snippet:

```
IEnumerable<string> query =
  nameList.OrderBy(n => n);
```

The query expression syntax we have for the sequence is shown in the following code snippet:

```
IEnumerable<string> query =
  from n in nameList
  orderby n
  select n;
```

We can create our own comparer as the key selector to sort the sequence by the last character in each element; here is the code we can use to achieve this using the `IComparer<T>` interface. Suppose we want to sort our previous sequence:

```
public partial class Program
{
  public static void OrderByOperatorWithComparer()
  {
    IEnumerable<string> query =
      nameList.OrderBy(
        n => n,
        new LastCharacterComparer());
```

```
    foreach (string s in query)
    {
      Console.WriteLine(s);
    }
  }
}
```

We also create a new class, `LastCharacterComparer`, which inherits the `IComparer<string>` interface, as follows:

```
public class LastCharacterComparer : IComparer<string>
{
  public int Compare(string x, string y)
  {
    return string.Compare(
      x[x.Length - 1].ToString(),
       y[y.Length - 1].ToString());
  }
}
```

We will get the following output on the console when we run the preceding `OrderByOperatorWithComparer()` method:

As you can see, we have an ordered sequence now, but the sorting key is the last character of each element. This is achieved with the help of our custom comparer. Unfortunately, the custom comparer is only available using the fluent syntax. In other words, we can't use it in the query expression method.

When we sort the sequence, we can have more than one comparer as a condition. We can use the `ThenBy` extension method for the second condition after we call the `OrderBy` method. Let's take a look at the following code to demonstrate this:

```
public partial class Program
{
  public static void OrderByThenByOperator()
  {
```

```
        IEnumerable<string> query = nameList
          .OrderBy(n => n.Length)
          .ThenBy(n => n);
        foreach (string s in query)
        {
          Console.WriteLine(s);
        }
    }
}
```

From the preceding code, we sort the sequence by the length of each element, and then we sort the result alphabetically. If we call the `OrderByThenByOperator()` method, we will get the following output:

We can also use query expression syntax when we need to sort a sequence using two conditions, as shown in the following code snippet:

```
IEnumerable<string> query =
  from n in nameList
  orderby n.Length, n
  select n;
```

If we run `OrderByThenByOperator()` method again after replacing the query operation with the query expression syntax, we will get the exact same output as we get when we use the fluent syntax. However, there is no `ThenBy` keyword in the query expression syntax. What we need to do is just separate the condition using a comma.

We can use our custom comparer in the use of the `ThenBy` method as well. Let's take a look at the following code to try this:

```
public partial class Program
{
  public static void OrderByThenByOperatorWithComparer()
  {
    IEnumerable<string> query = nameList
      .OrderBy(n => n.Length)
```

```
        .ThenBy(n => n, new LastCharacterComparer());
      foreach (string s in query)
      {
        Console.WriteLine(s);
      }
    }
  }
```

In this code, we use the same `LastCharacterComparer` class that we use in the `OrderByOperatorWithComparer()` method. If we call the `OrderByThenByOperatorWithComparer()` method, the following is the output we will get on the console:

Besides ascending sorting, we also have descending sorting. In fluent syntax, we can simply use `OrderByDescending()` and `ThenByDescending()` methods. The usage in code is exactly the same, as the code for sorting in an ascending order. However, in the query expression syntax, we have the descending keyword to achieve this goal. We use this keyword just after we define the condition in the `orderby` keyword, as shown in the following code:

```
public partial class Program
{
  public static void OrderByDescendingOperator()
  {
    IEnumerable<string> query =
      from n in nameList
      orderby n descending
      select n;
    foreach (string s in query)
    {
      Console.WriteLine(s);
    }
  }
}
```

As you can see, there is a descending keyword in the as well code. Actually, we can replace the descending keyword with the ascending keyword in order to sort the sequence in an ascending manner. However, ascending sorting is the default sorting in LINQ, so the ascending keyword can be omitted. The following is the output if we run the code and invoke the `OrderByDescendingOperator()` method:

Grouping

Grouping is an operation that will generate a sequence of `IGrouping<TKey, TElement>` objects, which are grouped by the `TKey` key value. For instance, we will group a sequence of path address files in one directory by their first letters. The following code can be found in the `Grouping.csproj` project file and will search all file in `G:\packages`, which is the setup files of Visual Studio 2015 Community Edition. You can adjust the drive letter and folder name based on the drive letter and folder name on your computer.

```
public partial class Program
{
  public static void GroupingByFileNameExtension()
  {
    IEnumerable<string> fileList =
      Directory.EnumerateFiles(
        @"G:\packages", "*.*",
        SearchOption.AllDirectories);
    IEnumerable<IGrouping<string, string>> query =
      fileList.GroupBy(f =>
      Path.GetFileName(f)[0].ToString());
    foreach (IGrouping<string, string> g in query)
    {
      Console.WriteLine();
      Console.WriteLine(
        "File start with the letter: " +
          g.Key);
      foreach (string filename in g)
      Console.WriteLine(
        "..." + Path.GetFileName(filename));
```

[168]

```
        }
    }
}
```

The preceding code will find all files in the `G:\packages` folder (including all the subdirectories) then group them based on the first letter in their filenames. As you can see when we enumerate a query using the `foreach` loop, we have `g.Key`, which is the key selector for grouping that string list. If we run the `GroupingByFileNameExtension()` method, we will get the following output on the console:

The `GroupBy` extension method also has a clause in order to be used in the query expression syntax. The clauses we can use are `group` and `by`. The following code snippet can replace the query in our previous code:

```
IEnumerable<IGrouping<string, string>> query =
    from f in fileList
    group f by Path.GetFileName(f)[0].ToString();
```

We will still have the same output as the fluent syntax output, although we replace the query using the query expression syntax. As you can see, the grouping operation in LINQ only groups the sequence; it does not sort. We can sort the result using the `OrderBy` operator provided by LINQ.

In the preceding query expression syntax, we see that we do not need the select clause again since the group clause will end the query as well. However, we still need the select clause when using the group clause if we add a query continuation clause. Now let's we take a look at the following code, which applies the query continuation clause to sort the sequence:

```
public partial class Program
{
    public static void GroupingByInto()
    {
```

```
IEnumerable<string> fileList =
  Directory.EnumerateFiles(
    @"G:\packages", "*.*",
    SearchOption.AllDirectories);
IEnumerable<IGrouping<string, string>> query =
  from f in fileList
  group f
    by Path.GetFileName(f)[0].ToString()
    into g
  orderby g.Key
  select g;
foreach (IGrouping<string, string> g in query)
{
  Console.WriteLine(
    "File start with the letter: " + g.Key);
  //foreach (string filename in g)
  Console.WriteLine(          "..." + Path.GetFileName(filename));
}
  }
}
```

As you can see in the preceding code, we modify the query by adding the query continuation clause and the `orderby` operator to sort the sequence result. The query continuation clause we use is the `into` keyword. Using the `into` keyword, we store the grouping result, and then we manipulate the grouping again. If we run the preceding code, we will get the following output on the console:

We deliberately remove the elements of each group since what we want to examine now is the key itself. Now, we can see that the key is in the ascending order. This happens since we first store the result of the grouping then we sort the key in an ascending manner.

The set operation

The set operation is an operation that returns a result set that is based on the presence or the absence of equivalent elements within the same or separate collection. There are four set operators that LINQ provides; they are Concat, Union, Intersect, and Except. For all the four set operators, there is no query expression keyword.

Let's start with Concat and Union. Using the Concat operator, we will get all the elements of first sequence followed by all the elements of the second sequence as a result. Union does this with the Concat operator but returns only one element for the duplicate elements. The following code, which we can find in the SetOperation.csproj project, demonstrates the difference between Concat and Union:

```
public partial class Program
{
  public static void ConcatUnionOperator()
  {
    IEnumerable<int> concat = sequence1.Concat(sequence2);
    IEnumerable<int> union = sequence1.Union(sequence2);
    Console.WriteLine("Concat");
    foreach (int i in concat)
    {
      Console.Write(".." + i);
    }
    Console.WriteLine();
    Console.WriteLine();
    Console.WriteLine("Union");
    foreach (int i in union)
    {
      Console.Write(".." + i);
    }
    Console.WriteLine();
    Console.WriteLine();
  }
}
```

The two sequences we have as as follows:

```
public partial class Program
{
  static int[] sequence1 = { 1, 2, 3, 4, 5, 6 };
  static int[] sequence2 = { 3, 4, 5, 6, 7, 8 };
}
```

Our preceding code tries to use the `Concat` and `Union` operators. And as per our discussion, the following is the output we will get if we run the `ConcatUnionOperator()` method:

```
C:\WINDOWS\system32\cmd.exe                              —    □    ×
Concat
..1..2..3..4..5..6..3..4..5..6..7..8

Union
..1..2..3..4..5..6..7..8

Press any key to continue . . .
```

The `Intersect` and `Except` are set operators as well. `Intersect` returns the elements that are present in both of the input sequences. `Except` returns the elements of the first input sequence, which are not present in the second. The following code explains the difference between `Intersect` and `Except`:

```csharp
public partial class Program
{
  public static void IntersectExceptOperator()
  {
    IEnumerable<int> intersect = sequence1.Intersect(sequence2);
    IEnumerable<int> except1 = sequence1.Except(sequence2);
    IEnumerable<int> except2 = sequence2.Except(sequence1);
    Console.WriteLine("Intersect of Sequence");
    foreach (int i in intersect)
    {
      Console.Write(".." + i);
    }
    Console.WriteLine();
    Console.WriteLine();
    Console.WriteLine("Except1");
    foreach (int i in except1)
    {
      Console.Write(".." + i);
    }
    Console.WriteLine();
    Console.WriteLine();
    Console.WriteLine("Except2");
    foreach (int i in except2)
    {
      Console.Write(".." + i);
    }
    Console.WriteLine();
    Console.WriteLine();
  }
```

```
}
```

If we invoke the `IntersectExceptOperator()` method, the following output will be
displayed on the console screen:

We apply the two sequences we used earlier in the `ConcatUnionOperator()` method as
an input. As you can see from the preceding console screenshot, in the `Intersect`
operation, only duplication elements are returned. In the `Except` operation, only the unique
element will be returned.

Conversion methods

The main role of conversion methods is to convert one type of collections to other types of
collection. Here, we will discuss the conversion methods provided by LINQ; they are
`OfType`, `Cast`, `ToArray`, `ToList`, `ToDictionary`, and `ToLookup`.

The `OfType` and `Cast` methods have a similar function; they convert `IEnumerable` into
`IEnumerable<T>`. The difference is that `OfType` will discard the wrong type elements, if
any, and `Cast` will throw an exception if there is any wrong type element. Let's take a look
at the following code, which we can find in the `ConversionMethods.csproj` project:

```
public partial class Program
{
  public static void OfTypeCastSimple()
  {
    ArrayList arrayList = new ArrayList();
    arrayList.AddRange(new int[] { 1, 2, 3, 4, 5 });

    IEnumerable<int> sequenceOfType = arrayList.OfType<int>();
    IEnumerable<int> sequenceCast = arrayList.Cast<int>();

    Console.WriteLine(
      "OfType of arrayList");
```

```
      foreach (int i in sequenceOfType)
      {
        Console.Write(".." + i);
      }
      Console.WriteLine();
      Console.WriteLine();

      Console.WriteLine(
        "Cast of arrayList");
      foreach (int i in sequenceCast)
      {
        Console.Write(".." + i);
      }
      Console.WriteLine();
      Console.WriteLine();
    }
  }
```

The preceding code is a simple example of using the `OfType` and `Cast` conversions. We have an array that contains only `int` elements. Indeed, they can be converted easily. The following will be the output if we run the `OfTypeCastSimple()` method:

 In .NET Core, `ArrayList` definition lies in `System.Collections.NonGeneric.dll`. Hence, we have to download the NuGet package on `https://www.nuget.org/packages/System.Colle ctions.NonGeneric/`

Now let's add several lines of code to the preceding code. The code will now be as follows:

```
public partial class Program
{
  public static void OfTypeCastComplex()
  {
    ArrayList arrayList = new ArrayList();
    arrayList.AddRange(
      new int[] { 1, 2, 3, 4, 5 });

    arrayList.AddRange(
      new string[] {"Cooper", "Shawna", "Max"});
```

```
IEnumerable<int> sequenceOfType =
    arrayList.OfType<int>();
IEnumerable<int> sequenceCast =
    arrayList.Cast<int>();

Console.WriteLine(
  "OfType of arrayList");
foreach (int i in sequenceOfType)
{
  Console.Write(".." + i);
}
Console.WriteLine();
Console.WriteLine();

Console.WriteLine(
    "Cast of arrayList");
foreach (int i in sequenceCast)
{
  Console.Write(".." + i);
}
Console.WriteLine();
Console.WriteLine();
  }
}
```

From the preceding code, we can see that we changed the method name to `OfTypeCastComplex` and inserted the code to add a string element to `arrayList`. If we run the method, the `OfType` conversion will run successfully and return only the `int` element, while the `Cast` conversion will throw an exception since there are some string elements in the input sequence.

The others conversion methods are `ToArray()` and `ToList()`. The difference between them is that `ToArray()` will convert the sequence into an array and `ToList()` into a generic list. Also, `ToDictionary()` and `ToLookup()` method names are available for conversion. `ToDictionary()` will create `Dictionary<TKey, TValue>` from the sequence based on a specified key selector function, and `ToLookup()` will create `Lookup<TKey, TElement>` from the sequence based on the specified key selector and element selector functions.

Element operation

Element operation is an operation that extracts individual elements from the sequence according to their index or using a predicate. There are several element operators that exist in LINQ; they are `First`, `FirstOrDefault`, `Last`, `Single`, `SingleOrDefault`, `ElementAt`, and `DefaultIfEmpty`. Let's use the sample code to understand the function of all these element operators.

The following is the code to demonstrate the element operator, which we can find in the `ElementOperation.csproj` project:

```
public partial class Program
{
  public static void FirstLastOperator()
  {
    Console.WriteLine(
      "First Operator: {0}",
      numbers.First());
    Console.WriteLine(
      "First Operator with predicate: {0}",
      numbers.First(n => n % 3 == 0));
    Console.WriteLine(
      "Last Operator: {0}",
      numbers.Last());
    Console.WriteLine(
      "Last Operator with predicate: {0}",
      numbers.Last(n => n % 4 == 0));
  }
}
```

The preceding code demonstrates the use of the `First` and `Last` operators. The numbers array is as follows:

```
public partial class Program
{
  public static int[] numbers = {
    1, 2, 3,
    4, 5, 6,
    7, 8, 9
  };
}
```

Before we move further, let's take a moment to look at the following output on the console if we run the `FirstLastOperator()` method:

From the output, we can find that the `First` operator will return the first element of the sequence, and the `Last` operator will return the last element. We can also use a lambda expression for the `First` and `Last` operators to filter the sequence. In the preceding example, we filtered the sequence to numbers that can be divided only by four.

Unfortunately, the `First` and `Last` operators cannot return an empty value; instead, they throw an exception. Let's examine the following code regarding the use of the `First` operator, which will return an empty sequence:

```
public partial class Program
{
  public static void FirstOrDefaultOperator()
  {
    Console.WriteLine(
      "First Operator with predicate: {0}",
      numbers.First(n => n % 10 == 0));
    Console.WriteLine(
      "First Operator with predicate: {0}",
      numbers.FirstOrDefault(n => n % 10 == 0));
  }
}
```

If we uncomment all commented code lines in the preceding code, the method will throw an exception since there's no number that can be divided by `10`. To solve this problem, we can use the `FirstOrDefault` operator instead, and it will return the default value because the numbers are in the sequence of integers. So, it will return the default value of the integer, which is `0`.

We also have `Single` and `SingleOrDefault` as element operators, and we can take a look at their use in the following code:

```
public partial class Program
{
  public static void SingleOperator()
  {
```

```
Console.WriteLine(
  "Single Operator for number can be divided by 7: {0}",
  numbers.Single(n => n % 7 == 0));
Console.WriteLine(
  "Single Operator for number can be divided by 2: {0}",
  numbers.Single(n => n % 2 == 0));

Console.WriteLine(
  "SingleOrDefault Operator: {0}",
  numbers.SingleOrDefault(n => n % 10 == 0));

Console.WriteLine(
  "SingleOrDefault Operator: {0}",
  numbers.SingleOrDefault(n => n % 3 == 0));
    }
  }
```

If we run the preceding code, an exception is thrown due to the following code snippet:

```
Console.WriteLine(
  "Single Operator for number can be divided by 2: {0}",
  numbers.Single(n => n % 2 == 0));
```

Also, the following code snippet causes an error:

```
Console.WriteLine(
  "SingleOrDefault Operator: {0}",
  numbers.SingleOrDefault(n => n % 3 == 0));
```

The error occurs because the `Single` operator can only have one matching element. In the first code snippet, we have 2, 4, 6, and 8 as the result. In the second code snippet, we have 3, 6, and 9 as the result.

The `Element` operation also has `ElementAt` and `ElementAtOrDefault` operators to get the nth element from the sequence. Let's take a look at the following code to demonstrate the operators:

```
public partial class Program
{
  public static void ElementAtOperator()
  {
    Console.WriteLine(
      "ElementAt Operator: {0}",
      numbers.ElementAt(5));

    //Console.WriteLine(
      //"ElementAt Operator: {0}",
      //numbers.ElementAt(11));
```

```
      Console.WriteLine(
        "ElementAtOrDefault Operator: {0}",
        numbers.ElementAtOrDefault(11));
    }
  }
```

Like the `First` and `Last` operators, `ElementAt` has to return the value as well. The commented code lines in the preceding code will throw an exception since there's no element in index `11`. However, we can overcome this problem using `ElementAtOrDefault`, and then the commented lines will return the default value of `int`.

The last in element operation is the `DefaultIfEmpty` operator, which will return the default value in a sequence if no element is found in the input sequence. The following code will demonstrate the `DefaultIfEmpty` operator:

```
public partial class Program
{
  public static void DefaultIfEmptyOperator()
  {
    List<int> numbers = new List<int>();

    //Console.WriteLine(
      //"DefaultIfEmpty Operator: {0}",
      //numbers.DefaultIfEmpty());

    foreach (int number in numbers.DefaultIfEmpty())
    {
      Console.WriteLine(
        "DefaultIfEmpty Operator: {0}", number);
    }
  }
}
```

Since the return of the `DefaultIfEmpty` operator is `IEnumerable<T>`, we have to enumerate it, although it contains only one element. As you can see in the preceding code, we comment the direct access of the numbers variable because it will return the type of variable, not the value of the variable. Instead, we have to enumerate the numbers query to get the one and only value stored in the `IEnumerable<T>` variable.

Summary

LINQ has made our task of querying a collection easier because we don't need to learn much syntax to access different types of collections. It implements a deferred execution concept, which means that the query will not be executed in the constructor time but in the enumeration process. Almost all query operators provide the deferred execution concept; however, there are exceptions for the operators that do the following:

Return a scalar value or single element, such as `Count` and `First`.

Convert the result of query; they are `ToList`, `ToArray`, `ToDictionary`, and `ToLookup`. They are also called conversion operators.

In other words, methods that return a sequence implement deferred execution for instance, the `Select` method (`IEnumerable<X>-> Select -> IEnumerable<Y>`) and methods that return a single object don't implement deferred execution, for instance, the `First` method (`IEnumerable<X>-> First -> Y`).

There are two types of LINQ querying syntaxes; they are the fluent syntax and the query expression syntax. The former takes a lambda expression for the parameter to represent the logic that will be performed in the sequence enumeration. The latter is a shorthand syntax that we can use in order to perform LINQ queries. In the query expression syntax, .NET Framework provides the keywords for each query operator but not all operators. Our code will be more readable and required less coding when we use the query expression syntax. However, both fluent and query syntax will do the same thing. The difference between them is only the syntax. Each keyword in the query expression syntax has its own extension method in the `Enumerable` class.

By understanding LINQ, we now have had enough knowledge to create functional programming. In the next chapter, we will discuss asynchronous programming in order to enhance code responsiveness in order to build user-friendly application.

6
Enhancing the Responsiveness of the Functional Program with Asynchronous Programming

Responsive applications are a must in today's programming approach. They can improve the performance of the application itself and make our application have a user-friendly interface. We need to asynchronously run the code execution process in our program to have a responsive application. To achieve this goal, in this chapter, we will discuss the following topics:

- Using thread and thread pool to build a responsive application
- Learning about asynchronous programming model patterns
- Learning about task-based asynchronous patterns
- Using the async and await keywords to build asynchronous programming
- Applying an asynchronous method in a functional approach

Building a responsive application

The first time .NET Framework was announced, the flow of the program was executed sequentially. The drawback of this execution flow is that our application has to wait for the operation to finish before executing the next operation. It will freeze our application, and that will be an unpleasant user experience.

To minimize this problem, .NET Framework introduces thread, the smallest unit of execution, which can be scheduled independently by the OS. And the asynchronous programming means that you run a piece of code on a separate thread, freeing up the original thread and doing other things while the task is completed.

Running a program synchronously

Let's start our discussion by creating a program that will run all operations synchronously. The following is the code that demonstrates the synchronous operation that we can find in the `SynchronousOperation.csproj` project:

```
public partial class Program
{
  public static void SynchronousProcess()
  {
    Stopwatch sw = Stopwatch.StartNew();
    Console.WriteLine(
      "Start synchronous process now...");
    int iResult = RunSynchronousProcess();
    Console.WriteLine(
      "The Result = {0}",iResult);
    Console.WriteLine(
      "Total Time = {0} second(s)!",
      sw.ElapsedMilliseconds/1000);
  }
  public static int RunSynchronousProcess()
  {
    int iReturn = 0;
    iReturn += LongProcess1();
    iReturn += LongProcess2();
    return iReturn;
  }
  public static int LongProcess1()
  {
    Thread.Sleep(5000);
    return 5;
  }
  public static int LongProcess2()
  {
    Thread.Sleep(7000);
    return 7;
  }
}
```

As we can see in the preceding code, the `RunSynchronousProcess()` method executes two methods; they are the `LongProcess1()` and `LongProcess2()` methods. Now let's call the preceding `RunSynchronousProcess()` method, and we will get the following output on the console:

These two methods, `LongProcess1()` and `LongProcess2()`, are independent, and each method takes a particular time to finish. Since it is executed synchronously, it takes 12 seconds to finish these two methods. The `LongProcess1()` method needs 5 seconds to finish, and the `LongProcess2()` method needs 7 seconds to finish.

Applying threads in the program

We can improve our previous code so that it can be the responsive program by refactoring some of the code and adding threads to the code. The refactored code would be as follows, which we can find in the `ApplyingThreads.csproj` project:

```
public partial class Program
{
  public static void AsynchronousProcess()
  {
    Stopwatch sw = Stopwatch.StartNew();
    Console.WriteLine(
      "Start asynchronous process now...");
    int iResult = RunAsynchronousProcess();
    Console.WriteLine(
      "The Result = {0}",
      iResult);
    Console.WriteLine(
      "Total Time = {0} second(s)!",
      sw.ElapsedMilliseconds / 1000);
  }
  public static int RunAsynchronousProcess()
  {
    int iResult1 = 0;
    // Creating thread for LongProcess1()
    Thread thread = new Thread(
```

```
          () => iResult1 = LongProcess1());
      // Starting the thread
      thread.Start();
      // Running LongProcess2()
      int iResult2 = LongProcess2();
      // Waiting for the thread to finish
      thread.Join();
      // Return the the total result
      return iResult1 + iResult2;
  }
  public static int LongProcess1()
  {
    Thread.Sleep(5000);
    return 5;
  }
  public static int LongProcess2()
  {
    Thread.Sleep(7000);
    return 7;
  }
}
```

As we can see, we refactor the RunSynchronousProcess() method in the previous code into the RunAsynchronousProcess() method. And if we run the RunAsynchronousProcess() method, we will get the following output on the console:

Compared to the RunSynchronousProcess() method, we now have a faster process in the RunAsynchronousProcess() method. We create a new thread that will run the LongProcess1() method. The thread will not run until it has started using the Start() method. Take a look at the following code snippet, in which we create and run the thread:

```
// Creating thread for LongProcess1()
Thread thread = new Thread(
  () =>
  iResult1 = LongProcess1());
// Starting the thread
thread.Start();
```

After the thread is run, we can run the other operation, in this case, the `LongProcess2()` method. When this operation is done, we have to wait for the thread to be finished so that we use the `Join()` method from the thread instance. The following code snippet will explain this:

```
// Running LongProcess2()
int iResult2 = LongProcess2();
// Waiting for the thread to finish
thread.Join();
```

The `Join()` method will block the current thread until the other thread that's being executed is finished. After the other thread finishes, the `Join()` method will return, and then the current thread will be unblocked.

Creating threads using thread pool

Besides using the thread itself, we can also precreate some threads using the `System.Threading.ThreadPool` class. We use this class if we need to work with threads from the thread pool. When using thread pool, you are more likely to use only the `QueueUserWorkItem()` method. This method will add an execution request to the thread pool queue. If any threads are available in the thread pool, the request will execute right away. Let's take a look at the following code in order to demonstrate the use of thread pool, which we can find in the `UsingThreadPool.csproj` project:

```
public partial class Program
{
  public static void ThreadPoolProcess()
  {
    Stopwatch sw = Stopwatch.StartNew();
    Console.WriteLine(
      "Start ThreadPool process now...");
    int iResult = RunInThreadPool();
    Console.WriteLine("The Result = {0}",
      iResult);
    Console.WriteLine("Total Time = {0} second(s)!",
      sw.ElapsedMilliseconds / 1000);
  }
  public static int RunInThreadPool()
  {
    int iResult1 = 0;
    // Assignin work LongProcess1() to idle thread
    // in the thread pool
    ThreadPool.QueueUserWorkItem((t) =>
      iResult1 = LongProcess1());
```

```
        // Running LongProcess2()
        int iResult2 = LongProcess2();
        // Waiting the thread to be finished
        // then returning the result
        return iResult1 + iResult2;
    }
    public static int LongProcess1()
    {
        Thread.Sleep(5000);
        return 5;
    }
    public static int LongProcess2()
    {
        Thread.Sleep(7000);
        return 7;
    }
}
```

In the thread pool, we can invoke the `QueueUserWorkItem()` method to put a new work item in a queue, which is managed by the thread pool when we need to run the long running process instead of creating a new thread. There are three possibilities of how the work is treated when we send it to thread pool; they are as follows:

- The thread has one or more available threads idle in the thread pool so that the work can be handled by the idle thread and run immediately.
- No threads are available, but the `MaxThreads` property has not been reached yet so the thread pool will create a new thread, assign the work, and run the work immediately.
- There is no available thread in the thread pool and the total number of threads in the thread pool has reached the `MaxThreads`. In this situation, the work item will wait in the queue for the first available thread.

Now, let's run the `ThreadPoolProcess()` method, and we will get the following output on the console:

As we can see in the preceding screenshot, we get the same result with the similar process time we get when we apply the new thread that we discussed in the previous section.

The asynchronous programming model pattern

The **asynchronous programming model (APM)** is an asynchronous operation that uses the IAsyncResult interface as its design pattern. It's also called the IAsyncResult pattern. For this purpose, the framework has provided the method named BeginXx and EndXx, in which Xx is the operation name, for instance, BeginRead and EndRead provided by the FileStream class to read bytes from a file asynchronously.

The difference in the synchronous Read() method with BeginRead() and EndRead() can be recognized from the method's declaration, as follows:

```
public int Read(
  byte[] array,
  int offset,
  int count
)
public IAsyncResult BeginRead(
  byte[] array,
  int offset,
  int numBytes,
  AsyncCallback userCallback,
  object stateObject
)
public int EndRead(
  IAsyncResult asyncResult
)
```

As we can see, in the synchronous Read() method, we need three parameters; they are array, offset, and numBytes. In the BeginRead() method, there are two more parameter additions; they are userCallback, the method that will be called when the asynchronous read operation is completed, and stateObject, an object provided by the user that distinguishes the asynchronous read request from other requests.

Using the synchronous Read() method

Now, let's take a look at the following code, which we can find in the APM.csproj project, in order to distinguish the asynchronous BeginRead() method from the synchronous Read() method in a clearer way:

```
public partial class Program
{
```

```
public static void ReadFile()
{
  FileStream fs =
    File.OpenRead(
      @"..\..\..\LoremIpsum.txt");
  byte[] buffer = new byte[fs.Length];
  int totalBytes =
    fs.Read(buffer, 0, (int)fs.Length);
  Console.WriteLine("Read {0} bytes.", totalBytes);
  fs.Dispose();
}
}
```

The preceding code will synchronously read the `LoremIpsum.txt` file (included in the `APM.csproj` project), which means that the reading process has to be completed before executing the next process. If we run the preceding `ReadFile()` method, we will get the following output on the console:

Using the BeginRead() and EndRead() methods

Now, let's compare the synchronous reading process using the `Read()` method with the asynchronous reading process using the `BeginRead()` and `EndRead()` methods from the following code:

```
public partial class Program
{
  public static void ReadAsyncFile()
  {
    FileStream fs =
      File.OpenRead(
        @"..\..\..\LoremIpsum.txt");
    byte[] buffer = new byte[fs.Length];
    IAsyncResult result = fs.BeginRead(buffer, 0, (int)fs.Length,
      OnReadComplete, fs);
    //do other work while file is read
    int i = 0;
    do
    {
      Console.WriteLine("Timer Counter: {0}", ++i);
    }
```

```
      while (!result.IsCompleted);
      fs.Dispose();
    }
    private static void OnReadComplete(IAsyncResult result)
    {
      FileStream fStream = (FileStream)result.AsyncState;
      int totalBytes = fStream.EndRead(result);
      Console.WriteLine("Read {0} bytes.", totalBytes);fStream.Dispose();
    }
  }
```

As we can see, we have two methods named `ReadAsyncFile()` and `OnReadComplete()`. The `ReadAsyncFile()` method will read the `LoremIpsum.txt` file asynchronously and then invoke the `OnReadComplete()` method just after finishing reading the file. We have additional code to make sure that the asynchronous operation runs properly using the following `do-while` looping code snippet:

```
//do other work while file is read
int i = 0;
do
{
  Console.WriteLine("Timer Counter: {0}", ++i);
}
while (!result.IsCompleted);
```

The preceding `do-while` loop will iterate until the asynchronous operation is completed, as indicated in the `IsComplete` property of `IAsyncResult`. The asynchronous operation is started when the `BeginRead()` method is invoked, as shown in the following code snippet:

```
IAsyncResult result =
  fs.BeginRead(
    buffer, 0, (int)fs.Length, OnReadComplete, fs);
```

After that, it will continue with the next process while it reads the file. The `OnReadComplete()` method will be invoked when the reading process is finished, and since the implementation of the `OnReadComplete()` method set the `IsFinish` variable to true, it will stop our `do-while` looping.

The output we will get by running the `ReadAsyncFile()` method is as follows:

From the screenshot of the preceding output, we can see that the iteration of the `do-while` loop is successfully executed when the reading process is run as well. The reading process is finished in the 64th iteration of the `do-while` loop.

Adding LINQ to the BeginRead() method invocation

We can also use LINQ to define the `OnReadComplete()` method so that we can replace that method using the anonymous method, as follows:

```
public partial class Program
{
  public static void ReadAsyncFileAnonymousMethod()
  {
    FileStream fs =
      File.OpenRead(
        @"..\..\..\LoremIpsum.txt");
    byte[] buffer = new byte[fs.Length];
    IAsyncResult result = fs.BeginRead(buffer, 0, (int)fs.Length,
      asyncResult => { int totalBytes = fs.EndRead(asyncResult);
    Console.WriteLine("Read {0} bytes.", totalBytes);
      }, null);
    //do other work while file is read
    int i = 0;
    do
    {
      Console.WriteLine("Timer Counter: {0}", ++i);
    }
```

```
     while (!result.IsCompleted);
     fs.Dispose();
   }
 }
```

As we can see, we replace the invocation of the `BeginRead()` method with the following code snippet:

```
IAsyncResult result =
  fs.BeginRead(
    buffer,
    0,
    (int)fs.Length,
    asyncResult =>
    {
      int totalBytes =
        fs.EndRead(asyncResult);
      Console.WriteLine("Read {0} bytes.", totalBytes);
    },
  null);
```

From the preceding code, we can see that we don't have the `OnReadComplete()` method anymore since it has been represented by the anonymous method. We remove the `FileStream` instance in the callback because the anonymous method in lambda will access it using the closure. And if we invoke the `ReadAsyncFileAnonymousMethod()` method, we will get the exact same output as the `ReadAsyncFile()` method except the iteration count, since it depends on the CPU speed.

Besides the `IsCompleted` property, which is used to fetch the value that indicates whether the asynchronous operation is complete, there are three more properties we can use when dealing with `IAsyncResult`; they are as follows:

- `AsyncState`: This is used to retrieve an object defined by the user that qualifies or contains information about an asynchronous operation
- `AsyncWaitHandle`: This is used to retrieve `WaitHandle` (an object from the operating system that waits for exclusive access to shared resources), which indicates the completeness of the asynchronous operation
- `CompletedSynchronously`: This is used to retrieve a value that indicates whether the asynchronous operation completed synchronously

Unfortunately, there are several shortages when applying APM, such as the inability to do a cancelation. This means that we cannot cancel the asynchronous operator because from the invocation of `BeginRead` until the callback is triggered, there is no way to cancel the background process. If `LoremIpsum.txt` is a gigabyte file, we have to wait until the asynchronous operation is finished instead of canceling the operation.

The APM pattern is no longer recommended in a new development due to its obsolete technology.

The task-based asynchronous pattern

The **task-based asynchronous pattern** (**TAP**) is a pattern that's used to represent arbitrary asynchronous operations. The concept of this pattern is to represent asynchronous operations in a method and combine the status of the operation and the API that is used to interact with these operators for them to become a single object. The objects are the `Task` and `Task<TResult>` types in the `System.Threading.Tasks` namespace.

Introducing the Task and Task<TResult> classes

The `Task` and `Task<TResult>` classes were announced in .NET Framework 4.0 in order to represent an asynchronous operation. It uses threads that are stored in the thread pool but offers the flexibility of how the task is created. We use the `Task` class when we need to run a method as a task but don't need the return value; otherwise, we use the `Task<TResult>` class when we need to get the return value.

We can find a complete reference, including methods and properties, inside `Task` and `Task<TResult>` on the MSDN site at `https://msdn.mic rosoft.com/en-us/library/dd321424(v=vs.110).aspx`.

Applying a simple TAP model

Let's start our discussion on TAP by creating the following code, which we can find in the TAP.csproj project, and use it to read a file asynchronously:

```
public partial class Program
{
  public static void ReadFileTask()
  {
    bool IsFinish = false;
    FileStream fs = File.OpenRead(
      @"..\..\..\LoremIpsum.txt");
    byte[] readBuffer = new byte[fs.Length];
    fs.ReadAsync(readBuffer, 0, (int)fs.Length)
      .ContinueWith(task => {
      if (task.Status ==
        TaskStatus.RanToCompletion)
        {
          IsFinish = true;
          Console.WriteLine(
          "Read {0} bytes.",
          task.Result);
        }
        fs.Dispose();});
    //do other work while file is read
    int i = 0;
    do
    {
      Console.WriteLine("Timer Counter: {0}", ++i);
    }
    while (!IsFinish);
    Console.WriteLine("End of ReadFileTask() method");
  }
}
```

As we can see in the preceding code, the ReadAsync() method inside the FileStream class will return Task<int>, which in this case will indicate the number of bytes that have been read from the file. After invoking the ReadAsync() method, we invoke the ContinueWith() extension method using method chaining, as discussed in Chapter 1, *Tasting Functional Type in C#*. It allows us to specify Action<Task<T>>, which will be run after the asynchronous operation is completed.

By invoking the `ContinueWith()` method after the task is completed, the delegate will be run in a synchronous operation immediately. And if we run the preceding `ReadFileTask()` method, we get the following output on the console:

Using the WhenAll() extension method

We successfully applied a simple TAP in the previous section. Now, we will continue by asynchronously reading two files and then processing the other operation only when both the reading operations have been completed. Let's take a look at the following code, which will demonstrate our need:

```
public partial class Program
{
  public static void ReadTwoFileTask()
  {
    bool IsFinish = false;
    Task readFile1 =
      ReadFileAsync(
      @"..\..\..\LoremIpsum.txt");
    Task readFile2 =
      ReadFileAsync(
      @"..\..\..\LoremIpsum2.txt");
    Task.WhenAll(readFile1, readFile2)
      .ContinueWith(task =>
      {
        IsFinish = true;
        Console.WriteLine(
        "All files have been read successfully.");
      });
    //do other work while file is read
    int i = 0;
    do
    {
```

```
      Console.WriteLine("Timer Counter: {0}", ++i);
    }
    while (!IsFinish);
    Console.WriteLine("End of ReadTwoFileTask() method");
  }
  public static Task<int> ReadFileAsync(string filePath)
  {
    FileStream fs = File.OpenRead(filePath);
    byte[] readBuffer = new byte[fs.Length];
    Task<int> readTask =
      fs.ReadAsync(
      readBuffer,
      0,
      (int)fs.Length);
    readTask.ContinueWith(task =>
    {
      if (task.Status == TaskStatus.RanToCompletion)
      Console.WriteLine(
        "Read {0} bytes from file {1}",
        task.Result,
        filePath);
      fs.Dispose();
    });
    return readTask;
  }
}
```

As we can see, we use the `Task.WhenAll()` method to wrap the two tasks that are passed in as parameters into a larger asynchronous operation. It then returns a task that represents the combination of these two asynchronous operations. We don't need to wait for the completeness of both files' reading operations but it adds a continuation for when these two files have been read successfully.

If we run the preceding `ReadTwoFileTask()` method, we get the following output on the console:

```
Timer Counter: 55
Timer Counter: 56
Timer Counter: 57
Timer Counter: 58
Timer Counter: 59
Timer Counter: 60
Timer Counter: 61
Timer Counter: 62
Timer Counter: 63
Timer Counter: 64
Timer Counter: 65
Read 67189244 bytes from file ..\..\..\LoremIpsum2.txt
Read 67189244 bytes from file ..\..\..\LoremIpsum.txt
Timer Counter: 66
All files have been read successfully.
End of ReadTwoFileTask() method
Press any key to continue . . .
```

As we have discussed earlier that the drawback of APM pattern is that we cannot cancel the background process, now let's try to cancel the list of tasks in TAP by refactoring the preceding code we have. The complete code will become like the following:

```csharp
public partial class Program
{
  public static void ReadTwoFileTaskWithCancellation()
  {
    bool IsFinish = false;

    // Define the cancellation token.
    CancellationTokenSource source =
      new CancellationTokenSource();
    CancellationToken token = source.Token;

    Task readFile1 =
      ReadFileAsync(
      @"..\..\..\LoremIpsum.txt");
    Task readFile2 =
      ReadFileAsync(
      @"..\..\..\LoremIpsum2.txt");

    Task.WhenAll(readFile1, readFile2)
      .ContinueWith(task =>
      {
        IsFinish = true;
```

```
                Console.WriteLine(
                    "All files have been read successfully.");
            }
            , token
        );

        //do other work while file is read
        int i = 0;
        do
        {
          Console.WriteLine("Timer Counter: {0}", ++i);
          if (i > 10)
          {
            source.Cancel();
            Console.WriteLine(
                "All tasks are cancelled at i = " + i);
             break;
          }
        }
        while (!IsFinish);

        Console.WriteLine(
            "End of ReadTwoFileTaskWithCancellation() method");
    }
}
```

As we can see from the preceding code, we add `CancellationTokenSource` and `CancellationToken` to inform the cancellation process. We then pass token to the `Task.WhenAll()` function. After the tasks have run, we can cancel the tasks using the `source.Cancel()` method.

The following is the output we will get on the console if we run the preceding code:

The preceding output tells us that the tasks have been canceled successfully in the 11th counter because the counter has been higher than 10.

Wrapping an APM into a TAP model

If the framework doesn't offer a TAP model for asynchronous operation, we can, if we want, wrap APM `BeginXx` and `EndXx` methods into the TAP model using the `Task.FromAsync` method. Let's take a look at the following code in order to demonstrate the wrapping process:

```
public partial class Program
{
  public static bool IsFinish;
  public static void WrapApmIntoTap()
  {
    IsFinish = false;
    ReadFileAsync(
      @"..\..\..\LoremIpsum.txt");
      //do other work while file is read
      int i = 0;
    do
    {
      Console.WriteLine("Timer Counter: {0}", ++i);
    }
    while (!IsFinish);
    Console.WriteLine(
      "End of WrapApmIntoTap() method");
  }
```

```
private static Task<int> ReadFileAsync(string filePath)
{
  FileStream fs = File.OpenRead(filePath);
  byte[] readBuffer = new Byte[fs.Length];
  Task<int> readTask =
    Task.Factory.FromAsync(
    (Func<byte[],
    int,
    int,
    AsyncCallback,
    object,
    IAsyncResult>)
  fs.BeginRead,
  (Func<IAsyncResult, int>)
  fs.EndRead,
  readBuffer,
  0,
  (int)fs.Length,
  null);
  readTask.ContinueWith(task =>
  {
    if (task.Status == TaskStatus.RanToCompletion)
    {
      IsFinish = true;
      Console.WriteLine(
        "Read {0} bytes from file {1}",
        task.Result,
        filePath);
    }
    fs.Dispose();
  });
  return readTask;
}
}
```

From the preceding code, we can see that we use the `BeginRead()` and `EndRead()` methods, which are actually APM patterns, but we use them in the TAP model, as shown in the following code snippet:

```
Task<int> readTask =
  Task.Factory.FromAsync(
    (Func<byte[],
    int,
    int,
    AsyncCallback,
    object,
    IAsyncResult>)
    fs.BeginRead,
```

```
    (Func<IAsyncResult, int>)
    fs.EndRead,
    readBuffer,
    0,
    (int)fs.Length,
null);
```

And if we run the preceding `WrapApmIntoTap()` method, we will get the following output on the console:

As we can see in the screenshot of the output result, we have successfully read the `LoremIpsum.txt` file using the `BeginRead()` and `EndRead()` methods wrapped into the TAP model.

Asynchronous programming with the async and await keywords

The `async` and `await` keywords were announced in C# 5.0 and became the latest and greatest things in C# asynchronous programming. Developed from the TAP pattern, C# integrates these two keywords into the language itself so that it makes it simple and easy to read. Using these two keywords, the `Task` and `Task<TResult>` classes still become the core building blocks of asynchronous programming. We will still build a new `Task` or `Task<TResult>` data type using the `Task.Run()` method, as discussed in the previous section.

Now let's take a look at the following code, which demonstrates the `async` and `await` keywords, which we can find in the `AsyncAwait.csproj` project:

```
public partial class Program
{
```

```
static bool IsFinish;
public static void AsyncAwaitReadFile()
{
  IsFinish = false;
  ReadFileAsync();
  //do other work while file is read
  int i = 0;
  do
  {
    Console.WriteLine("Timer Counter: {0}", ++i);
  }
  while (!IsFinish);
  Console.WriteLine("End of AsyncAwaitReadFile() method");
}
public static async void ReadFileAsync()
{
  FileStream fs =
    File.OpenRead(
    @"..\..\..\LoremIpsum.txt");
  byte[] buffer = new byte[fs.Length];
  int totalBytes =
    await fs.ReadAsync(
    buffer,
    0,
    (int)fs.Length);
  Console.WriteLine("Read {0} bytes.", totalBytes);
  IsFinish = true;
  fs.Dispose();
}
}
```

As we can see in the preceding code, we refactor the code from our previous topic by adding the `await` keyword when we read the file stream, as shown in the following code snippet:

```
int totalBytes =
  await fs.ReadAsync(
    buffer,
    0,
    (int)fs.Length);
```

Also, we use the `async` keyword in front of the method name, as shown in the following code snippet:

```
public static async void ReadFileAsync()
{
  // Implementation
}
```

From the preceding two code snippets, we can see that the `await` keyword can only be called inside a method that is marked with the `async` keyword. And when `await` is reached–in this case, it is in await `fs.ReadAsync()`–the thread that called the method will jump out of the method and continue on its way to something else. The asynchronous code then takes place on a separate thread (like how we use the `Task.Run()` method). However, everything after await is scheduled to be executed when the task is finished. And if we run the preceding `AsyncAwaitReadFile()` method, we will get the following output on the console:

```
C:\WINDOWS\system32\cmd.exe                                    —  □  ×
Timer Counter: 50
Timer Counter: 51
Timer Counter: 52
Timer Counter: 53
Timer Counter: 54
Timer Counter: 55
Timer Counter: 56
Timer Counter: 57
Timer Counter: 58
Timer Counter: 59
Timer Counter: 60
Timer Counter: 61
Timer Counter: 62
Timer Counter: 63
Timer Counter: 64
Timer Counter: 65
Timer Counter: 66
Read 67189244 bytes.
Timer Counter: 67
End of AsyncAwaitReadFile() method
Press any key to continue . . .
```

As with the TAP model, we obtain the asynchronous result here as well.

Asynchronous functions in functional programming

Now, using the chaining method, we are going to use the `async` and `await` keywords in functional programming. Suppose we have three tasks, as shown in the following code snippet, and we need to chain them together:

```
public async static Task<int> FunctionA(
  int a) => await Task.FromResult(a * 1);
public async static Task<int> FunctionB(
  int b) => await Task.FromResult(b * 2);
public async static Task<int> FunctionC(
  int c) => await Task.FromResult(c * 3);
```

For that purpose, we have to create a new extension method for `Task<T>` named `MapAsync`, with the following implementation:

```
public static class ExtensionMethod
{
  public static async Task<TResult> MapAsync<TSource, TResult>(
    this Task<TSource> @this,
    Func<TSource, Task<TResult>> fn) => await fn(await @this);
}
```

The `MapAsync()` method allows us to define the method as `async`, accept the task returned from the `async` method, and `await` the call to the delegate. The following is the complete code we use to chain the three tasks that we can find in the `AsyncChain.csproj` project:

```
public partial class Program
{
  public async static Task<int> FunctionA(
    int a) => await Task.FromResult(a * 1);
  public async static Task<int> FunctionB(
    int b) => await Task.FromResult(b * 2);
  public async static Task<int> FunctionC(
    int c) => await Task.FromResult(c * 3);
  public async static void AsyncChain()
  {
    int i = await FunctionC(10)
    .MapAsync(FunctionB)
    .MapAsync(FunctionA);
    Console.WriteLine("The result = {0}", i);
  }
}
```

If we run the preceding `AsyncChain()` method, we will get the following output on the console:

Summary

Asynchronous programming is a way that we can use to develop a responsive application, and we successfully applied `Thread` and `ThreadPool` to achieve this goal. We can create a new thread to run the work, or we can reuse the available threads in thread pool.

We also learned about the asynchronous programming model pattern, which is an asynchronous operation that uses the `IAsyncResult` interface as its design pattern. In this pattern, we used the two methods that are preceded by `Begin` and `End`; for instance, in our discussion, these were the `BeginRead()` and `EndRead()` methods. The `BeginRead()` method started the asynchronous operation when invoked, and then the `EndRead()` method stopped the operation so that we could fetch the return value of the operation.

Besides the asynchronous programming model pattern, .NET Framework also has a task-based asynchronous pattern to run the asynchronous operation. The concept of this pattern is to represent asynchronous operations in a method and combine the status of the operation and the API that is used to interact with these operators to become a single object. The objects we used in this pattern are `Task` and `Task<TResult>`, which we can find in the `System.Threading.Tasks` namespace. In this pattern, we can also cancel the active tasks running as background processes.

Then, C# announced `async` and `await` to complete the asynchronous technique, which we can choose. It was developed from the task-based asynchronous pattern, where the `Task` and `Task<TResult>` classes became the core building blocks of asynchronous programming. The last thing we did in this chapter is that we tried to chain the three tasks using our extension method based on the use of the `async` and `await` keywords.

In the next chapter, we will discuss the recursion that is useful in functional programming in order to simplify the code. We will learn about the usage of recursion and how to reduce the lines of code based on the recursion.

7
Learning Recursion

In the first announcement of functional programming, many functional languages didn't have the loop feature to iterate the sequence. All we had to do was construct the recursion process to iterate the sequence. Although C# has iteration features such as `for` and `while`, it is better if we discuss recursion in the functional approach. Recursion will also simplify our code. To do that, in this chapter, we will discuss the following topics:

- Understanding how the recursive routine works
- Refactoring an iteration into a recursion
- Distinguishing tail recursion between the accumulator-passing style and the continuation-passing style
- Understanding indirect recursion over direct recursion
- Applying recursion in the functional approach using the Aggregate LINQ operator

Exploring recursion

A recursive function is a function that calls itself. Like the iteration loop, for instance, the `while` and `for` loop–it is used to solve a complicated task one piece at a time and combine the results. However, there is a difference between the `for` loop and `while` loop. The iteration will keep repeating until the task is done, while the recursion will break the task up into smaller pieces in order to solve the larger problem and then combine the result. In the functional approach, the recursion is closer to the mathematical approach since it is often shorter than iteration, although it's somehow more difficult to design and test.

In Chapter 1, *Tasting Functional Style in C#*, we were acquainted with recursive functions, when we discussed the concepts of functional programming. There, we analyzed the factorial function named GetFactorial() in the imperative and functional approach. To refresh our memory, following is the GetFactorial() function implementation, which we can find in the SimpleRecursion.csproj project:

```
public partial class Program
{
  private static int GetFactorial(int intNumber)
  {
    if (intNumber == 0)
    {
      return 1;
    }
    return intNumber * GetFactorial(intNumber - 1);
  }
}
```

From our discussion in Chapter 1, *Tasting Functional Style in C#* we know that the factorial of the non-negative integer N is the multiplication of all positive integers less than or equal to N. So, suppose we have the following function to calculate the factorial of five:

```
private static void GetFactorialOfFive()
{
  int i = GetFactorial(5);
  Console.WriteLine("5! is {0}",i);
}
```

As we can predict, if we invoke the preceding GetFactorialOfFive() method, we will get the following output on the console:

Back to the GetFactorial() method again; we see in the implementation of this method there is code that will end the recursion, as shown in the following code snippet:

```
if (intNumber == 0)
{
  return 1;
}
```

We can see that the preceding code is the base case of the recursion and the recursion usually has the base case. This base case will define the end of the recursion chain since, in this case, the method will change the state of `intNumber` every time the recursion is run, and the chain will be stopped if `intNumber` is zero.

Working of the recursive routine

In order to understand how the recursive routine works, let's examine the state of `intNumber` if we find the factorial of five, as shown in the following flow of the program:

```
int i = GetFactorial(5)
  (intNumber = 5) != 0
  return (5 * GetFactorial(4))
    (intNumber = 4) != 0
    return (4 * GetFactorial(3))
      (intNumber = 3) != 0
      return (3 * GetFactorial(2))
        (intNumber = 2) != 0
        return (2 * GetFactorial(1))
          (intNumber = 1) != 0
          return (1 * GetFactorial(0))
            (intNumber = 0) == 0
            return 1
          return (1 * 1 = 1)
        return (2 * 1 = 2)
      return (3 * 2 = 6)
    return (4 * 6 = 24)
  return (5 * 24 = 120)
i = 120
```

Using the preceding flow, it becomes clearer how the recursion works. The base case we have defines the end of the recursion chain. A programming language compiler converts the specific case of recursion into an iteration when applicable because a loop-based implementation becomes more efficient by eliminating the need for a function call.

Be careful when applying the recursion in your program logic. If you miss a base case or give a wrong value to it, you may go off into an infinite recursion. For instance, in the preceding `GetFactorial()` method, if we pass `intNumber < 0`, then our program will never end.

Refactoring an iteration to the recursion

Recursion makes our programs more readable, and it is essential in the functional programming approach. Here, we are going to refactor the for loop iteration to the recursion method. Let's take a look at the following code, which we can find in the `RefactoringIterationToRecursion.csproj` project:

```
public partial class Program
{
  public static int FindMaxIteration(
      int[] intArray)
  {
    int iMax = 0;
    for (int i = 0; i < intArray.Length; i++)
    {
      if (intArray[i] > iMax)
      {
        iMax = intArray[i];
      }
    }
    return iMax;
  }
}
```

The preceding `FindMaxIteration()` method is used to pick the maximum number in the array of numbers. Consider that we have the following code in order to run the `FindMaxIteration()` method:

```
public partial class Program
{
  static void Main(string[] args)
  {
    int[] intDataArray =
        {8, 10, 24, -1, 98, 47, -101, 39 };
    int iMaxNumber = FindMaxIteration(intDataArray);
    Console.WriteLine(
        "Max Number (using FindMaxRecursive) = " +
          iMaxNumber);
  }
}
```

As we can expect, we will have the following output in the console window:

```
Max Number (using FindMaxIteration) = 98
Press any key to continue . . .
```

Now, let's refactor the `FindMaxIteration()` method to the recursive function. The following is the implementation of the `FindMaxRecursive()` method, which is the recursion version of the `FindMaxIteration()` method:

```
public partial class Program
{
  public static int FindMaxRecursive(
      int[] intArray,
      int iStartIndex = 0)
  {
    if (iStartIndex == intArray.Length - 1)
    {
      return intArray[iStartIndex];
    }
    else
    {
      return Math.Max(intArray[iStartIndex],
        FindMaxRecursive(intArray, iStartIndex + 1));
    }
  }
}
```

We can invoke the preceding `FindMaxRecursive()` method using the same code as we did in the `FindMaxIteration()` method, as follows:

```
public partial class Program
{
  static void Main(string[] args)
  {
    int[] intDataArray = {8, 10, 24, -1, 98, 47, -101, 39 };
    int iMaxNumber = FindMaxRecursive(intDataArray);
    Console.WriteLine"Max Number(using FindMaxRecursive) = " +
        iMaxNumber);
  }
}
```

As we can see in the preceding method, we have the following base case to define the end of the recursion chain:

```
if (iStartIndex == intArray.Length - 1)
```

```
  {
    return intArray[iStartIndex];
  }
```

If we run the preceding code, we will get the same result as the one we got in our previous method, as shown in the following console screenshot:

Now, let's take a look at the following flow to know how we can get this result when we use the recursion function:

```
Array = { 8, 10, 24, -1, 98, 47, -101, 39 };
Array.Length - 1 = 7
int iMaxNumber = FindMaxRecursive(Array, 0)
  (iStartIndex = 0) != 7
  return Max(8, FindMaxRecursive(Array, 1))
    (iStartIndex = 1) != 7
    return Max(10, FindMaxRecursive(Array, 2))
      (iStartIndex = 2) != 7
      return Max(24, FindMaxRecursive(Array, 3))
        (iStartIndex = 3) != 7
        return Max(-1, FindMaxRecursive(Array, 4))
          (iStartIndex = 4) != 7
          return Max(98, FindMaxRecursive(Array, 5))
           (iStartIndex = 5) != 7
           return Max(47, FindMaxRecursive(Array, 6))
             (iStartIndex = 6) != 7
             return Max(-101, FindMaxRecursive(Array, 7))
               (iStartIndex = 7) == 7
               return 39
             return Max(-101, 39) = 39
           return Max(47, 39) = 47
          return Max(98, 47) = 98
        return Max(-1, 98) = 98
      return Max(24, 98) = 98
    return Max(10, 98) = 98
  return Max(8, 98) = 98
iMaxNumber = 98
```

Using the preceding flow, we can distinguish every state change in the maximum number we get every time the `FindMaxRecursive()` method is called. Then, we can prove that the maximum number in the given array is 98.

Using tail recursion

In the `GetFactorial()` method we discussed previously, traditional recursion is used to calculate the factorial number. This recursion model performs the recursive call first and returns the value, and then it calculates the result. Using this recursion model, we won't get the result until the recursive call is finished.

Besides the traditional recursion model, we have another recursion called tail recursion. The tail call becomes the last thing in the function and it doesn't do anything after the recursion at all. Let's look at the following code, which we can find in the `TailRecursion.csproj` project:

```
public partial class Program
{
  public static void TailCall(int iTotalRecursion)
  {
    Console.WriteLine("Value: " + iTotalRecursion);
    if (iTotalRecursion == 0)
    {
      Console.WriteLine("The tail is executed");
      return;
    }
    TailCall(iTotalRecursion - 1);
  }
}
```

From the preceding code, the tail is executed when `iTotalRecursion` has reached 0, as shown in the following code snippet:

```
if (iTotalRecursion == 0)
{
  Console.WriteLine("The tail is executed");
  return;
}
```

If we run the preceding `TailCall()` method and pass 5 for the `iTotalRecursion` argument, we will get the following output on the console:

Now, let's examine the state change every time the function is called recursively in this code:

```
TailCall(5)
   (iTotalRecursion = 5) != 0
   TailCall(4)
      (iTotalRecursion = 4) != 0
      TailCall(3)
        iTotalRecursion = 3) != 0
        TailCall(2)
           iTotalRecursion = 2) != 0
           TailCall(1)
              iTotalRecursion = 1) != 0
              TailCall(0)
                 iTotalRecursion = 0) == 0
                 Execute the process in tail
           TailCall(1) => nothing happens
        TailCall(2) => nothing happens
     TailCall(3) => nothing happens
   TailCall(4) => nothing happens
TailCall(5) => nothing happens
```

From the preceding flow of recursion, the process is only run in the last recursion call. After that, nothing happens to the other recursive calls. In other words, we can conclude that the flow will actually be as follows:

```
TailCall(5)
   (iTotalRecursion = 5) != 0
   TailCall(4)
      (iTotalRecursion = 4) != 0
      TailCall(3)
        iTotalRecursion = 3) != 0
        TailCall(2)
           iTotalRecursion = 2) != 0
           TailCall(1)
              iTotalRecursion = 1) != 0
              TailCall(0)
                 iTotalRecursion = 0) == 0
                 Execute the process in tail
   Finish!
```

Now, the flow of our tail recursion is obvious and clear. The idea of tail recursion is to minimize the use of the stack that is sometimes the expensive resource we have. Using tail recursion, the code doesn't need to remember the last state it has to come back to when the next step returns, since it has the temporary result in the accumulator parameter in this case. The following topic is the two styles that follow tail recursion; they are **accumulator-passing style (APS)** and **continuation-passing style (CPS)**.

Accumulator-passing style

In the **accumulator-passing style** (**APS**), the recursion performs the calculation first, executes the recursive call, and then passes the result of the current step to the next recursive step. Let's take a look at the following accumulator passing style of the tail recursive code we refactor from the GetFactorial() method, which we can find in the AccumulatorPassingStyle.csproj project:

```
public partial class Program
{
  public static int GetFactorialAPS(int intNumber,
    int accumulator = 1)
  {
    if (intNumber == 0)
    {
      return accumulator;
    }
    return GetFactorialAPS(intNumber - 1,
        intNumber * accumulator);
  }
}
```

Compared to the GetFactorial() method, we now have a second parameter named accumulator in the GetFactorialAPS() method. Since the result of the factorial 0 is 1, we give the default value of 1 to the accumulator parameter. Instead of just returning a value, it now returns the calculation of the factorial every time the recursive function is called. To prove this, consider that we have the following code in order to invoke the GetFactorialAPS() method:

```
public partial class Program
{
  private static void GetFactorialOfFiveUsingAPS()
  {
    int i = GetFactorialAPS(5);
    Console.WriteLine(
        "5! (using GetFactorialAPS) is {0}",i);
  }
}
```

If we run the preceding method, we will get the following output on the console:

Now, let's examine every call of the `GetFactorialAPS()` method to see the state change inside the method from the following flow of the program:

```
int i = GetFactorialAPS(5, 1)
  accumulator = 1
  (intNumber = 5) != 0
  return GetFactorialAPS(4, 5 * 1)
    accumulator = 5 * 1 = 5
    (intNumber = 4) != 0
    return GetFactorialAPS(3, 4 * 5)
      accumulator = 4 * 5 = 20
      (intNumber = 3) != 0
      return GetFactorialAPS(2, 3 * 20)
        accumulator = 3 * 20 = 60
        (intNumber = 2) != 0
        return GetFactorialAPS(1, 2 * 60)
          accumulator = 2 * 60 = 120
          (intNumber = 1) != 0
          return GetFactorialAPS(0, 1 * 120)
            accumulator = 1 * 120 = 120
            (intNumber = 0) == 0
            return accumulator
          return 120
        return 120
      return 120
    return 120
  return 120
i = 120
```

As we can see from the preceding flow, since it performs the calculation every time it's called, we now have the result of the calculation in the last call of the function, when the `intNumber` parameter has reached `0`, as shown in the following code snippet:

```
return GetFactorialTailRecursion(0, 1 * 120)
  accumulator = 1 * 120 = 120
  (intNumber = 0) == 0
  return accumulator
return 120
```

We can also refactor the preceding `GetFactorialAPS()` method into the `GetFactorialAPS2()` method in order to not return any value, so it will become more obvious how the APS of tail recursion works. The code will be as follows:

```
public partial class Program
{
  public static void GetFactorialAPS2(
      int intNumber, int accumulator = 1)
```

```
  {
    if (intNumber == 0)
    {
      Console.WriteLine("The result is " + accumulator);
      return;
    }
    GetFactorialAPS2(intNumber - 1, intNumber * accumulator);
  }
}
```

Suppose we have the following `GetFactorialOfFiveUsingAPS2()` method to call the `GetFactorialAPS2()` method:

```
public partial class Program
{
  private static void GetFactorialOfFiveUsingAPS2()
  {
    Console.WriteLine("5! (using GetFactorialAPS2)");
    GetFactorialAPS2(5);
  }
}
```

So, we will get the following output on the console if we invoke the preceding `GetFactorialOfFiveUsingAPS2()` method:

Now, the flow of the `GetFactorialAPS2()` method becomes clearer, as shown in the following flow of the program:

```
GetFactorialAPS2(5, 1)
  accumulator = 1
  (intNumber = 5) != 0
  GetFactorialAPS2(4, 5 * 1)
    accumulator = 5 * 1 = 5
    (intNumber = 4) != 0
    GetFactorialAPS2(3, 4 * 5)
      accumulator = 4 * 5 = 20
      (intNumber = 3) != 0
      GetFactorialAPS2(2, 3 * 20)
        accumulator = 3 * 20 = 60
        (intNumber = 2) != 0
        GetFactorialAPS2(1, 2 * 60)
```

```
            accumulator = 2 * 60 = 120
            (intNumber = 1) != 0
            GetFactorialAPS2(0, 1 * 120)
              accumulator = 1 * 120 = 120
              (intNumber = 0) == 0
              Show the accumulator value
      Finish!
```

From the preceding flow, we can see that we calculate the accumulator every time the `GetFactorialAPS2()` method is invoked. The result of this recursion type is that we do not need to use the stack anymore since the function doesn't need to memorize its start position when it calls the function itself.

Continuation-passing style

The **continuation-passing style** (**CPS**) has the same purpose as APS in implementing the recursive function using a tail call, but it has explicit continuation in processing the operation. The return of the CPS function will be passed on to the continuation function.

Now, let's refactor the `GetFactorial()` method into the following `GetFactorialCPS()` method, which we can find in the `ContinuationPassingStyle.csproj` project:

```
public partial class Program
{
  public static void GetFactorialCPS(int intNumber, Action<int>
        actCont)
  {
    if (intNumber == 0)
      actCont(1);
    else
      GetFactorialCPS(intNumber - 1,x => actCont(intNumber * x));
  }
}
```

As we can see, instead of using the accumulator, as we did in the `GetFactorialAPS()` method, we now use `Action<T>` to delegate an anonymous method, which we use as a continuation. Suppose we have the following code to invoke the `GetFactorialCPS()` method:

```
public partial class Program
{
  private static void GetFactorialOfFiveUsingCPS()
  {
    Console.Write("5! (using GetFactorialCPS) is ");
    GetFactorialCPS(5,  x => Console.WriteLine(x));
```

```
        }
    }
```

If we run the preceding `GetFactorialOfFiveUsingCPS()` method, we will get the following output on the console:

Indeed, we get the same result compared to the `GetFactorial()` method or the `GetFactorialAPS2()` method. However, the flow of recursion now becomes a little bit different, as shown in the following explanation:

```
GetFactorialCPS(5, Console.WriteLine(x))
   (intNumber = 5) != 0
  GetFactorialCPS(4, (5 * x))
    (intNumber = 4) != 0
   GetFactorialCPS(3, (4 * x))
     (intNumber = 3) != 0
    GetFactorialCPS(2, (3 * x))
      (intNumber = 2) != 0
     GetFactorialCPS(1, (2 * x))
       (intNumber = 1) != 0
      GetFactorialCPS(0, (1 * x))
        (intNumber = 0) != 0
       GetFactorialCPS(0, (1 * 1))
      (1 * 1 = 1)
     (2 * 1 = 2)
    (3 * 2 = 6)
   (4 * 6 = 24)
  (5 * 24 = 120)
Console.WriteLine(120)
```

The return of each recursion now is passed to the continuation process, in this case, the `Console.WriteLine()` function.

Indirect recursion over direct recursion

We have discussed recursion methods earlier. Actually, in our previous discussion, we applied direct recursion since we only dealt with a single method and we invoked it over and over again until the base case was executed. However, there's another recursive type, which is called indirect recursion. Indirect recursion involves at least two functions, for instance, function A and function B. In the application of an indirect recursion, function A calls function B, and then function B makes a call back to function A. It's considered a recursion because when method B calls method A, function A is actually active when it calls function B. In other words, the invocation of function A has not finished when function B calls function A again. Let's take a look at the following code, which demonstrates the indirect recursion that we can find in the `IndirectRecursion.csproj` project:

```
public partial class Program
{
  private static bool IsOdd(int targetNumber)
  {
    if (targetNumber == 0)
    {
      return false;
    }
    else
    {
      return IsEven(targetNumber - 1);
    }
  }
  private static bool IsEven(int targetNumber)
  {
    if (targetNumber == 0)
    {
      return true;
    }
    else
    {
      return IsOdd(targetNumber - 1);
    }
  }
}
```

We have two functions in the preceding code: IsOdd() and IsEven(). Each function calls the other function every time the comparison results false. The IsOdd() function will call IsEven() when targetNumber is not zero and so will the IsEven() function. The logic of each function is simple. For instance, the IsOdd() method decides whether or not targetNumber is odd by investigating whether or not the previous number, which is targetNumber - 1, is even. Likewise, the IsEven() method decides whether or not targetNumber is even by investigating whether or not the previous number is odd. They all subtract targetNumber by one until it becomes zero, and since zero is an even number, it's now quite easy to determine whether targetNumber is odd or even. Now, we add the following code to examine whether the number 5 is even or not:

```
public partial class Program
{
  private static void CheckNumberFive()
  {
    Console.WriteLine("Is 5 even number? {0}", IsEven(5));
  }
}
```

If we run the preceding CheckNumberFive() method, we will get the following output on the console:

Now, to make this clearer, let's take a look at the following indirect recursion flow involving the IsOdd() and IsEven() methods:

```
IsEven(5)
  (targetNumber = 5) != 0
  IsOdd(4)
    (targetNumber = 4) != 0
    IsEven(3)
      (targetNumber = 3) != 0
      IsOdd(2)
        (targetNumber = 2) != 0
        IsEven(1)
          (targetNumber = 1) != 0
            IsOdd(0)
            (targetNumber = 0) == 0
              Result = False
```

From the preceding flow, we can see that when we check whether number 5 is even or not, we move down to number 4 and check whether it is odd. We then check number 3 and so on, until we reach 0. By reaching 0, we can easily determine whether it's odd or even.

Recursion in a functional approach using LINQ Aggregate

When we deal with a factorial formula, we can use LINQ Aggregate to refactor our recursive function into a functional approach. LINQ Aggregate will accumulate the given sequence, and then we will have the result of the recursion from the accumulator. In Chapter 1, *Tasting Functional Style in C#* we have already done this refactoring. Let's borrow the code from the chapter to analyze the use of the Aggregate method. The following code will use the Aggregate method, which we can find in the RecursionUsingAggregate.csproj project:

```
public partial class Program
{
    private static void GetFactorialAggregate(int intNumber)
    {
        IEnumerable<int> ints =
            Enumerable.Range(1, intNumber);
        int factorialNumber =
            ints.Aggregate((f, s) => f * s);
        Console.WriteLine("{0}! (using Aggregate) is {1}",
            intNumber, factorialNumber);
    }
}
```

If we run the preceding GetFactorialAggregate() method and pass 5 as the parameter, we will get the following output on the console:

As we can see in the preceding console screenshot, we get the exact same result compared to what we get with the use of nonaggregate recursion.

Delving into the Aggregate method

As we discussed earlier, the `Aggregate` method will accumulate the given sequence. Let's take a look at the following code, which we can find in the `AggregateExample.csproj` project file, to demonstrate how the `Aggregate` method works:

```
public partial class Program
{
  private static void AggregateInt()
  {
    List<int> listInt = new List<int>() { 1, 2, 3, 4, 5, 6 };
    int addition = listInt.Aggregate(
        (sum, i) => sum + i);
    Console.WriteLine("The sum of listInt is " + addition);
  }
}
```

From the preceding code, we can see that we have a list of `int` data types, which contains numbers from 1 to 6. We then invoke the `Aggregate` method to sum up the members of `listInt`. Here is the flow of the preceding code:

```
(sum, i) => sum + i
sum = 1
sum = 1 + 2
sum = 3 + 3
sum = 6 + 4
sum = 10 + 5
sum = 15 + 6
sum = 21
addition = sum
```

If we run the preceding `AggregateInt()` method, we will get the following output on the console:

Actually, the `Aggregate` method not only adds the number, but it also adds the string. Let's examine the following code, which demonstrates the `Aggregate` method used to add the string sequence:

```
public partial class Program
{
  private static void AggregateString()
  {
    List<string> listString = new List<string>()
      {"The", "quick", "brown", "fox", "jumps", "over",
            "the", "lazy", "dog"};
    string stringAggregate = listString.Aggregate((strAll, str) =>
            strAll + " " + str);
    Console.WriteLine(stringAggregate);
  }
}
```

If we run the preceding `AggregateString()` method, we will get the following output on the console:

The following is a declaration of the `Aggregate` method that we can find in MSDN:

```
public static TSource Aggregate<TSource>(
  this IEnumerable<TSource> source,
  Func<TSource, TSource, TSource> func
)
```

The following is the flow of the `AggregateUsage()` method based on the previous declaration:

```
(strAll, str) => strAll + " " + str
strAll = "The"
strAll = strAll + " " + str
strAll = "The" + " " + "quick"
strAll = "The quick" + " " + "brown"
strAll = "The quick brown" + " " + "fox"
strAll = "The quick brown fox" + " " + "jumps"
strAll = "The quick brown fox jumps" + " " + "over"
strAll = "The quick brown fox jumps over" + " " + "the"
strAll = "The quick brown fox jumps over the" + " " + "lazy"
strAll = "The quick brown fox jumps over the lazy" + " " + "dog"
```

```
strAll = "The quick brown fox jumps over the lazy dog"
stringAggregate = str
```

From the preceding flow, we can concatenate all strings in listString using the Aggregate method. This proves that not only can the int data type be handled, but the string data type can be handled as well.

Summary

Although C# has a feature to iterate a sequence using the for or while loop, it's better for us to approach functional programming using recursion to iterate the sequence. We already discussed how the recursion routine works and refactored the iteration into recursion. We know that in the recursion, we have a base case that will define the end of the recursion chain.

In the traditional recursion model, the recursive call performs first then returns the value and then calculates the result. The result won't be displayed until the recursive call is finished. Whereas, the tail recursion doesn't do anything after recursion at all. There are two styles in tail recursion; they are APS and CPS.

Besides direct recursion, we also discussed indirect recursion. Indirect recursion involves at least two functions. Then, we applied recursion into the functional approach using the **Aggregrate LINQ** operator. We also delved into the Aggregate operator and discussed how it works.

In the next chapter, we will discuss optimizing techniques to make our code more efficient. We will use laziness thinking so the code will be executed at the perfect time and also caching techniques so the code doesn't need to execute every time it's required.

8

Optimizing the Code using Laziness and Caching Techniques

We discussed recursion, which help us to iterate sequences easily, in the previous chapter. Furthermore, we need to discuss about optimizing code since it is an essential technique if we want to develop a good program. In a functional approach, we can use laziness and caching techniques to make our code efficient so that it will run faster. By discussing laziness and caching techniques, we will be able to develop efficient code. To learn more about laziness and caching techniques, in this chapter, we will discuss the following topics:

- Implementing laziness in our code: lazy enumeration, lazy evaluation, nonstrict evaluation, and lazy initialization
- The benefit of being lazy
- Caching expensive resources using precomputation and memoization

Introduction to laziness

When we talk about being lazy in our daily activity, we might think about something we don't do but we actually have to do. Or, we might put off doing something just because we are lazy. In functional programming, laziness is analogous to our laziness in daily activities. The execution of particular code is deferred due to the concept of laziness thinking. In `Chapter 5`, *Querying Any Collection Easily with LINQ* we mentioned that LINQ implemented deferred execution when querying data from a collection.

The query will be executed only when it's enumerated. Now, let's discuss the laziness concept we can use in the functional approach.

Lazy enumeration

In the .NET framework, there are some techniques to enumerate a collection of data, such as array and `List<T>`. However, implicitly, they are eager evaluations since in an array, we have to define its size first and then fill in the allocated memory before we use it. `List<T>` has a similar concept compared to array. It adopts the array mechanism. The difference between these two enumeration techniques is that we can easily expand the size in `List<T>` rather than array.

In contrast, the .NET framework has `IEnumerable<T>` to enumerate data collection, and fortunately, it will be evaluated lazily. Actually, array and `List<T>` implement the `IEnumerable<T>` interface, but because it has to be filled by data it has to be eagerly evaluated. We used this `IEnumerable<T>` interface when we dealt with LINQ in `Chapter 5`, *Querying Any Collection Easily with LINQ*.

The `IEnumerable<T>` interface implements the `IEnumerable` interface, which is defined like this:

```
public interface IEnumerable<out T> : IEnumerable
```

There is only a single method that the `IEnumerable<T>` interface has: `GetEnumerator()`. The definition of this method is similar to what is shown in the following code:

```
IEnumerator<T> GetEnumerator()
```

As you can see, the `GetEnumerator()` method returns the `IEnumerator<T>` data type. This type has only three methods and a single property. Here are the methods and properties it has:

- `Current`: This is a property that stores the element of the collection for the current position of the enumerator.
- `Reset()`: This is a method that sets the enumerator to the initial position, which is before the first element of the collection. The index of the initial position is usually *-1* (minus one).
- `MoveNext()`: This is a method to move the enumerator to the next collection element.

- `Dispose()`: This is a method to free, release, or reset unmanaged resources. It's inherited from the `IDisposable` interface.

Now, let's play with the Fibonacci algorithm, which will generate infinite numbers. The algorithm will generate sequences by adding the previous two elements. In mathematical terms, the formula can be defined as follows:

```
Fn = Fn-1 + Fn-2
```

The first two numbers for the calculation of this algorithm can be 0 and 1 or 1 and 1.

Using this algorithm, we are going to prove that the `IEnumerable` interface is a lazy evaluation. So, we create a class named `FibonacciNumbers`, which implements the `IEnumerable<Int64>` interface that we can find in the `LazyEnumeration.csproj` project, as shown in the following code:

```
public partial class Program
{
  public class FibonacciNumbers
    : IEnumerable<Int64>
  {
    public IEnumerator<Int64> GetEnumerator()
    {
      return new FibEnumerator();
    }
    IEnumerator IEnumerable.GetEnumerator()
    {
      return GetEnumerator();
    }
  }
}
```

Since the `FibonacciNumbers` class implements the `IEnumerable<T>` interface, it has the `GetEnumerator()` method, as we discussed earlier, to enumerate the data collection. And because the `IEnumerable<T>` interface implements the `IEnumerator<T>` interface, we create the `FibEnumerator` class, as shown in the following code:

```
public partial class Program
{
  public class FibEnumerator
    : IEnumerator<Int64>
  {
    public FibEnumerator()
    {
      Reset();
    }
```

```csharp
    // To get the current element
    public Int64 Current { get; private set; }
    // To get the last element
    Int64 Last { get; set; }
    object IEnumerator.Current
    {
      get
      {
        return Current;
      }
    }
    public void Dispose()
    {
      ; // Do Nothing
    }
    public bool MoveNext()
    {
      if (Current == -1)
      {
        // Fibonacci algorithm
        // F0 = 0
        Current = 0;
      }
      else if (Current == 0)
      {
        // Fibonacci algorithm
        // F1 = 1
        Current = 1;
      }
      else
      {
        // Fibonacci algorithm
        // Fn = F(n-1) + F(n-2)
        Int64 next = Current + Last;
        Last = Current;
        Current = next;
      }
      // It's never ending sequence,
      // so the MoveNext() always TRUE
      return true;
    }
    public void Reset()
    {
      // Back to before first element
      // which is -1
      Current = -1;
    }
}
```

```
    }
```

Now, we have the `FibEnumerator` class that implements the `IEnumerator<T>` interface. Since the class implements `IEnumerator<T>`, it has the `Reset()`, `MoveNext()`, and `Dispose()` methods, as we have discussed already. It also has the `Current` property from the implementation of the `IEnumerator<T>` interface. We add the `Last` property to save the last current number.

Now, it's time to create the caller to instantiate the `FibonacciNumbers` class. We can create the `GetFibonnacciNumbers()` function, which has an implementation similar to what is shown in the following code:

```
public partial class Program
{
  private static void GetFibonnacciNumbers(
    int totalNumber)
  {
    FibonacciNumbers fibNumbers =
      new FibonacciNumbers();
    foreach (Int64 number in
      fibNumbers.Take(totalNumber))
    {
      Console.Write(number);
      Console.Write("\t");
    }
    Console.WriteLine();
  }
}
```

Because the `FibonacciNumbers` class will enumerate infinite numbers, we have to use the `Take()` method, as shown in the following code snippet, in order not to create an infinite loop:

```
foreach (Int64 number in
  fibNumbers.Take(totalNumber))
```

Suppose we need to enumerate 40 numbers from the sequence; we can pass 40 as an argument to the `GetFibonnacciNumbers()` function, as follows:

```
GetFibonnacciNumbers(40)
```

And if we run the preceding function, we will get the following output on the console:

We can get the preceding output on the console since `IEnumerable` is a lazy evaluation. This is because the `MoveNext()` method will only be called to calculate the result if it's asked to do so. Imagine if it's not lazy and is always called; then, our previous code will spin and result in an infinite loop.

Lazy evaluation

The simple example we have on lazy evaluation is when we deal with two Boolean statements and need to compare them. Let's take a look at the following code, which demonstrates lazy evaluation, which we can find in the `SimpleLazyEvaluation.csproj` project:

```
public partial class Program
{
  private static MemberData GetMember()
  {
    MemberData member = null;
    try
    {
      if (member != null || member.Age > 50)
      {
        Console.WriteLine("IF Statement is TRUE");
        return member;
      }
      else
      {
        Console.WriteLine("IF Statement is FALSE");
        return null;
      }
    }
    catch (Exception e)
    {
      Console.WriteLine("ERROR: " + e.Message);
      return null;
    }
```

```
    }
  }
```

And here is the `MemberData` class we use in the preceding code:

```
public class MemberData
{
  public string Name { get; set; }
  public string Gender { get; set; }
  public int Age { get; set; }
}
```

And if we run the preceding `GetMember()` method, we will get the following output on the console:

As we know, when we use the `||` (OR) operator in the Boolean expression, it will result in TRUE if at least one expression is TRUE. Now take a look at the following code snippet:

```
if (member != null || member.Age > 50)
```

In the preceding example, when the compiler finds that member `!= null` is FALSE, it then evaluates the other expression, which is `member.Age > 50`. Since the member is null, it has no `Age` property; so, when we try to access this property, it will throw an exception.

Now, let's refactor the preceding code snippet into the following code using the `&&` (AND) operator:

```
if (member != null && member.Age > 50)
```

The complete method named `GetMemberANDOperator()` will be as follows:

```
public partial class Program
{
  private static MemberData GetMemberANDOperator()
  {
    MemberData member = null;
    try
    {
      if (member != null && member.Age > 50)
      {
        Console.WriteLine("IF Statement is TRUE");
```

```
      return member;
    }
    else
    {
      Console.WriteLine("IF Statement is FALSE");
      return null;
    }
  }
  catch (Exception e)
  {
    Console.WriteLine("ERROR: " + e.Message);
    return null;
  }
  }
}
```

If we run the preceding `GetMemberANDOperator()` method, we will get the following output on the console:

Now, the `if` statement has been successfully executed and it results in `FALSE` after being evaluated. However, the `member.Age > 50` expression is never evaluated in this case so that the exception is not thrown. The reason why the `member.Age > 50` expression is not evaluated is that the compiler is too lazy to do it since the first expression, `member != null`, is `FALSE` and the result of this `&&` logical operation will result in `FALSE` regardless of the result of other expression. We can now say that laziness is ignoring another expression when it can decide the result using only one expression.

Nonstrict evaluation

Some people may think that lazy evaluation is synonymous with nonstrict evaluation. However, it's not actually synonymous since the evaluation of a particular expression will be ignored if it's not needed in the lazy evaluation, while the reduction of evaluation will be applied in a nonstrict evaluation. Let's take a look at the following code in order to distinguish strict and nonstrict evaluation, which we can find in the `NonStrictEvaluation.csproj` project:

```
public partial class Program
{
  private static int OuterFormula(int x, int yz)
```

```
  {
    Console.WriteLine(
      String.Format(
        "Calculate {0} + InnerFormula({1})",
        x,
        yz));
    return x * yz;
  }
  private static int InnerFormula(int y, int z)
  {
    Console.WriteLine(
      String.Format(
        "Calculate {0} * {1}",
        y,
        z
        ));
    return y * z;
  }
}
```

In the preceding code, we are going to calculate the formula of `x + (y * z)`. The `InnerFormula()` function will calculate the multiplication of `y` and `z`, while the `OuterFormula()` function will calculate the addition of `x` and the result of `y * z`. When evaluating the formula in strict evaluation, we first calculate the `(y * z)` expression to retrieve the value and then add the result to the `x`. The code will be like the following `StrictEvaluation()` function:

```
public partial class Program
{
  private static void StrictEvaluation()
  {
    int x = 4;
    int y = 3;
    int z = 2;
    Console.WriteLine("Strict Evaluation");
    Console.WriteLine(
      String.Format(
        "Calculate {0} + ({1} * {2})",x, y, z));
    int result = OuterFormula(x, InnerFormula(y, z));
    Console.WriteLine(
      String.Format(
        "{0} + ({1} * {2}) = {3}",x, y, z, result));
    Console.WriteLine();
  }
}
```

As you can see, in the preceding code we invoke the `OuterFormula()` function like the following code snippet:

```
int result = OuterFormula(x, InnerFormula(y, z));
```

And for the strict evaluation we discussed earlier, the output we get on the console will be as follows:

As you can see in the preceding figure, when we calculate `4 + (3 * 2)`, we first calculate the result of `(3 * 2)` and then after getting the result, we add it to `4`.

Now, let's compare it with nonstrict evaluation. In nonstrict evaluation, the + operator is reduced first and then we reduce the inner formula, which is `(y * z)`. We will see that the evaluation will be started from the outside to the inside. Now let's refactor the preceding `OuterFormula()` function to the `OuterFormulaNonStrict()` function, as shown in the following code:

```
public partial class Program
{
  private static int OuterFormulaNonStrict(
    int x,
    Func<int, int, int> yzFunc)
  {
    int y = 3;
    int z = 2;
    Console.WriteLine(
      String.Format(
        "Calculate {0} + InnerFormula ({1})",
        x,
        y * z
        ));
    return x * yzFunc(3, 2);
  }
}
```

As you can see, we modify the second parameter of the function into the `Func<int, int, int>` delegate. We will call `OuterFormulaNonStrict()` from the `NonStrictEvaluation()` function, as follows:

```
public partial class Program
{
  private static void NonStrictEvaluation()
  {
    int x = 4;
    int y = 3;
    int z = 2;
    Console.WriteLine("Non-Strict Evaluation");
    Console.WriteLine(
      String.Format(
        "Calculate {0} + ({1} * {2})",x, y, z));
    int result = OuterFormulaNonStrict(x, InnerFormula);
    Console.WriteLine(
      String.Format(
        "{0} + ({1} * {2}) = {3}",x, y, z, result));
    Console.WriteLine();
  }
}
```

In the preceding code, we can see that we pass the `InnerFormula()` function into the second parameter of the `OuterFormulaNonStrict()` function, as shown in the following code snippet:

```
int result = OuterFormulaNonStrict(x, InnerFormula);
```

The expression in the preceding code snippet will be evaluated using nonstrict evaluation. To prove this, let's run the `NonStrictEvaluation()` function, and we will get the following output on the console:

We can see that our expression is evaluated from the outside to the inside. The `OuterFormulaNonStrict()` function is run first even though the result of the `InnerFormula()` function is not retrieved yet. And if we run the `OuterFormula()` function and the `OuterFormulaNonStrict()` function consecutively, we will get a clear difference in the order of the evaluation, as shown in the following output screenshot:

Now, we can compare the difference. In strict evaluation, the calculation of `(3 * 2)` is run first and then fed to the `(4 + InnerFormula())` expression, while in nonstrict evaluation, the `(4 + InnerFormula())` expression is run before the calculation of `(3 * 2)`.

Lazy initialization

Lazy initialization is an optimizing technique where the object creation is deferred until it is used. It means that we can define an object but it won't be initialized if the member of the object is not accessed yet. C# introduced the `Lazy<T>` class in C# 4.0, and we can use to lazily initialize the object. Now, let's take a look at the following code in order to demonstrate the lazy initialization that we can find in the `LazyInitialization.csproj` project:

```
public partial class Program
{
  private static void LazyInitName(string NameOfPerson)
  {
    Lazy<PersonName> pn =
      new Lazy<PersonName>(
        () =>
          new PersonName(NameOfPerson));
    Console.WriteLine(
      "Status: PersonName has been defined.");
    if (pn.IsValueCreated)
```

[236]

```
    {
      Console.WriteLine(
        "Status: PersonName has been initialized.");
    }
    else
    {
      Console.WriteLine(
        "Status: PersonName hasn't been initialized.");
    }
    Console.WriteLine(
      String.Format(
        "Status: PersonName.Name = {0}",
        (pn.Value as PersonName).Name));
    if (pn.IsValueCreated)
    {
      Console.WriteLine(
        "Status: PersonName has been initialized.");
    }
    else
    {
      Console.WriteLine(
        "Status: PersonName hasn't been initialized.");
    }
  }
}
```

We define the `PersonName` class as follows:

```
public class PersonName
{
  public string Name { get; set; }
  public PersonName(string name)
  {
    Name = name;
    Console.WriteLine(
      "Status: PersonName constructor has been called."
      );
  }
}
```

As you can see in the preceding `LazyInitName()` function implementation, we lazily initialize the `PersonName` object using the `Lazy<T>` class, as shown in the following code snippet:

```
Lazy<PersonName> pn =
  new Lazy<PersonName>(
    () =>
      new PersonName(NameOfPerson));
```

By doing this, `PersonName` isn't actually initialized after we define the `pn` variable, like what we usually get when we define the class directly using the following code:

```
PersonName pn =
  new PersonName(
    NameOfPerson);
```

Instead, using lazy initialization we access the object's member in order to initialize it, as discussed earlier. `Lazy<T>` has a property named `Value`, which gets the value for the `Lazy<T>` instance. It also has the `IsValueCreated` property to indicate whether a value has been created for this `Lazy<T>` instance. In the `LazyInitName()` function, we use the `Value` property, as shown in the following code snippet:

```
Console.WriteLine(
  String.Format(
    "Status: PersonName.Name = {0}",
    (pn.Value as PersonName).Name));
```

We use `(pn.Value as PersonName).Name` to access the `Name` property of the `PersonName` class, which has been instantiated by the `pn` variable. We use the `IsValueCreated` property to prove whether or not the `PersonName` class has been initialized, as shown in the following code snippet:

```
if (pn.IsValueCreated)
{
  Console.WriteLine(
    "Status: PersonName has been initialized.");
}
else
{
  Console.WriteLine(
    "Status: PersonName hasn't been initialized.");
}
```

Now let's run the `LazyInitName()` function and pass `Matthew Maxwell` as its argument, as shown in the following code:

```
LazyInitName("Matthew Maxwell");
```

We will get the following output on the console:

From the preceding screenshot, we have five lines of information. The first line we get is when `PersonName` is defined. We then check the value of the `IsValueCreated` property to find whether `PersonName` has been initialized. We get the `FALSE` result, which means that it's not initialized yet; so we have the second line of the information on the console. The next two lines are the interesting things we get from lazy initialization. When we access the `Value` property of the `Lazy<T>` class to retrieve the `Name` property of the `PersonName` instance, the code calls the constructor of `PersonName` before it accesses the `Name` property of `PersonName` class. This is why we have lines 3 and 4 in the preceding console. And after we check the `IsValueCreated` property again, we find that `PersonName` has now been initialized and the `pn` variable has an instance of `PersonName`.

The advantages and disadvantages of being lazy

We have learned about laziness so far. We can also elaborate the advantages of being lazy, such as:

- We don't need to pay the initialization time for features we don't use
- The program execution becomes more efficient because sometimes, in the functional approach, the order of the execution is not important compared to the imperative approach
- Being lazy will make a programmer write better code by writing efficient code

Besides the advantages, being lazy also has disadvantages, such as:

- The flow of the application is hard to predict and we can lose control over our application sometimes
- The code complexity in laziness can cause a bookkeeping overhead

Caching expensive resources

Sometimes, we have to create an expensive resource in our program. It's not a problem if we only do it once. It will be a big problem if we do it over and over for the same function. Fortunately, in a functional approach, we will get the same output if we pass the exact same input or arguments. We can then cache this expensive resource and use it again when the passed argument is the same. Now we are going to discuss precomputation and memoization in order to cache the resources.

Performing initial computation

One of the caching techniques we have is precomputation, which performs an initial computation in order to create a lookup table. This lookup table is used to avoid repetitive computation when a particular process is executed. Now we are going to create code to compare the difference in the process with and without precomputation. Let's take a look at the following code, which we can find in the `Precomputation.csproj` project:

```
public partial class Program
{
  private static void WithoutPrecomputation()
  {
    Console.WriteLine("WithoutPrecomputation()");
    Console.Write(
      "Choose number from 0 to 99 twice ");
    Console.WriteLine(
      "to find the power of two result: ");
    Console.Write("First Number: ");
    int iInput1 = Convert.ToInt32(Console.ReadLine());
    Console.Write("Second Number: ");
    int iInput2 = Convert.ToInt32(Console.ReadLine());
    int iOutput1 = (int) Math.Pow(iInput1, 2);
    int iOutput2 = (int)Math.Pow(iInput2, 2);
    Console.WriteLine(
      "2 the power of {0} is {1}",
      iInput1,
      iOutput1);
    Console.WriteLine(
      "2 the power of {0} is {1}",
      iInput2,
      iOutput2);
  }
}
```

The preceding simple `WithoutPrecomputation()` function will calculate the square of the two numbers that we input from 0 to 99. Suppose we want to calculate the number `19` and `85`; we will get the following output on the console window:

As you can see, the function has done its job well. It asks for two input numbers from the user with the following code snippet:

```
Console.Write("First Number: ");
int iInput1 = Convert.ToInt32(Console.ReadLine());
Console.Write("Second Number: ");
int iInput2 = Convert.ToInt32(Console.ReadLine());
```

It uses the `Math.Pow()` method in the `System` namespace in order to get to the power of n, as shown in the following code snippet:

```
int iOutput1 = (int) Math.Pow(iInput1, 2);
int iOutput2 = (int)Math.Pow(iInput2, 2);
```

We can refactor the `WithoutPrecomputation()` function to use precomputation techniques so that it doesn't need any repetition calculation every time the user asks to calculate the power of the same numbers by two. The function we are going to have will be as follows:

```
public partial class Program
{
  private static void WithPrecomputation()
  {
    int[]powerOfTwos = new int[100];
    for (int i = 0; i < 100; i++)
    {
      powerOfTwos[i] = (int)Math.Pow(i, 2);
    }
    Console.WriteLine("WithPrecomputation()");
    Console.Write(
      "Choose number from 0 to 99 twice ");
    Console.WriteLine(
      "to find the power of two result: ");
```

```
      Console.Write("First Number: ");
      int iInput1 = Convert.ToInt32(Console.ReadLine());
      Console.Write("Second Number: ");
      int iInput2 = Convert.ToInt32(Console.ReadLine());
      int iOutput1 = FindThePowerOfTwo(powerOfTwos, iInput1);
      int iOutput2 = FindThePowerOfTwo(powerOfTwos, iInput2);
      Console.WriteLine(
        "2 the power of {0} is {1}",
        iInput1,
        iOutput1);
      Console.WriteLine(
        "2 the power of {0} is {1}",
        iInput2,
        iOutput2);
   }
 }
```

As you can see in the preceding code, we create a lookup table named `powerOfTwos` in the beginning of the function, as shown in the following code snippet:

```
int[] powerOfTwos = new int[100];
for (int i = 0; i < 100; i++)
{
  powerOfTwos[i] = (int)Math.Pow(i, 2);
}
```

Since we ask the user to input a number from 0 to 99, the lookup table will store the database of the power of two numbers from the range numbers. Moreover, the difference between the `WithPrecomputation()` function and the `WithoutPrecomputation()` function is that we have the collection of the power of two result. Now we use the `FindThePowerOfTwo()` function, as shown in the following code snippet:

```
int iOutput1 = FindThePowerOfTwo(squares, iInput1);
int iOutput2 = FindThePowerOfTwo(squares, iInput2);
```

The `FindThePowerOfTwo()` function will look for the selected number in the lookup table, which in this case is `powerOfTwos`. And the implementation of the `FindThePowerOfTwo()` function will be as follows:

```
public partial class Program
{
  private static int FindThePowerOfTwo (
    int[] precomputeData,
    int baseNumber)
  {
    return precomputeData[baseNumber];
  }
```

}

As you can see, the `FindThePowerOfTwo()` function returns the value of the lookup table, whose index we specify with the `baseNumber` parameter. We will get the following output on the console if we run the `WithPrecomputation()` function:

Again, we calculate the square of 19 and 85 and, indeed, we have the exact same result as what we get when we run the `WithoutPrecomputation()` function. Now, we have a lookup table of squared numbers from 0 to 99. The advantages in our program are more effective since every time we ask to calculate the same number (19 and 85), it will not need to run the calculation but will look for the result in the lookup table.

However, the precomputation code we explored earlier is not a functional approach since, each time the `FindThePowerOfTwo()` function is called, it will iterate the squares again. We can refactor it so that it will be functional using the power of currying, a technique to change structure arguments by sequence, which we discussed in Chapter 1, *Tasting Functional Style in C#*. Now let's take a look at the following code:

```
public partial class Program
{
    private static void WithPrecomputationFunctional()
    {
        int[]powerOfTwos = new int[100];
        for (int i = 0; i < 100; i++)
        {
            powerOfTwos[i] = (int) Math.Pow(i, 2);
        }
        Console.WriteLine("WithPrecomputationFunctional()");
        Console.Write(
            "Choose number from 0 to 99 twice ");
        Console.WriteLine(
            "to find the power of two result: ");
        Console.Write("First Number: ");
        int iInput1 = Convert.ToInt32(Console.ReadLine());
        Console.Write("Second Number: ");
        int iInput2 = Convert.ToInt32(Console.ReadLine());
        var curried = CurriedPowerOfTwo(powerOfTwos);
```

```
    int iOutput1 = curried(iInput1);
    int iOutput2 = curried(iInput2);
    Console.WriteLine(
      "2 the power of {0} is {1}",
      iInput1,
      iOutput1);
    Console.WriteLine(
      "2 the power of {0} is {1}",
      iInput2,
      iOutput2);
  }
}
```

If we compare the preceding WithPrecomputationFunctional() function with the
WithPrecomputation() function, we can see that it uses the CurriedPowerOfTwo()
function now, as shown in the following code snippet:

```
var curried = CurriedSquare(squares);
int iOutput1 = curried(iInput1);
int iOutput2 = curried(iInput2);
```

Using the CurriedPowerOfTwo() function, we split the function argument so that the
curried variable can now handle the lookup table and we can call
the WithPrecomputationFunctional() function as many times as we want with no need
to iterate the lookup table again. The CurriedPowerOfTwo() function implementation can
be found in the following code:

```
public partial class Program
{
  public static Func<int, int>
  CurriedPowerOfTwo(int[] intArray)
      => i => intArray[i];
}
```

If we run the WithPrecomputationFunctional() function, the following output will be
displayed in our console window:

Again, we have the exact same output compared to our previous functions: the `WithoutPrecomputation()` function and the `WithPrecomputation()` function. We have successfully refactored the function and the functional approach has been fulfilled in this precomputation technique.

Memoization

Besides performing precomputation techniques to optimize the code, we can also use memoization techniques to make our code more optimal. Memoization is the process of remembering the result of the function with a specific input. Each time we execute a particular function with a specific input argument, the code will remember the result. So, each time we call the function with the exact same input argument again, the code doesn't need to run the code; instead. it will get it from the place it stores the result in.

Let's borrow the repetitive `GetFactorial()` function we discussed in Chapter 5, *Querying Any Collection Easily with LINQ* and then refactor it in order to use the memoization technique. As we know, the implementation of the `GetFactorial()` function is as follows:

```
public partial class Program
{
  private static int GetFactorial(int intNumber)
  {
    if (intNumber == 0)
    {
      return 1;
    }
    return intNumber * GetFactorial(intNumber - 1);
  }
}
```

To make the `GetFactorial()` function use memoization, we have to save the result every time the `GetFactorial()` function returns a value. The refactoring code of the preceding `GetFactorial()` function will be as follows and we can find it in the `Memoization.csproj` project:

```
public partial class Program
{
  private static Dictionary<int, int>
    memoizeDict = new Dictionary<int, int>();
  private static int GetFactorialMemoization(int intNumber)
  {
    if (intNumber == 0)
    {
      return 1;
```

```
        }
        if (memoizeDict.ContainsKey(intNumber))
        {
            return memoizeDict[intNumber];
        }
        int i = intNumber * GetFactorialMemoization(
            intNumber - 1);
        memoizeDict.Add(intNumber, i);
        return i;
    }
}
```

As you can see, we have a `Dictionary` class named `memoizeDict` to store all the results when the particular arguments have been passed to the `GetFactorialMemoization()` function. The definition of this dictionary is like what is shown in the following code snippet:

```
private static Dictionary<int, int>
    memoizeDict = new Dictionary<int, int>();
```

Another difference when we compare the `GetFactorialMemoization()` function to the `GetFactorial()` function is that it now saves the result when the `GetFactorialMemoization()` function is run with the particular arguments that have been called so far. The following code snippet shows the code for this algorithm:

```
private static int GetFactorialMemoization(int intNumber)
{
    if (intNumber == 0)
    {
        return 1;
    }
    if (memoizeDict.ContainsKey(intNumber))
    {
        return memoizeDict[intNumber];
    }
    int i = intNumber * GetFactorialMemoization(
        intNumber - 1);
    memoizeDict.Add(intNumber, i);
    return i;
}
```

First, we check whether the particular argument has been passed to the function. If so, it doesn't need to run the function; instead, it just retrieves the result from the dictionary. If the parameter arguments haven't been passed yet, the function is run and we save the result in the dictionary. Using memoization, we can optimize the code since we don't need to run the function over and over again if the arguments are exactly the same. Suppose we pass 10 to the `GetFactorialMemoization()` function. If we run the function again and pass 10 again, the processing speed time will increase since it doesn't need to run the repetitive `GetFactorialMemoization()` function. Fortunately, by passing 10 to the function parameter, it will also run the function with the 1-9 argument since it's a recursive function. The effect and the result of the invocation of these 10 items will be saved in the directory and calling the function using these arguments will be much faster.

Now let's compare the performance of the `GetFactorial()` function with the `GetFactorialMemoization()` function. We will pass `9216` as an argument and run them it times. The following is the `RunFactorial()` function used to call the `GetFactorial()` function:

```
public partial class Program
{
  private static void RunFactorial()
  {
    Stopwatch sw = new Stopwatch();
    int factorialResult = 0;
    Console.WriteLine(
      "RunFactorial() function is called");
    Console.WriteLine(
      "Get factorial of 9216");
    for (int i = 1; i <= 5; i++)
    {
      sw.Restart();
      factorialResult = GetFactorial(9216);
      sw.Stop();
      Console.WriteLine(
        "Time elapsed ({0}): {1,8} ns",
        i,
        sw.ElapsedTicks *
          1000000000 /
          Stopwatch.Frequency);
    }
  }
}
```

If we run the `RunFactorial()` function, we will get the following output on the console:

As you can see from the output, we need `281461 ns` in the first invocation of the `GetFactorial()` function and about 75,000- 98,000 nanoseconds in the remaining invocations. The process speed is almost the same for all invocations since the recursive `GetFactorial()` function is invoked everytime. Now let's move on to the following `RunFactorialMemoization()` function in order to call the `GetFactorialMemoization()` function:

```
public partial class Program
{
  private static void RunFactorialMemoization()
  {
    Stopwatch sw = new Stopwatch();
    int factorialResult = 0;
    Console.WriteLine(
      "RunFactorialMemoization() function is called");
    Console.WriteLine(
      "Get factorial of 9216");
    for (int i = 1; i <= 5; i++)
    {
      sw.Restart();
      factorialResult = GetFactorialMemoization(9216);
      sw.Stop();
      Console.WriteLine(
        "Time elapsed ({0}): {1,8} ns",
        i,
        sw.ElapsedTicks *
          1000000000 /
          Stopwatch.Frequency);
    }
  }
}
```

If we run the `RunFactorialMemoization()` function, we will get the following output on the console:

Now we can see that, by using memoization, the process speed has increased to a great extent. Even though it needs the extra time in the first invocation of `GetFactorialMemoization()`, in the invocation 3 to 5, the process becomes faster.

Summary

We discussed that, by being lazy, we can create efficient code. Lazy enumeration is useful when we need to iterate an infinite loop so that it will not overflow since the `MoveNext()` method in `IEnumerator` will be run only if asked. Also, lazy evaluation makes our code run faster because the compiler does not need to check all Boolean expressions if one of them has given the result.

In nonstrict evaluation, we treat a function in programming like we treat a mathematical function. Using this evaluation technique, we use the functional approach to solve the function.

We have also become acquainted with the lazy initialization provided by the `Lazy<T>` class to defer the object's initialization, which means that we can define an object but it won't be initialized if the member of the object has not been accessed yet.

To optimize our code, we discussed caching techniques using precomputation and memoization. In precomputation, we prepare something like a lookup table so we don't need to run the function with the exact argument; instead, we just need to get the result from the table. We also have memoization in order to remember the result of the function with a specific input. Using memoization, every time we call the function with the exact same input argument again, the code doesn't need to run the code; instead, it will get it from the place where it stores the result.

In the next chapter, we will discuss monads and their use in functional programming.

9

Working with Pattern

In the previous chapter, we discussed optimizing code to develop efficient code. Now, we are going to discuss the pattern that will make our code flow in a regular order so that it will be easier to maintain and understand the flow of the program. The main topics we are going to discuss in this chapter are pattern matching and Monad as a design pattern. Pattern matching will match the condition using a mathematical approach so that we will get a functional taste of things. And Monad is an inseparable part of the functional programming since it's a design pattern for complex problems in software design. Using Monad, we can give more power to existing data types by amplifying their behavior. This chapter will look further into pattern matching and `Monad`, and we will discuss the following topics:

- Understanding pattern matching in functional programming
- Transforming data and switching decisions using pattern matching
- Simplifying pattern matching in order to make it more functional
- Testing pattering matching feature in C# 7
- Finding out which C# types implement Monad naturally
- Generating monadic types
- Understanding the rules of Monad

Dissecting pattern matching in functional programming

In functional programming, pattern matching is a form of dispatch to choose the correct variant of the functions to be called. It's actually inspired by a standard mathematical notation with the syntax to express conditional execution. We can start our discussion on matching pattern by borrowing the code from Chapter 1, *Tasting Functional Style in C#*, when we talked about recursion. The following is the GetFactorial() functional we used to retrieve a factorial value:

```
public partial class Program
{
  private static intGetFactorial(intintNumber)
  {
    if (intNumber == 0)
    {
      return 1;
    }
    returnintNumber * GetFactorial(intNumber - 1);
  }
}
```

As we can see in the preceding code, it gives us two definitions. In this case, the dispatcher is chosen based on whether the actual intNumber parameter pattern matches 0 or not. The use of the pattern matching are closer to this if conditional expression since we have to decide which section will be selected by providing a specific input.

Transforming data using pattern matching

Pattern matching is somehow transforming data. Let's borrow another function from the previous chapter to continue the discussion. As we might remember, we had a function in the extension method called IsPrime() to check whether or not it is a prime number. We will use it again to demonstrate pattern matching to transform data. For those who have forgotten the implementation of the IsPrime() function, here is the code:

```
public static class ExtensionMethods
{
  public static bool IsPrime(this int i)
  {
    if ((i % 2) == 0)
    {
      return i == 2;
```

```
      }
      int sqrt = (int)Math.Sqrt(i);
      for (int t = 3; t <= sqrt; t = t + 2)
      {
        if (i % t == 0)
        {
          return false;
        }
      }
      return i != 1;
    }
  }
```

Again, we use pattern matching to determine whether the number is a prime number, composite number, or neither. However, now we will transform the `int` number into text, as we can see in the following `NumberFactorType()` function, which we can find in the `MatchingPattern.csproj` project:

```
  public partial class Program
  {
    public static string NumberFactorType(
      int intSelectedNumber)
    {
      if (intSelectedNumber < 2)
      {
        return "neither prime nor composite number";
      }
      else if (intSelectedNumber.IsPrime())
      {
        return "prime number";
      }
      else
      {
        return "composite number";
      }
    }
  }
```

As we can see in the preceding code, we use the `if...else` conditional statement to match the condition instead of the `if` conditional statement we used in the previous example. Now, let's call the `NumberFactorType()` function to match the int number we give and transform it into text using the following `TransformIntIntoText()` function:

```
  public partial class Program
  {
    public static void TransformIntIntoText()
    {
```

```
    for (int i = 0; i < 10; i++)
    {
      Console.WriteLine(
        "{0} is {1}", i, NumberFactorType(i));
    }
  }
}
```

We pass the number 0 to 9 into the `NumberFactorType()` function to get a matching result. And if we run the `TransformIntIntoText()` function, we get the following output on the console:

As you can see from the preceding screenshot, we have successfully used pattern matching to transform `int` into text.

Switching for pattern matching

We know that pattern matching can transform data into another form. This is actually similar to the `Select()` method in LINQ and conceptually similar to the switch case statement. Now let's take a look at the following `HexCharToByte()` function to convert a hexadecimal character into `byte`:

```
public partial class Program
{
  public static byte HexCharToByte(
    char c)
  {
    byte res;

    switch (c)
    {
      case '1':
        res = 1;
        break;
      case '2':
```

```
    res = 2;
  break;
case '3':
  res = 3;
  break;
case '4':
  res = 4;
  break;
case '5':
  res = 5;
  break;
case '6':
  res = 6;
  break;
case '7':
  res = 7;
  break;
case '8':
  res = 8;
  break;
case '9':
  res = 9;
  break;
case 'A':
case 'a':
  res = 10;
  break;
case 'B':
case 'b':
  res = 11;
  break;
case 'C':
case 'c':
  res = 12;
  break;
case 'D':
case 'd':
  res = 13;
  break;
case 'E':
case 'e':
  res = 14;
  break;
case 'F':
case 'f':
  res = 15;
  break;
default:
```

```
        res = 0;
        break;
    }

    return res;
  }
}
```

Then, we add a wrapper to convert the hexadecimal in string into int, as shown in the following `HexStringToInt()` function:

```
public partial class Program
{
  public static intHexStringToInt(
    string s)
  {
    int iCnt = 0;
    int retVal = 0;
    for (inti = s.Length - 1; i>= 0; i--)
    {
      retVal += HexCharToByte(s[i]) *
        (int) Math.Pow(0x10, iCnt++);
    }
    return retVal;
  }
}
```

From the preceding code, we can see that we call the `HexCharToByte()` function to get each int value for each hexadecimal character. Then, we use the power of 16 to get all the hexadecimal values. Suppose we have the following `GetIntFromHexString()` function to convert several hexadecimal digits in a string into int:

```
public partial class Program
{
  private static void GetIntFromHexString()
  {
    string[] hexStrings = {
      "FF", "12CE", "F0A0", "3BD",
      "D43", "35", "0", "652F",
      "8DCC", "4125"
    };
    for (int i = 0; i < hexStrings.Length; i++)
    {
      Console.WriteLine(
        "0x{0}\t= {1}",
        hexStrings[i],
        HexStringToInt(hexStrings[i]));
```

```
        }
      }
   }
```

If we run the `GetIntFromHexString()` function, we get the following output on the console:

```
0xFF    = 255
0x12CE  = 4814
0xF0A0  = 61600
0x3BD   = 957
0xD43   = 3395
0x35    = 53
0x0     = 0
0x652F  = 25903
0x8DCC  = 36300
0x4125  = 16677
Press any key to continue . . .
```

As you can see in the preceding screenshot, each hexadecimal character in the string is converted into the `int` value and then it sums up all the results.

> **TIP**
>
> To convert a hexadecimal character into a byte, we can use the `Parse` and `TryParse` methods or format it using the `String.Format`. `HexCharToByte()` function we discussed earlier, which is for sample purposes only.

Simplifying pattern matching

We have successfully used the `switch` statement to implement pattern matching. However, the example doesn't apply a functional approach since the `res` variable in the `HexCharToByte()` function is mutated during execution. Now, we are going to refactor the `HexCharToByte()` function in order to apply a functional approach. Let's take a look at the following `HexCharToByteFunctional()` function, which can be found in the `SimplifyingPatternMatching.csproj` project:

```
public partial class Program
{
  public static byte HexCharToByteFunctional(
    char c)
  {
    return c.Match()
      .With(ch =>ch == '1', (byte)1)
      .With(ch =>ch == '2', 2)
      .With(ch =>ch == '3', 3)
      .With(ch =>ch == '4', 4)
```

```
            .With(ch =>ch == '5', 5)
            .With(ch =>ch == '6', 6)
            .With(ch =>ch == '7', 7)
            .With(ch =>ch == '8', 8)
            .With(ch =>ch == '9', 9)
            .With(ch =>ch == 'A', 10)
            .With(ch =>ch == 'a', 10)
            .With(ch =>ch == 'B', 11)
            .With(ch =>ch == 'b', 11)
            .With(ch =>ch == 'C', 12)
            .With(ch =>ch == 'c', 12)
            .With(ch =>ch == 'D', 13)
            .With(ch =>ch == 'd', 13)
            .With(ch =>ch == 'E', 14)
            .With(ch =>ch == 'e', 14)
            .With(ch =>ch == 'F', 15)
            .With(ch =>ch == 'f', 15)
            .Else(0)
            .Do();
    }
}
```

The preceding `HexCharToByteFunctional()` function is refactored from the `HexCharToByte()` function and now implements the functional approach. As you can see, we have four methods similar to the `switch` statement or the `if...else` condition statement: `Match()`, `With()`, `Else()`, and `Do()`. Let's take a look at the following `Match()` function used by the preceding `HexCharToByteFunctional()` function:

```
public static class PatternMatch
{
  public static PatternMatchContext<TIn> Match<TIn>(
    this TIn value)
  {
    return new PatternMatchContext<TIn>(value);
  }
}
```

As you can see, the `Match()` function returns the new `PatternMatchContext` data type. The `PatternMatchContext` class implementation is as follows:

```
public class PatternMatchContext<TIn>
{
  private readonlyTIn _value;
  internal PatternMatchContext(TIn value)
  {
    _value = value;
  }
```

```
public PatternMatchOnValue<TIn, TOut> With<TOut>(
  Predicate<TIn> condition,
  TOut result)
{
  return new PatternMatchOnValue<TIn, TOut>(_value)
    .With(condition, result);
}
}
```

When the `Match()` function generates a new instance of `PatternMatchContext`, its constructor stores the value passed as an argument to the _value private variable, as shown in the following code snippet:

```
internal PatternMatchContext(TIn value)
{
  _value = value;
}
```

In this `PatternMatchContext` class, there is also a method called `With()`, which we can compare with the _value value. The method will invoke the `With()` method inside the `PatternMatchOnValue` class, the implementation of which is as follows:

```
public class PatternMatchOnValue<TIn, TOut>
{
  private readonlyIList<PatternMatchCase> _cases =
    new List<PatternMatchCase>();
  private readonlyTIn _value;
  private Func<TIn, TOut> _elseCase;

  internal PatternMatchOnValue(TIn value)
  {
    _value = value;
  }

  public PatternMatchOnValue<TIn, TOut> With(
    Predicate<TIn> condition,
    Func<TIn, TOut> result)
  {
    _cases.Add(new PatternMatchCase
    {
      Condition = condition,
      Result = result
    });

    return this;
  }
}
```

```
public PatternMatchOnValue<TIn, TOut> With(
  Predicate<TIn> condition,
  TOut result)
{
  return With(condition, x => result);
}

public PatternMatchOnValue<TIn, TOut> Else(
Func<TIn, TOut> result)
{
  if (_elseCase != null)
  {
    throw new InvalidOperationException(
      "Cannot have multiple else cases");
  }
  _elseCase = result;
  return this;
}

public PatternMatchOnValue<TIn, TOut> Else(
  TOut result)
{
  return Else(x => result);
}

public TOut Do()
{
  if (_elseCase != null)
  {
    With(x => true, _elseCase);
    _elseCase = null;
  }

  `foreach (var test in _cases)
  {
    if (test.Condition(_value))
    {
      returntest.Result(_value);
    }
  }

  throw new IncompletePatternMatchException();
}

private structPatternMatchCase
{
  public Predicate<TIn> Condition;
  publicFunc<TIn, TOut> Result;
```

```
    }
  }
```

As you can see from the preceding code, when the `With()` method, which is a member of the `PatternMatchContext` class, returns a new instance of `PatternMatchOnValue`, its constructor also stores the value to the `_value` private variable, as shown in the following code snippet:

```
internal PatternMatchOnValue(TIn value)
{
  _value = value;
}
```

It then calls the `With()` method, which is passed an anonymous method as `condition` and an expected value as `result`, as shown in the following code snippet:

```
public PatternMatchOnValue<TIn, TOut> With(
  Predicate<TIn> condition,
  TOut result)
{
  return With(condition, x => result);
}
```

This `With()` method then calls another `With()` method, which passes `Predicate<T>` and `Func<T1, T2>` as shown in the following code snippet:

```
public PatternMatchOnValue<TIn, TOut> With(
  Predicate<TIn> condition,
  Func<TIn, TOut> result)
{
  _cases.Add(new PatternMatchCase
  {
    Condition = condition,
    Result = result
  });

  return this;
}
```

This `With()` method collects all cases and stores them in the `_cases` list typed as `PatternMatchCase`, the implementation of which is as follows:

```
private structPatternMatchCase
{
  public Predicate<TIn> Condition;
  publicFunc<TIn, TOut> Result;
}
```

Once we have provided all the conditions, we call the `Else()` method, which contains the default result. The implementation of the `Else()` method is as shown in the following code snippet:

```
public PatternMatchOnValue<TIn, TOut> Else(
  TOut result)
{
  return Else(x => result);
}
```

We then invoke another `Else()` method passing `Func<T1, T2>`, as shown in the following code snippet:

```
public PatternMatchOnValue<TIn, TOut> Else(
  Func<TIn, TOut> result)
{
  if (_elseCase != null)
  {
    throw new InvalidOperationException(
      "Cannot have multiple else cases");
  }
  _elseCase = result;
  return this;
}
```

After we collect all _cases and _elseCase variables, we have to invoke the `Do()` method to compare all cases. The implementation of the `Do()` method can be seen in the following code snippet:

```
public TOut Do()
{
  if (_elseCase != null)
  {
    With(x => true, _elseCase);
    _elseCase = null;
  }
  foreach (var test in _cases)
  {
    if (test.Condition(_value))
    {
      returntest.Result(_value);
    }
  }
  throw new IncompletePatternMatchException();
}
```

As you can see, the Do() method will assign the _elseCase variable, if any, to the _cases list using the With() method, as shown in the following code snippet:

```
if (_elseCase != null)
{
  With(x => true, _elseCase);
  _elseCase = null;
}
```

It then compares all _cases list members using the foreach loop to find the correct _value value using the following code snippet:

```
foreach (var test in _cases)
{
  if (test.Condition(_value))
  {
    return test.Result(_value);
  }
}
```

Although invoking the Else() method is optional, it's mandatory to match one of all the With() method invocations. If not, the Do() method will throw an IncompletePatternMatchException exception, as shown in the following code snippet:

```
throw new IncompletePatternMatchException();
```

For now, we don't need to implement anything in the IncompletePatternMatchException exception, so we just need to create a new class implementation Exception class, as shown in the following code:

```
public class IncompletePatternMatchException :
  Exception
{
}
```

Until here, we have successfully refactored the HexCharToByte() function into the HexCharToByteFunctional() function. We can modify the HexStringToInt() function to invoke the HexCharToByteFunctional() function, as shown in the following code:

```
public partial class Program
{
  public static intHexStringToInt(
    string s)
  {
    int iCnt = 0;
    int retVal = 0;
    for (int i = s.Length - 1; i >= 0; i--)
```

```
      {
        retVal += HexCharToByteFunctional(s[i]) *
        (int)Math.Pow(0x10, iCnt++);
      }

      return retVal;
    }
}
```

However, the `HexStringToInt()` function does not implement the functional approach. We can refactor it to the `HexStringToIntFunctional()` function, as shown in the following code:

```
public partial class Program
{
  public static intHexStringToIntFunctional(
    string s)
  {
    returns.ToCharArray()
      .ToList()
      .Select((c, i) => new { c, i })
      .Sum((v) =>
        HexCharToByteFunctional(v.c) *
          (int)Math.Pow(0x10, v.i));
  }
}
```

From the preceding `HexStringToIntFunctional()` function, we can see that, first, we convert the strings into a list of characters by reversing the order of the list. This is because we need to assign the least significant byte with the lowest index. We then select each member of the list and create a new class that contains the character itself and the index. Afterwards, we sum them up based on their index and value. Now, we have the following `GetIntFromHexStringFunctional()` function, and it invokes the `HexStringToIntFunctional()` function:

```
public partial class Program
{
  private static void GetIntFromHexStringFunctional()
  {
    string[] hexStrings = {
      "FF", "12CE", "F0A0", "3BD",
      "D43", "35", "0", "652F",
      "8DCC", "4125"
    };
    Console.WriteLine(
      "Invoking GetIntFromHexStringFunctional() function");
    for (int i = 0; i<hexStrings.Length; i++)
```

```
        {
          Console.WriteLine(
            "0x{0}\t= {1}",
            hexStrings[i],
            HexStringToIntFunctional(
              hexStrings[i]));
        }
      }
    }
```

This is actually similar to the GetIntFromHexString() function in the MatchingPattern.csproj project. If we run the GetIntFromHexStringFunctional() function, we will get the following output on the console:

```
C:\WINDOWS\system32\cmd.exe                                    —    □    ×
Invoking GetIntFromHexStringFunctional() function
0xFF     = 255
0x12CE   = 4814
0xF0A0   = 61600
0x3BD    = 957
0xD43    = 3395
0x35     = 53
0x0      = 0
0x652F   = 25903
0x8DCC   = 36300
0x4125   = 16677
Press any key to continue . . .
```

As you can see, we get the exact same output compared to the GetIntFromHexString() function in the MatchingPattern.csproj project since we have successfully refactored it to functional pattern matching.

 For a simpler method in pattern matching, we can use the Simplicity NuGet package, which we can download directly from Visual Studio using **Package Manager Console** and typing Install-PackageSimplicity.

Welcoming the coming of pattern matching feature in C# 7

The planned language features in C# 7 includes pattern matching which has the extensions to the `is` operator. We now can introduce a new variable after the type and this variable is assigned to the left-hand side operand of the `is` operator but with the type specified as the right-hand side operand. Let's make it clear using the following code snippet which we can find in `MatchingPatternCSharp7.csproj` project:

```
public partial class Program
{
  private static void IsOperatorBeforeCSharp7()
  {
    object o = GetData();
    if (o is String)
    {
      var s = (String)o;
      Console.WriteLine(
        "The object is String. Value = {0}",
          s);
    }
  }
}
```

And the `GetData()` function implementation is as follow:

```
public partial class Program
{
  private static object GetData(
      bool objectType = true)
  {
    if (objectType)
        return "One";
    else
        return 1;
  }
}
```

In the preceding `IsOperatorBeforeCSharp7()` function, we should assign `s` variable with the value of `o` after we check the content of the `o` object variable in `if` statement. It is what we can do before C# 7 introduce pattern matching feature. Now, let's compare the preceding code with the following `IsOperatorInCSharp7()` function:

```
public partial class Program
{
  private static void IsOperatorInCSharp7()
```

```
  {
    object o = GetData();
    if (o is String s)
    {
      Console.WriteLine(
          "The object is String. Value = {0}",
          s);
    }
  }
}
```

As we can see, we now can assign `s` variable with the content of `o` variable but with the string data type, as we have discussed earlier. We assign the `s` variable inside the `if` statement when the condition is checked.

Fortunately, this feature can also be applied in switch statement as we can see in the following code snippet:

```
public partial class Program
{
  private static void SwitchCaseInCSharp7()
  {
    object x = GetData(
        false);
    switch (x)
    {
      case string s:
          Console.WriteLine(
              "{0} is a string of length {1}",
              x,
              s.Length);
          break;
      case int i:
          Console.WriteLine(
              "{0} is an {1} int",
              x,
              (i % 2 == 0 ? "even" : "odd"));
          break;
      default:
          Console.WriteLine(
              "{0} is something else",
              x);
          break;
    }
  }
}
```

As we can see in the preceding `SwitchCaseInCSharp7()` function, we can assign `s` and `i` variable with the content of `x` variable in the `case` checking so we don't need to assign the variable again.

 For more information about pattern matching feature in C# 7, we can find it in official Roslyn GitHub page on `https://github.com/dotnet/roslyn/blob/features/patterns/docs/features/patterns.md`

Introducing Monad as a design pattern

It's quite difficult to explain **Monad** in an **object-oriented programming** (OOP) language such as C#. However, in OOP, there is one useful idea to explain Monad: design patterns. A design pattern is a reusable solution for complex problems in software design. Imagine a design pattern in architecture. Many buildings in this world must have the same pattern: doors, windows, walls, and so on. If we compare design patterns in architecture with design patterns in software design, we'll realize that they both have the same idea. In a design pattern for software design, we have functions, types, variables, and so on. These design pattern have been available in the C# language and will come together to build an application.

Considering this design pattern definition, we now have a definition of Monad itself. Monad is a type that uses a Monad pattern. And the Monad pattern is a design pattern for types.

In C#, there are some types that have actually implemented Monad naturally; they are `Nullable<T>`, `IEnumerable<T>`, `Func<T>`, `Lazy<T>`, and `Task<T>`. Some of these types had been discussed in the previous chapter. However, we will discuss them again in correlation with an explanation of Monad.

These five types have several things in common; obviously, they are generic types that take only one parameter, `T`. They implement monad naturally since they have certain rules that have certain operations provided; in other words, they are amplifiers of types. They can take a type and turn it into a special type.

We can say that `Nullable<T>`is an amplifier of types because it can turn, for instance, `int` to null, which is impossible without the use of `Nullable<T>` since `int` can only handle $-2,147,483,648$ to $2,147,483,647$.

Let's take a look at the following code, which we can find in the
`AmplifierOfTypes.csproj` project:

```
public partial class Program
{
  private static Nullable<int> WordToNumber(string word)
  {
    Nullable<int> returnValue;
    if (word == null)
    {
      return null;
    }
    switch (word.ToLower())
    {
      case "zero":
        returnValue = 0;
        break;
      case "one":
        returnValue = 1;
        break;
      case "two":
        returnValue = 2;
        break;
      case "three":
        returnValue = 3;
        break;
      case "four":
        returnValue = 4;
        break;
      case "five":
        returnValue = 5;
        break;
      default:
        returnValue = null;
        break;
    }

    return returnValue;
  }
}
```

The preceding code will convert the number in the `string` type into the `int` type.
However, since the `string` type is allowed to be null, the `int` type will not be able to
handle this data type. For this purpose, we use `Nullable<int>` as a return type; so now,
the returning value can be null, as shown in the following code snippet:

```
if (word == null)
```

```
  {
    return null;
  }
```

Then, we can invoke the preceding `WordToNumber()` function using the following `PrintStringNumber()` function:

```
public partial class Program
{
  private static void PrintStringNumber(
    string stringNumber)
  {
    if (stringNumber == null &&
      WordToNumber(stringNumber) == null)
    {
      Console.WriteLine(
        "Word: null is Int: null");
    }
    else
    {
      Console.WriteLine(
        "Word: {0} is Int: {1}",
        stringNumber.ToString(),
        WordToNumber(stringNumber));
    }
  }
}
```

Now, we can return `null` to the `int` data type since it has become a `Nullable` type, as shown in the following code snippet:

```
if (stringNumber == null &&
  WordToNumber(stringNumber) == null)
```

The preceding code snippet will handle the null string input that is passed to the `WordToNumber()` function. And now we can invoke the preceding `PrintStringNumber()` function using the following code:

```
public partial class Program
{
  private static void PrintIntContainingNull()
  {
    PrintStringNumber("three");
    PrintStringNumber("five");
    PrintStringNumber(null);
    PrintStringNumber("zero");
    PrintStringNumber("four");
  }
```

```
}
```

If we run the `PrintIntContainingNull()` function, we will get the following output on the console:

```
C:\WINDOWS\system32\cmd.exe                              —    □    ✕
Word: three is Int: 3
Word: five is Int: 5
Word: null is Int: null
Word: zero is Int: 0
Word: four is Int: 4
Press any key to continue . . .
```

From the preceding screenshot, you can see that we now can give the int data types' null value since it has implemented monad naturally and has been amplified using the amplifier of types.

IEnumerable<T> also implements monad because it can amplify the type of T we pass to IEnumerable<T>. Suppose we want to amplify the string type using IEnumerable<T> in order for it to be enumerated and sorted; we can use the following code:

```
public partial class Program
{
  private static void AmplifyString()
  {
    IEnumerable<string> stringEnumerable
      = YieldNames();
    Console.WriteLine(
      "Enumerate the stringEnumerable");

    foreach (string s -> in stringEnumerable)
    {
      Console.WriteLine(
        "- {0}", s);
    }

    IEnumerable<string>stringSorted =
      SortAscending(stringEnumerable);

    Console.WriteLine();
    Console.WriteLine(
      "Sort the stringEnumerable");

    foreach (string s -> in stringSorted)
    {
      Console.WriteLine(
```

```
        "- {0}", s);
    }
  }
}
```

In the `AmplifyString()` function, we are going to show that we can leverage the `string` type to store multiple values and represent the enumeration and sorting, as shown in the following code snippet, to initialize the enumerable string:

```
IEnumerable<string> stringEnumerable
  = YieldNames();
```

We can use the following code snippet to sort the enumerable string:

```
IEnumerable<string> stringSorted =
  SortAscending(stringEnumerable);
```

The implementation of the `YieldNames()` function we use to initialize the enumerable string is as follows:

```
public partial class Program
{
  private static IEnumerable<string> YieldNames()
  {
    yield return "Nicholas Shaw";
    yield return "Anthony Hammond";
    yield return "Desiree Waller";
    yield return "Gloria Allen";
    yield return "Daniel McPherson";
  }
}
```

And the implementation of the `SortAscending()` function that we use to sort the enumerable string will be as follows:

```
public partial class Program
{
  private static IEnumerable<string> SortAscending(
    IEnumerable<string> enumString)
  {
    returnenumString.OrderBy(s => s);
  }
}
```

As you can see, in the `YieldNames()` function implementation, the function will yield five people-name-typed strings. These people names will be kept in the `stringEnumerable` variable typed `IEnumerable<string>`. It becomes obvious that `stringEnumerable` has now been leveraged so that it can handle multiple values. And in the `SortAscending()` function, we can see that `stringEnumerable` has been leveraged so that it can be sorted and ordered. If we run the preceding `AmplifyString()` function, we will get the following output on the console:

From the preceding screenshot, we can see that we have successfully amplified the `string` type so it can now enumerate multiple `string` values and can sort their values.

As we have discussed in many ways in the previous chapter, `Func<T>` is an encapsulate method that returns a value of the type specified by the `T` parameter with no need to pass any parameter. For this purpose, we will create the following `Func<T>` method in our `AmplifiedFuncType.csproj` project:

```
public partial class Program
{
    Func<int> MultipliedFunc;
}
```

`MultipliedFunc` is a delegate that will take care of a function that returns the `int` value with no passing argument. Now, the following code will explain that `Func<T>` also implements monad naturally. However, before we go through with the `Func<T>` explanation, we are going to create a wrapper using the `Nullable` type we discussed earlier. Let's take a look at the following `MultipliedByTwo()` function:

```
public partial class Program
{
    private static Nullable<int>MultipliedByTwo(
        Nullable<int>nullableInt)
    {
```

```
      if (nullableInt.HasValue)
      {
        int unWrappedInt =
          nullableInt.Value;
        int multipliedByTwo =
          unWrappedInt * 2;
        return GetNullableFromInt(
          multipliedByTwo);
      }
      else
      {
        return new Nullable<int>();
      }
    }
  }
```

The GetNullableFromInt() function in the MultipliedByTwo() function has the following implementation:

```
public partial class Program
{
  private static Nullable<int> GetNullableFromInt(
    int iNumber)
  {
    return new Nullable<int>(
      iNumber);
  }
}
```

The MultipliedByTwo() function is simple. Obviously, it will wrap the unwrapped value after we perform the multiplication operator on that unwrapped value. Suppose we have the following RunMultipliedByTwo() function:

```
public partial class Program
{
  private static void RunMultipliedByTwo()
  {
    for (int i = 1; i <= 5; i++)
    {
      Console.WriteLine(
        "{0} multiplied by to is equal to {1}",
        i, MultipliedByTwo(i));
    }
  }
}
```

If we run the preceding `RunMultipliedByTwo()` function, we will have the following output on the console:

From the preceding screenshot, you can see that there's a general pattern provided by the function. The unwrapped 1, 2, 3, 4, 5 will be multiplied by two and will be wrapped into 2, 4, 6, 8, 10.

Now, we are going to explain `Func<T>`. Let's create the following `GetFuncFromInt()` function, which will return the value typed `Func<int>`:

```
public partial class Program
{
  private static Func<int> GetFuncFromInt(
    int iItem)
  {
    return () => iItem;
  }
}
```

The preceding `GetFuncFromInt()` function will generate a brand new `Func<T>` method from the `int` value. Again, we will create the `MultipliedByTwo()` function but with a different signature, as follows:

```
public partial class Program
{
  private static Func<int> MultipliedByTwo(
   Func<int> funcDelegate)
  {
    int unWrappedFunc =
      funcDelegate();
    int multipliedByTwo =
      unWrappedFunc* 2;
    return GetFuncFromInt(
      multipliedByTwo);
  }
}
```

The preceding will successfully compile. However, suppose we have the following code:

```
public partial class Program
{
  private static void RunMultipliedByTwoFunc()
  {
    Func<int> intFunc = MultipliedByTwo(
    () => 1 + 1);
  }
}
```

If we run the preceding `RunMultipliedByTwoFunc()` function, we will get the fixed result 4 rather that the formula `(1 + 1) * 4`. To solve this problem, we can create new code as follows:

```
public partial class Program
{
  private static Func<int> MultipliedByTwoFunction(
    Func<int> funcDelegate)
  {
    return () =>
    {
      int unWrappedFunc =
        funcDelegate();
      int multipliedByTwo =
        unWrappedFunc * 2;
      return multipliedByTwo;
    };
  }
}
```

Using the preceding `MultipliedByTwoFunction()` function, the original function delegate value is kept every time the new value is requested. And now we can conclude that our previous code will use the unwrapped value and then perform some operation on it. There are differences between using the `Nullable<int>` operation and the `Func<int>`operation, such as how the wrapped type result is created. Using the `Nullable` monad, we can directly use the unwrapped value , perform a computation, and then produce the wrapped value. Using `Func` Monad, however, we have to be smarter since, as we discussed earlier, we have to produce a delegate in order to keep the previous `Func` Monad.

And in Monad, we can see that by multiplying two into the wrapped `int`, the function can produce another wrapped `int` so that we can call it *amplification*.

Creating the Monadic M<T> type

Now, we are going to implement higher-order programming in monad by refactoring our previous code. Let's take a look at the following `MultipliedByTwoFunction()` function, which we can find in the `GeneratingMonadInCSharp.csproj` project:

```
public partial class Program
{
  private static Nullable<int> MultipliedByTwoFunction(
    Nullable<int> iNullable,
    Func<int,int> funcDelegate)
  {
    if (iNullable.HasValue)
    {
      int unWrappedInt =
        iNullable.Value;
      int multipliedByTwo =
        funcDelegate(unWrappedInt);
      return new Nullable<int>(
        multipliedByTwo);
    }
    else
    {
      return new Nullable<int>();
    }
  }
}
```

From the preceding `MultipliedByTwoFunction()` function, you can see that we now use `Func<int, int>`, which passes an integer argument to produce an integer result. We also get the `Nullable<int>` parameter directly from the argument now. And we can have the following `MultipliedByTwo()` function get the value of multiplying by two:

```
public partial class Program
{
  private static Nullable<int> MultipliedByTwo(
    Nullable<int> iNullable)
  {
    return MultipliedByTwoFunction(
      iNullable,
      (int x) => x * 2);
  }
}
```

In the preceding `MultipliedByTwo()` function, we see that we define the `iNullable` value and the anonymous method, as shown in the following code snippet:

```
return MultipliedByTwoFunction(
    iNullable,
    (int x) => x * 2);
```

And suppose we have the following `RunMultipliedByTwo()` function to call the `MultipliedByTwo()` function:

```
public partial class Program
{
    private static void RunMultipliedByTwo()
    {
        Console.WriteLine(
            "RunMultipliedByTwo() implementing " +
            "higher-order programming");

        for (int i = 1; i <= 5; i++)
        {
            Console.WriteLine(
                "{0} multiplied by to is equal to {1}",
                i, MultipliedByTwo(i));
        }
    }
}
```

If we run the preceding `RunMultipliedByTwo()` function, we will get the following output on the console screen:

As you can see from the preceding screen shot, we have successfully refactored our `MultipliedByTwo()` function in the `AmplifiedFuncType.csproj` project.

Implementing the generic data type to Monad

We can also make our previous `MultipliedByTwo()` function more general by implementing generics, as shown in the following code:

```
public partial class Program
{
  private static Nullable<T> MultipliedByTwoFunction<T>(
    Nullable<T> iNullable,
    Func<T,T> funcDelegate)
    where T : struct
  {
    if (iNullable.HasValue)
    {
      T unWrappedInt = iNullable.Value;
      T multipliedByTwo = funcDelegate(unWrappedInt);
      return new Nullable<T>(
        multipliedByTwo);
    }
    else
    {
      return new Nullable<T>();
    }
  }
}
```

And if for some reason we need to have a function that passes an integer value but results in a double-for instance, and we want to divide an integer number, we can amplify that function so that it can modify the value from `int` to `double`, as shown in the following code:

```
public partial class Program
{
  private static Nullable<R> MultipliedByTwoFunction<V, R>(
    Nullable<V> iNullable,
    Func<V,R> funcDelegate)
  where V : struct
  where R : struct
  {
    if (iNullable.HasValue)
    {
      V unWrappedInt = iNullable.Value;
      R multipliedByTwo = funcDelegate(unWrappedInt);
      return new Nullable<R>(multipliedByTwo);
    }
    else
    {
```

```
        return new Nullable<R>();
    }
  }
}
```

And since `Nullable` is a amplification of type in the preceding
`MultipliedByTwoFunction()` method, we can modify it to any other types, as follows:

```
public partial class Program
{
  static Lazy<R> MultipliedByTwoFunction<V,R>(
    Lazy<V> lazy,
  Func<V, R> function)
  where V : struct
  where R : struct
  {
    return new Lazy<R>(() =>
    {
      V unWrappedInt = lazy.Value;
      R multipliedByTwo = function(unWrappedInt);
      return multipliedByTwo;
    });
  }
}
```

As we discussed earlier, `MultipliedByTwoFunction()` has a monad pattern since it
passes a value of a particular type and turns it into a value of the amplified type. In other
words, we have a function that has a pattern to turn a function from V to R into a function
from M<V> to M<R>, where M<R> is an amplified type. This is so that we can write a method
that has a Monad pattern like this:

```
public partial class Program
{
  private static M<R> MonadFunction<V, R>(
    M<V> amplified,
    Func<V, R> function)
  {
    // Implementation
  }
}
```

Now, we have a monadic M<T> type, which is to be used if we need to implement a Monad
pattern in our function. However, if we take a look at our previous
`MultipliedByTwoFunction<V, R>()` method, we can see that there is something we can
improve in it, as shown in the following code:

```
public partial class Program
```

```
{
  private static Nullable<R>
  MultipliedByTwoFunctionSpecial<V, R>(
    Nullable<V> nullable,
    Func<V, Nullable<R>> function)
  where V : struct
  where R : struct
  {
    if (nullable.HasValue)
    {
      V unWrappedInt = nullable.Value;
      Nullable<R >multipliedByTwo = function(unWrappedInt);
      return multipliedByTwo;
    }
    else
    {
      return new Nullable<R>();
    }
  }
}
```

We have modified the second parameter from `Func<V, R>` to `Func<V, Nullable<R>>`. This is done to prevent an inappropriate result, such as `Nullable<Nullable<double>>`, if we expect the return type `Nullable<double>`. We can also implement it to another type, such as `Func<T>`, as shown in the following code:

```
public partial class Program
{
  private static Func<R>
  MultipliedByTwoFunctionSpecial<V, R>(
    Func<V> funcDelegate,
    Func<V, Func<R>> function)
  {
    return () =>
    {
      V unwrappedValue = funcDelegate();
      Func<R> resultValue = function(unwrappedValue);
      return resultValue();
    };
  }
}
```

Implementing Monad to Lazy<T> and Task<T>

Besides type `Func<T>`, we can also implement Monad to `Lazy<T>` and `Task<T>`, as shown in the following code:

```
public partial class Program
{
  private static Lazy<R>
  MultipliedByTwoFunctionSpecial<V, R>(
    Lazy<V> lazy,
    Func<V, Lazy<R>> function)
  {
    return new Lazy<R>(() =>
    {
      V unwrappedValue = lazy.Value;
      Lazy<R>resultValue = function(unwrappedValue);
      return resultValue.Value;
    });
  }

  Private static async Task<R>
  MultipliedByTwoFunctionSpecial<V, R>(
    Task<V> task,
    Func<V, Task<R>> function)
  {
    V unwrappedValue = await task;
    Task<R>resultValue = function(unwrappedValue);
    return await resultValue;
  }
}
```

Also, we can implement it for `IEnumerable<T>`. The code will be as follows:

```
public partial class Program
{
  staticIEnumerable<R>
  MultipliedByTwoFunctionSpecial<V, R>(
    IEnumerable<V> sequence,
    Func<V, IEnumerable<R>> function)
  {
    foreach (V unwrappedValue in sequence)
    {
      IEnumerable<R> resultValue = function(unwrappedValue);
      foreach (R r in resultValue)
      yield return r;
    }
  }
}
```

After we dissect the `MultipliedByTwoFunctionSpecial()` function for various data types, such as `Nullable`, `Func`, `Lazy`, `Task`, and `IEnumerable`, we can see that a monadic type has flattened `M<M<R>>` into `M<R>`. We can see that, when using the `Nullable` type, we have to avoid making `Nullable<Nullable<R>>` by checking whether the passing `Nullable` type's argument has a value. If not, just return a null `Nullable<R>` type, as shown in the following code snippet:

```
if (nullable.HasValue)
{
  V unWrappedInt = nullable.Value;
  Nullable<R> multipliedByTwo = function(unWrappedInt);
  return multipliedByTwo;
}
else
{
  return new Nullable<R>();
}
```

When we use task, we also have to await the outer task and then await the inner task to avoid creating a `<Task<R>>` task, as shown in the following code snippet:

```
private static async Task<R>
MultipliedByTwoFunctionSpecial<V, R>(
  Task<V> task,
  Func<V, Task<R>> function)
{
  V unwrappedValue = await task;
  Task<R> resultValue = function(unwrappedValue);
  return await resultValue;
}
```

The other monadic types have the same pattern.

Rules of the Monad pattern

We have discussed that the Monad pattern will always wrap up a value typed `T` into an instance of `M<T>`, as shown in the following code snippet:

```
public partial class Program
{
  private static M<T> MonadFunction <T>(Titem)
  {
    // Implementation
  }
}
```

Also, in the monad pattern, we can transform the instance of M<V> to an instance of M<R> if we have a function from V to R, as shown in the following code snippet:

```
public partial class Program
{
  private static M<R> MultipliedByTwoFunction <V, R>(
    M<V> wrapped, Func<V, R> function)
  {
    // Implementation
  }
}
```

Another rule the Monad pattern has is that we can transform the type of V to an instance of M<R> and then apply it to an instance of M<V> if we have a function from V to M<R>, as shown in the following code snippet:

```
public partial class Program
{
  private static Func<R>
  MultipliedByTwoFunctionSpecial<V, R>(
    Func<V> funcDelegate,
    Func<V, Func<R>> function)
  {
    // Implementation
  }
}
```

Summary

Pattern matching is a form of dispatch to choose the correct variant of functions to be called. In other words, its concept is close to the `if` conditional expression because we have to decide the correct selection by providing specific input. The matching process can be simplified to make it implement a functional approach. We discussed the `switch` case and then refactored it using LINQ so it became functional.

We learned the definition of monad itself: a type that uses the Monad pattern, which is a design pattern for types. In C#, there are some types that have implemented Monad naturally; they are `Nullable<T>`, `IEnumerable<T>`, `Func<T>`, `Lazy<T>`, and `Task<T>`.

For now, we have enough knowledge about functional programming in C#. In the next chapter, we will use everything you learned in this and previous chapters to develop an application that implements a functional approach. In the upcoming chapter, we will transform imperative code into functional code.

10
Taking an Action in C# Functional Programming

This is the most important chapter of this book since we will create a new application using a functional approach. We have already discussed functional programming in depth in the previous chapters, including functional programming concepts, **Language Integrated Query** (**LINQ**), recursion, optimizing, and patterns. What we are going to do now is develop an application with an imperative approach and then refactor it into a functional approach.

In this chapter, we will create a Windows forms application and explore how to create a form and then add the code to it. After finishing this chapter, we will be able to refactor the Windows form application from an imperative approach into a functional approach.

In this chapter, we will cover the following topics:

- Creating a Windows forms application
- Exploring how to create a form and then add the code to it
- Creating engine code in an imperative approach
- Transform the engine code from an imperative to a functional approach

Developing functional programming in Windows forms

Now, we are going to develop a calculator application in a Windows forms application. For this purpose, we have to create a new Windows forms project and a new form with several buttons to contain the numbers 0 to 9 and additional functionality, such as the following screenshot:

As you can see, we have 10 buttons that represent the numbers 0 to 9 and standard mathematical operators such as add (**+**), subtract (**–**), multiply (*****), and divide (**/**). We also have some additional function buttons; they are square root (**sqrt**), percent (**%**) and inverse (**1/x**). The rest includes these buttons: switch sign (**+/-**), decimal (**.**), Clear Entry (**CE**), Clear All (**C**), and Backspace (**del**). We also have a textbox to display the number we entered and set at the top of the form. Last but not least, there is always an equal button in all calculator applications. We give names to all these controls, as shown in the following code snippet:

```
namespace CalculatorImperative
{
  partial class Form1
  {
    private System.Windows.Forms.Button btn0;
    private System.Windows.Forms.Button btn1;
    private System.Windows.Forms.Button btn2;
    private System.Windows.Forms.Button btn3;
    private System.Windows.Forms.Button btn4;
    private System.Windows.Forms.Button btn5;
    private System.Windows.Forms.Button btn6;
    private System.Windows.Forms.Button btn7;
```

```
      private System.Windows.Forms.Button btn8;
      private System.Windows.Forms.Button btn9;
      private System.Windows.Forms.Button btnSwitchSign;
      private System.Windows.Forms.Button btnDecimal;
      private System.Windows.Forms.Button btnAdd;
      private System.Windows.Forms.Button btnDivide;
      private System.Windows.Forms.Button btnMultiply;
      private System.Windows.Forms.Button btnSubstract;
      private System.Windows.Forms.Button btnEquals;
      private System.Windows.Forms.Button btnSqrt;
      private System.Windows.Forms.Button btnPercent;
      private System.Windows.Forms.Button btnInverse;
      private System.Windows.Forms.Button btnDelete;
      private System.Windows.Forms.Button btnClearAll;
      private System.Windows.Forms.Button btnClearEntry;
      private System.Windows.Forms.TextBox txtScreen;
    }
  }
```

After we have all these controls, the following code snippet contains only the control's name and click events, if any, that we have to set in order to ease the creation of this app since the control's name is unchanged:

```
namespace CalculatorImperative
{
  partial class Form1
  {
    private void InitializeComponent()
    {
      this.btn0.Name = "btn0";
      this.btn0.Click +=
        new System.EventHandler(this.btnNumber_Click);
      this.btn1.Name = "btn1";

      // The rest of code can be found
      // in the downloaded source code
    }
  }
}
```

Additional settings, such as the control's axis location, font, or alignment, don't matter since the settings won't affect the entire code.

Creating the code behind a form

All controls in the form are set and we are now ready to add some code to it. As you can see in all the event clicks in the previous code snippet, there are five functions that will be called for a specific button when pressed: `btnNumber_Click()`, `btnFunction_Click()`, `btnEquals_Click()`, `btnClear_Click()`, and `btnOperator_Click()`.

The `btnNumber_Click()` function is for the 0 to 9 button. The `btnFunction_Click()` function is for the `btnSwitchSign`, `btnDecimal`, `btnSqrt`, `btnPercent`, `btnInverse`, and `btnDelete` button. The `btnEquals_Click()` function is for the `btnEquals` buttons. The `btnClear_Click()` function is for the `btnClearAll` and `btnClearEntry` buttons. And `btnOperator_Click()` is for the `btnAdd`, `btnSubstract`, `btnDivide`, and `btnMultiply` buttons. Also, there will be some helper functions that we will discuss.

Now let's look at the following code snippet, which contains the implementation of the `btnNumber_Click()` function:

```
namespace CalculatorImperative
{
  public partial class Form1 : Form
  {
    private void btnNumber_Click(object sender, EventArgs e)
    {
      Button btnNum = sender as Button;
      int numValue;
      switch (btnNum.Name)
      {
        case "btn1":
          numValue = 1;
          break;
        case "btn2":
          numValue = 2;
          break;
        case "btn3":
          numValue = 3;
          break;
        case "btn4":
          numValue = 4;
          break;
        case "btn5":
          numValue = 5;
          break;
        case "btn6":
          numValue = 6;
          break;
        case "btn7":
```

```
      numValue = 7;
      break;
    case "btn8":
      numValue = 8;
      break;
    case "btn9":
      numValue = 9;
      break;
    default:
      numValue = 0;
      break;
  }
  CalcEngine.AppendNum(numValue);
  UpdateScreen();
    }
  }
}
```

As you can see from the preceding code snippet, the btnNumber_Click() function will detect the pressed number button and then display it in the textbox. For now, let's skip the CalcEngine.AppendNum() and UpdateScreen() functions since we are going to discuss them later.

Let's move on to the btnFunction_Click() function, which will take an action if one of the functional buttons is pressed. The implementation of the function is as follows:

```
namespace CalculatorImperative
{
  public partial class Form1 : Form
  {
    private void btnFunction_Click(object sender, EventArgs e)
    {
      Button btnFunction = sender as Button;
      string strValue;
      switch (btnFunction.Name)
      {
        case "btnSqrt":
          strValue = "sqrt";
          break;
        case "btnPercent":
          strValue = "percent";
          break;
        case "btnInverse":
          strValue = "inverse";
          break;
        case "btnDelete":
          strValue = "delete";
```

```
              break;
           case "btnSwitchSign":
             strValue = "switchSign";
             break;
           case "btnDecimal":
             strValue = "decimal";
             break;
           default:
             strValue = "";
             break;
         }
         CalcEngine.FunctionButton(strValue);
         UpdateScreen();
       }
     }
   }
```

As you can see from the preceding code snippet, btnFunction_Click() will take action when the btnSqrt, btnPercent, btnInverse, btnDelete, btnSwitchSign, or btnDecimal buttons are pressed.

For the function that is responsible when one of the operator buttons is pressed, here is the code snippet of the btnOperator_Click() function implementation:

```
namespace CalculatorImperative
{
  public partial class Form1 : Form
  {
    private void btnOperator_Click(object sender, EventArgs e)
    {
      Button btnOperator = sender as Button;
      string strOperator = "";
      switch (btnOperator.Name)
      {
        case "btnAdd":
          strOperator = "add";
          break;
        case "btnSubtract":
          strOperator = "subtract";
          break;
        case "btnMultiply":
          strOperator = "multiply";
          break;
        case "btnDivide":
          strOperator = "divide";
          break;
      }
```

```
    CalcEngine.PrepareOperation(
      strOperator);
    UpdateScreen();
  }
 }
}
```

The preceding `btnOperator()` function will be used to run the operation of each operator: add, subtract, multiply, and divide. It then calls the `PrepareOperation()` method in the `CalcEngine` class, which we will discuss later.

To clear an entry or all entries, we have two buttons: `btnClearEntry` and `btnClearAll`. These two buttons will call the `btnClear_Click()` method every time the press event is generated. The implementation of this function is as follows:

```
namespace CalculatorImperative
{
  public partial class Form1 : Form
  {
    private void btnClear_Click(object sender, EventArgs e)
    {
      if (sender is System.Windows.Forms.Button)
      {
        Button btnClear = sender as Button;
        switch (btnClear.Name)
        {
          case "btnClearAll":
            CalcEngine.ClearAll();
            UpdateScreen();
            break;
          case "btnClearEntry":
            CalcEngine.Clear();
            UpdateScreen();
            break;
        }
      }
    }
  }
}
```

There are two methods in the `CalcEngine` class, as well, which are called when these two clearing buttons are pressed: `CalcEngine.Clear()` for the `btnClearEntry` button and `CalcEngine.ClearAll()` for the `btnClearAll` button.

The last button we have is the `btnEquals` button, which will call the `btnClear_Click()` method every time it is pressed; the implementation as follows:

```
namespace CalculatorImperative
{
  public partial class Form1 : Form
  {
    private void btnEquals_Click(object sender, EventArgs e)
    {
      //Attempt to solve the math
      if (!CalcEngine.Solve())
      {
        btnClearAll.PerformClick();
      }
      UpdateScreen();
    }
  }
}
```

From the preceding code snippet, when the `btnEquals` button is pressed, it tries to calculate the operation the user has given before calling the `CalcEngine.Solve()` method and then updating the textbox. If the calculation fails, it will clear the entries.

Now, let's create the `UpdateScreen()` method, which is used to display the current digit to the `txtScreen` textbox. The implementation is as follows:

```
namespace CalculatorImperative
{
  public partial class Form1 : Form
  {
    private void UpdateScreen()
    {
      txtScreen.Text = FormatDisplay(
        Convert.ToString(
        CalcEngine.GetDisplay()));
    }
  }
}
```

Inside the `UpdateScreen()` method, the `FormatDisplay()` method is called to form the display on `txtScreen`. The implementation of the `FormatDisplay()` method is as follows:

```
namespace CalculatorImperative
{
  public partial class Form1 : Form
  {
    private string FormatDisplay(
```

```
    string str)
{
  String dec = "";
  int totalCommas = 0;
  int pos = 0;
  bool addNegative = false;

  if (str.StartsWith("-"))
  {
    str = str.Remove(0, 1);
    addNegative = true;
  }

  if (str.IndexOf(".") > -1)
  {
    dec = str.Substring(
      str.IndexOf("."),
      str.Length - str.IndexOf("."));
    str = str.Remove(
      str.IndexOf("."),
      str.Length - str.IndexOf("."));
  }

  if (Convert.ToDouble(str) <
    Math.Pow(10, 19))
  {
    if (str.Length > 3)
    {
      totalCommas =
        (str.Length - (str.Length % 3)) / 3;

      if (str.Length % 3 == 0)
      {
        totalCommas--;
      }

      pos = str.Length - 3;
      while (totalCommas > 0)
      {
        str = str.Insert(pos, ",");
        pos -= 3;
        totalCommas--;
      }
    }
  }

  str += "" + dec;
  if (str.IndexOf(".") == -1)
```

```
    {
      str = str + ".";
    }

    if (str.IndexOf(".") == 0)
    {
      str.Insert(0, "0");
    }
    else if (str.IndexOf(".") ==
      str.Length - 2 &&
      str.LastIndexOf("0") ==
      str.Length - 1)
    {
      str = str.Remove(str.Length - 1);
    }

    if (addNegative)
    {
      str = str.Insert(0, "-");
    }

    return str;
  }
 }
}
```

Based on the preceding `FormatDisplay()` function implementation, the first thing that happens is that the function checks whether it is a negative number. If it does, the negative will be removed first and then the `addNegative` flag will be `true`, as shown in the following code snippet:

```
if (str.StartsWith("-"))
{
  str = str.Remove(0, 1);
  addNegative = true;
}
```

It then looks for the dot (.) character to indicate that it's a decimal number. If the dot is found, it will store the fraction in the `dec` variable and the rest in the `str` variable, as shown in the following code snippet:

```
if (str.IndexOf(".") > -1)
{
  dec = str.Substring(
    str.IndexOf("."),
    str.Length - str.IndexOf("."));
  str = str.Remove(
```

```
      str.IndexOf("."),
      str.Length - str.IndexOf("."));
}
```

Now, the function will make sure that the number is less than 10^{19}. If it is, the following code snippet will format the number:

```
if (Convert.ToDouble(str) <
  Math.Pow(10, 19))
{
  if (str.Length > 3)
  {
    totalCommas =
      (str.Length - (str.Length % 3)) / 3;

    if (str.Length % 3 == 0)
    {
      totalCommas--;
    }

    pos = str.Length - 3;
    while (totalCommas > 0)
    {
      str = str.Insert(pos, ",");
      pos -= 3;
      totalCommas--;
    }
  }
}
```

The result from the preceding format will be joined with the dec variable. If there's no fraction in the dec variable, the dot character will be added to the last position, as shown in the following code snippet:

```
str += "" + dec;
if (str.IndexOf(".") == -1)
{
  str = str + ".";
}
```

If only the fraction number is available, the 0 character will be added at the first position, as shown in the following code snippet:

```
if (str.IndexOf(".") == 0)
{
  str.Insert(0, "0");
}
else if (str.IndexOf(".") ==
```

```
    str.Length - 2 &&
    str.LastIndexOf("0") ==
    str.Length - 1)
{
    str = str.Remove(str.Length - 1);
}
```

Lastly, we check whether the `addNegative` flag is `true`. If it is, the negative mark (–) will be added at the first position, as follows:

```
if (addNegative)
{
    str = str.Insert(0, "-");
}
```

Creating the engine code in an imperative approach

We have successfully created the code behind the form. Now let's create the engine code in a wrapped class named `CalcEngine`. We will design it in a `CalcEngine.cs` file in the `CalculatorImperative.csproj` project.

Preparing class properties

In this calculator engine class, we need some properties to hold a particular value to be involved in the calculation process. The following code snippet is the class properties' declaration we are going to use in the calculation process:

```
namespace CalculatorImperative
{
    internal class CalcEngine
    {
        // This is the behind the scenes number
        // that represents what will be on the display
        // and what number to store as last input
        private static string m_input;

        // Sign of the number (positive or negative)
        private static string m_sign;

        // Current operator selected (+, -, * or /)
        public static String m_operator;
```

```
    // Last result displayed
    private static String m_lastNum;

    // Last input made
    private static String m_lastInput;

    // If the calculator should start a new input
    // after a number is hit
    public static bool m_wait;

    // If the user is entering in decimal values
    public static bool m_decimal;

    // If the last key that was hit was the equals button
    private static bool m_lastHitEquals;
  }
}
```

As you can see, we have eight properties that will be involved in the calculation process. The m_input property will hold all the values we have inputted and the formatting number m_sign will store whether the number is + or –. The m_operator property will store the operator, which is + for addition, – for subtraction, * for multiplication, and / for division. The m_lastNum property will hold the result of the calculation. The m_lastInput property will save the last number the user has inputted. The m_wait property is a flag that indicates that the number has been inputted and it's time to wait for the operator and the next number. The m_decimal property flag indicates whether or not it's a decimal number. And the m_lastHitEquals property flag indicates whether btnEquals has been pressed.

Constructing the constructor

In every class, it's best to have a constructor to prepare the properties of the class. It's the same with this class as well. The following is the code snippet of the class constructor implementation:

```
namespace CalculatorImperative
{
  internal class CalcEngine
  {
    static CalcEngine()
    {
      // "." is used to represent no input
      // which registers as 0
      m_input = ".";

      m_sign = "+";
```

```
        m_operator = null;
        m_lastNum = null;
        m_lastInput = null;
        m_wait = false;
        m_decimal = false;
        m_lastHitEquals = false;
      }
    }
  }
```

As you can see from the preceding code snippet, if we want to reset all the class properties we have to call the constructor, which is `CalcEngine()`. For `m_input`, we use the dot (.) character to indicate that there is no user inputted. We also use the `static` modifier since the class will be called directly by stating the class name instead of the instance of the class.

Clearing the properties

Earlier, we discussed that we have two clearing methods: `ClearAll()` and `Clear()`, as shown in the following code snippet:

```
switch (btnClear.Name)
{
  case "btnClearAll":
    CalcEngine.ClearAll();
    UpdateScreen();
    break;
  case "btnClearEntry":
    CalcEngine.Clear();
    UpdateScreen();
    break;
}
```

The preceding code snippet is extracted from the `btnClear_Click()` method. Here is the implementation of the `ClearAll()` method:

```
namespace CalculatorImperative
{
  internal class CalcEngine
  {
    // Resets all variables
    public static void ClearAll()
    {
      //Reset the calculator
      m_input = ".";
      m_lastNum = null;
      m_lastInput = null;
```

```
            m_operator = null;
            m_sign = "+";
            m_wait = false;
            m_decimal = false;
            m_lastHitEquals = false;
        }
    }
}
```

The `ClearAll()` method will reset all properties the `CalcEngine` class has. This is similar to the class constructor implementation. So, we can modify the class constructor implementation as follows:

```
namespace CalculatorImperative
{
    internal class CalcEngine
    {
        static CalcEngine()
        {
            ClearAll();
        }
    }
}
```

We also have the `Clear()` method to clear the last entry only. For this purpose, we just need to reset `m_sign`, `m_input`, and `m_decimal`. The implementation of the `Clear()` method is as follows:

```
namespace CalculatorImperative
{
    internal class CalcEngine
    {
        // For Clear Entry,
        // just reset appropriate variable
        public static void Clear()
        {
            //Just clear the current input
            m_sign = "+";
            m_input = ".";
            m_decimal = false;
        }
    }
}
```

Appending the number to the display box

As we know, we have a textbox to display the number we have inputted or to display the result of calculation. In the `btnNumber_Click()` method implementation, we call the `CalcEngine.AppendNum()` method, and here is its implementation:

```
namespace CalculatorImperative
{
  internal class CalcEngine
  {
    // Appends number to the input
    public static void AppendNum(
      double numValue)
    {
      if (numValue == Math.Round(numValue) &&
        numValue >= 0)
      {
        // The rest of code can be found
        // in the downloaded source code
      }
      // If they're trying to append a decimal or negative,
      // that's impossible so just replace the entire input
      // with that value
      else
      {
        // The rest of code can be found
        // in the downloaded source code
      }
    }
  }
}
```

From the preceding code, we can see that we have to distinguish the number with a negative sign or a decimal number with a dot mark. For this purpose, we use the following code snippet:

```
if (numValue == Math.Round(numValue) &&
    numValue >= 0)
```

If it's a pure number without a negative number or decimal mark, we check whether `m_input` is empty or whether the `m_wait` flag is `true`. If it is, we can continue the process. If the decimal flag is on, we don't need to insert the dot mark anymore; otherwise, we have to add the dot mark. The following code snippet will explain more about our explanation:

```
if (!IsEmpty())
{
  // if decimal is turned on
```

```
    if (m_decimal)
    {
      m_input += "" + numValue;
    }
    else
    {
      m_input = m_input.Insert(
        m_input.IndexOf("."), "" + numValue);
    }
  }
```

As you can see, we call the `IsEmpty()` function to check whether `m_input` is empty or the `m_wait` flag is true. The implementation of the function is as follows:

```
namespace CalculatorImperative
{
  internal class CalcEngine
  {
    // Indicate that user doesn't input value yet
    private static bool IsEmpty()
    {
      if (m_input.Equals(".") || m_wait)
        return true;
      else
        return false;
    }
  }
}
```

If `IsEmpty()` returns `true`, it will continue the process, as shown in the following code snippet:

```
if (m_lastHitEquals)
{
  ClearAll();
  m_lastHitEquals = false;
}

if (m_decimal)
{
  m_input = "." + numValue;
}
else
{
  m_input = numValue + ".";
}
m_wait = false;
```

From the preceding code, first, we check whether the `m_lastHitEquals` flag is on. If it is, we reset all class properties and then set `m_lastHitEquals` to off. Then, we check whether the `m_decimal` flag is on. If it is, insert the dot mark in front of the number. If not, insert the dot mark behind the number. After that, turn off the `m_wait` flag.

We also have to make sure there are no unnecessary zeroes that have been inserted using the following code snippet:

```
if (m_input.IndexOf("0", 0, 1) == 0 &&
  m_input.IndexOf(".") > 1)
{
  //Get rid of any extra zeroes
  //that may have been prepended
  m_input = m_input.Remove(0, 1);
}
```

The preceding code will handle the user input if it doesn't contain a negative mark (–) or dot mark. If it does, we have to check whether it has these marks or not using the following code snippet:

```
if (m_input.Contains(".") &&
  !(m_input.EndsWith("0") &&
  m_input.IndexOf(".") ==
  m_input.Length - 2))
{
  m_decimal = true;
}

if (m_input.Contains("-"))
{
  m_sign = "-";
}
else
{
  m_sign = "+";
}
```

However, before we perform the preceding process, we have to reset all the class properties and reformat the number as follows:

```
// Start over if the last key hit
// was the equals button
// and no operators were chosen
if (m_lastHitEquals)
{
  ClearAll();
  m_lastHitEquals = false;
```

```
    }
    m_input = "" + numValue;

    // Reformat
    m_input = FormatInput(m_input);
    if (!m_input.Contains("."))
    {
      m_input += ".";
    }
```

Again, we remove unnecessary zeroes and turn off the `m_wait` flag as follows:

```
    // Get rid of any extra zeroes
    // that may have been prepended or appended
    if (m_input.IndexOf("0", 0, 1) == 0 &&
      m_input.IndexOf(".") > 1)
    {
      m_input = m_input.Remove(0, 1);
    }

    if (m_input.EndsWith("0") &&
      m_input.IndexOf(".") == m_input.Length - 2)
    {
      m_input.Remove(m_input.Length - 1);
    }

    m_wait = false;
```

Preparing the mathematical operation

When we press one of the operator buttons, the `btnOperator_Click()` function will be fired; inside the function, there is a `CalcEngine.PrepareOperation()` function to prepare the calculation. The implementation of the `CalcEngine.PrepareOperation()` function is as follows:

```
    namespace CalculatorImperative
    {
      internal class CalcEngine
      {
        // Handles operation functions
        public static void PrepareOperation(
          string strOperator)
        {
          switch (strOperator)
          {
              // The rest of code can be found
```

```
        // in the downloaded source code
      }
    }
  }
}
```

The explanation of the preceding code is straightforward. We just need to know which button is pressed, +, -, *, or /. Then, we check whether it is the first number that the user inputs by checking whether m_lastNum is null or not or whether m_wait is on. If it is, we solve the calculation after we make sure that m_lastNum is not null, m_lastHitEquals is off, m_wait is off, and the current m_operator is different from the operator, which was just pressed by a user. After this, we replace m_operator with the current operator that the user inputs and fill m_lastNum with m_input that has been formatted. Also, other settings will have to be applied. The following code snippet will explain this better:

```
// If this is the first number
// that user inputs
if (m_lastNum == null ||
  m_wait)
{
  if (m_lastNum != null &&
    !m_operator.Equals("+") &&
    !m_lastHitEquals &&
    !m_wait)
  Solve();
  m_operator = "+";
  m_lastNum = "" + FormatInput(m_input);
  m_sign = "+";
  m_decimal = false;
  m_wait = true;
}
```

Otherwise, if it's not the first number the user inputs, we can perform the following process:

```
else
{
    if (!m_wait)
        Solve();
    m_operator = "+";
    m_sign = "+";
    m_wait = true;
}
```

Formatting the input

Before we go to the `Solve()` function implementation we discussed in the previous `PrepareOperation()` function, let's discuss the `FormatInput()` function first. The following is the implementation of the `FormatInput()` method:

```
namespace CalculatorImperative
{
    internal class CalcEngine
    {
        // Formats the input into a valid double format
        private static string FormatInput(
            string str)
        {
            // Format the input to something convertable
            // by Convert.toDouble

            // Prepend a Zero
            // if the string begins with a "."
            if (str.IndexOf(".") == 0)
            {
                str = "0" + str;
            }

            // Appened a Zero
            // if the string ends with a "."
            if (str.IndexOf(".") ==
                str.Length - 1)
            {
                str = str + "0";
            }

            // If negative is turned on
            // and there's no "-"
            // in the current string
            // then "-" is prepended
            if (m_sign.Equals("-") &&
                str != "0.0" &&
                str.IndexOf("-") == -1)
            {
                str = "-" + str;
            }

            return str;
        }
    }
}
```

The `FormatInput()` method is used to form the number that will be shown in the `txtScreen` textbox.

Solving the calculation

When we press the `btnEquals` button or the operator button that has the previous input, the `Solve()` method will be invoked to calculate the operation. The following is the implementation of the method:

```
namespace CalculatorImperative
{
    internal class CalcEngine
    {
        // Solve the currently stored expression
        public static bool Solve()
        {
            bool canSolve = true;
            // The rest of code can be found
            // in the downloaded source code

            return canSolve;
        }
    }
}
```

Calculating the additional operation

As we have discussed, we have other functional buttons: the `btnSqrt`, `btnPercent`, `btnInverse`, `btnDelete`, `btnSwitchSign`, and `btnDecimal` buttons. Here is the method that will be invoked if one of these buttons is pressed:

```
namespace CalculatorImperative
{
    internal class CalcEngine
    {
        // Handles decimal square roots,
        // decimal buttons, percents, inverse, delete,
        // and sign switching
        public static bool FunctionButton(
            string str)
        {
            bool success = false;
            switch (str)
            {
```

```
            // The rest of code can be found
            // in the downloaded source code
        }
        return success;
    }
  }
}
```

Creating the engine code in the functional approach

We have successfully created the calculator application in the imperative approach. Now, it's time to refactor all the imperative code into the functional code. We are going to refactor the engine first and then the code behind the form.

Adding several new properties

We will have exactly the same properties as with the imperative code, except that we add three new properties, as shown in the following code:

```
namespace CalculatorFunctional
{
    public class Calc
    {
        public string m_input { get; set; }
        public string m_sign { get; set; }
        public string m_operator { get; set; }
        public string m_lastNum { get; set; }
        public string m_lastInput { get; set; }
        public bool m_wait { get; set; }
        public bool m_decimal { get; set; }
        public bool m_lastHitEquals { get; set; }

        public bool m_solve { get; set; }
        public string m_answer { get; set; }
        public bool m_funcSuccess { get; set; }
    }
}
```

As you can see in the preceding code, m_solve, m_answer, and m_funcSuccess are the new properties we have just added. We will use these three additional properties in the Solve() function later.

Simplifying the pattern matching

As we discussed in Chapter 9, *Working with Pattern*, we will use the `Simplicity` class, which we can find in the `SimplicityLib.cs` file. The implementation of the class is as follows:

```
namespace CalculatorFunctional
{
    public static class CalcMethodsExtension
    {
        public static Calc AppendNum(
            this Calc calc,
            double numValue)
        {
            // The rest of code can be found
            // in the downloaded source code
        }

        public static Calc AppendNumWhenRound(
            this Calc calc,
            double numValue)
        {
            // The rest of code can be found
            // in the downloaded source code
        }
        // The rest of code can be found
        // in the downloaded source code
    }
}
```

Assigning the properties

To able to assign properties, we need to assign the properties' extension method. The following code will explain this better:

```
namespace CalculatorFunctional
{
    public static class CalcPropertiesExtension
    {
        public static Calc Input(
            this Calc calc,
            string input)
        {
            calc.m_input =
                input;
            return calc;
```

```
        }

        public static Calc LastNum(
            this Calc calc,
            string lastNum)
        {
            calc.m_lastNum =
                lastNum;
            return calc;
        }
        // The rest of code can be found
        // in the downloaded source code

        public static Calc ModifyCalcFuncSuccess(
            this Calc calc,
            bool val)
        {
            calc.m_funcSuccess = val;
            return calc;
        }

        public static Calc ModifyCalcFuncSuccessBasedOn(
            this Calc calc,
            Func<bool> predicate)
        {
            return predicate() ?
                calc.ModifyCalcFuncSuccess(true) :
                calc.ModifyCalcFuncSuccess(false);
        }
    }
}
```

Every time we invoke one of the preceding methods, the method will return the `Calc` class in which the target property has been changed.

Constructing the class by clearing the properties

We will not construct the class in this functional approach; we will clear properties to make all the properties ready to run the process. There are two clearing methods that we will use: the `Clear()` and `ClearAll()` methods. The following code snippet is the implementation of these two methods:

```
namespace CalculatorFunctional
{
    public static class CalcMethodsExtension
    {
```

```
        public static Calc Clear(
            this Calc calc)
        {
            return calc
                .ModifyCalcSign("+")
                .ModifyCalcInput(".")
                .ModifyCalcDecimal(false);
        }

        public static Calc ClearAll(
            this Calc calc)
        {
            return calc
                .Clear()
                .ModifyCalcLastNum(null)
                .ModifyCalcLastInput(null)
                .ModifyCalcOperator(null)
                .ModifyCalcWait(false)
                .ModifyCalcLastHitEquals(false);
        }
    }
}
```

As we discussed in the imperative approach, the `Clear()` method is for the `btnClearEntry` button and `ClearAll()` is for the `btnClearAll` button.

Appending the inputted number to the text box

In this functional approach, we will refactor the `AppendNum()` method in the imperative approach into the functional approach, as shown in the following code:

```
namespace CalculatorFunctional
{
    public static class CalcMethodsExtension
    {
        public static Calc AppendNum(
            this Calc calc,
            double numValue)
        {
            // The rest of code can be found
            // in the downloaded source code
        }

        public static Calc AppendNumWhenRound(
            this Calc calc,
            double numValue)
```

```
    {
        // The rest of code can be found
        // in the downloaded source code
    }
    // The rest of code can be found
    // in the downloaded source code
    }
}
```

Preparing the operation

To prepare the operation just after we press the operator button, here is the code that has been refactored from the `PreparingOperation()` method in the imperative approach:

```
namespace CalculatorFunctional
{
    public static class CalcMethodsExtension
    {
        public static Calc PrepareOperation(
            this Calc calc,
            string strOperator)
        {
            // The rest of code can be found
            // in the downloaded source code
        }

        public static Calc PrepareOperationAdd(
            this Calc calc)
        {
            // The rest of code can be found
            // in the downloaded source code
        }

        public static Calc
            PrepareOperationAddLastNumNull(
                this Calc calc)
        {
            // The rest of code can be found
            // in the downloaded source code
        }

        // The rest of code can be found
        // in the downloaded source code
    }
}
```

Formatting the input

To format the input that we use to form the input in `txtScreen`, we will use the following code:

```
namespace CalculatorFunctional
{
    public static class CalcMethodsExtension
    {
        public static String FormatInput(
            this Calc calc,
            String n)
        {
            return n
                .ModifyStringWhen(
                    () => n.IndexOf(".") == 0,
                    () => n = "0" + n)
                .ModifyStringWhen(
                    () => n.IndexOf(".") == n.Length - 1,
                    () => n = n + "0")
                .ModifyStringWhen(
                    () => calc.m_sign.Equals("-") &&
                        n != "0.0" &&
                        n.IndexOf("-") == -1,
                    () => n = "-" + n);
        }
    }
}
```

As you can see in the preceding code, we use the `ModifyStringWhen()` extension method, which has the following implementation:

```
namespace CalculatorFunctional
{
  public static class StringMethodsExtension
  {
    public static string ModifyStringWhen(
      this string @this,
      Func<bool> predicate,
      Func<string> modifier)
    {
      return predicate()
      ? modifier()
      : @this;
    }
  }
}
```

Solving the calculation

The solving calculation can be done using the `Solve()` method in the imperative approach. The following code is the refactoring `Solve()` method from the imperative approach:

```
namespace CalculatorFunctional
{
  public static class CalcMethodsExtension
  {
    public static Calc Solve(
      this Calc calc)
    {
      return calc.CleanUp()
      .Answer()
      .UpdateAnswerToCalc();
    }
  }
}
```

For the implementation of the `CleanUp()`, `Answer()`, and `UpdateAnswerToCalc()` methods, we can use the following code:

```
namespace CalculatorFunctional
{
    public static class CalcSolveMethodsExtension
    {
        public static Calc Answer(
            this Calc calc)
        {
            calc.m_answer = calc.m_operator.Match()
                .With(o => o == "+",
                    calc.m_lastNum.SolveAdd(
                        calc.m_lastInput))
                .With(o => o == "-",
                    calc.m_lastNum.SolveSubtract(
                        calc.m_lastInput))
                .With(o => o == "*",
                    calc.m_lastNum.SolveMultiply(
                        calc.m_lastInput))
                .With(o => o == "/",
                    !calc.FormatInput(
                        calc.m_lastInput).Equals(
                            "0.0") ?
                        calc.m_lastNum.SolveDivide(
                            calc.m_lastInput) :
                        "")
                .Else("")
                .Do();
```

```
                    calc.m_solve = calc.m_answer.Match()
                        .With(o => o.Equals(""), false)
                        .Else(true)
                        .Do();

                    return calc;
                }

            public static Calc CleanUp(
                this Calc calc)
            {
                return calc
                    .ModifyCalcInputWhen(
                        () => calc.m_input.Equals(""),
                        "0")
                    .ModifyCalcLastNumWhen(
                        () => calc.m_lastNum == null ||
                            calc.m_lastNum.Equals(""),
                        "0,0")
                    .ModifyCalcLastInputWhen(
                        () => !calc.m_wait,
                        "" + calc.FormatInput(
                            calc.m_input));
            }

            public static Calc UpdateAnswerToCalc(
                this Calc calc)
            {
                calc.m_lastNum = calc.m_answer;
                calc.m_input = calc.m_answer;
                calc.m_sign = "+";
                calc.m_decimal = false;
                calc.m_lastHitEquals = true;
                calc.m_wait = true;

                calc.m_solve = true;
                return calc;
            }
        }
    }
```

We also need to create the extension method for the `string` data type to accommodate the addition, subtraction, multiplication, and division operations, as follows:

```
namespace CalculatorFunctional
{
    public static class StringMethodsExtension
    {
```

```
        public static string SolveAdd(
            this string @string,
            string str)
        {
            return Convert.ToString(
                Convert.ToDouble(@string) +
                Convert.ToDouble(str));
        }

        public static string SolveSubtract(
            this string @string,
            string str)
        {
            return Convert.ToString(
                Convert.ToDouble(@string) -
                Convert.ToDouble(str));
        }

        public static string SolveMultiply(
            this string @string,
            string str)
        {
            return Convert.ToString(
                Convert.ToDouble(@string) *
                Convert.ToDouble(str));
        }

        public static string SolveDivide(
            this string @string,
            string str)
        {
            return Convert.ToString(
                Convert.ToDouble(@string) /
                Convert.ToDouble(str));
        }
    }
}
```

Calculating the additional operation

For the additional button, which will invoke the `FunctionButton()` method every time the additional button is pressed, here is the refactoring code from the imperative `FunctionButton()` method:

```
namespace CalculatorFunctional
{
```

```
public static class CalcMethodsExtension
{
    public static Calc PrepareOperation(
        this Calc calc,
        string strOperator)
    {
        // The rest of code can be found
        // in the downloaded source code
    }

    public static Calc PrepareOperationAdd(
        this Calc calc)
    {
        // The rest of code can be found
        // in the downloaded source code
    }
    // The rest of code can be found
    // in the downloaded source code
}
}
```

Summary

We successfully built a calculator application in Windows forms. We also refactored the imperative code into a functional approach. We created some extension methods to solve all refactoring processes so they can be functional.

In the next chapter, we will discuss code with best practices in the functional approach and perform a unit test for the application we built in this chapter.

11
Coding Best Practice and Testing the Functional Code

We developed a functional application in the previous chapter. To create better code in the functional approach, we have to follow the best practice rules and implement them in our code. In this chapter, we are going to discuss the concept of the functional approach, which is a pure function and makes our function similar to a mathematical function. The topics that will be covered in this chapter are as follows:

- Preventing dishonest signatures
- Creating immutable classes
- Avoiding `Temporal Coupling`
- Dealing with the side-effects
- Separating the code into a `Domain Logic` and the `Mutable Shell`
- Testing the functional code

Coding best practices in functional C#

The functional approach has the concept of a pure function. This means that the function will produce the same result as long as we pass the exact same input. Now, let's start our discussion to create the better functional code by following the coding best practices outlined here.

Preventing dishonest signatures

As we discussed in `Chapter 1`, *Tasting Functional Style in C#*, we use the mathematical approach to constructing our code in functional programming. In other words, functional programming is programming with mathematical functions. There are two requirements that mathematical functions must fit, they are:

- A mathematical function should always return the same result whenever we supply the same arguments.
- The signature of the mathematical function should deliver all the information for the possible accepted input values and the possible produced output.

Now let's take a look at the following code snippet, which we can find in the `HonestSignature.csproj` project:

```
public partial class Program
{
  public static int SumUp(
    int a, int b)
  {
    return a + b;
  }
}
```

By examining the preceding `SumUp()` function, we can say that we will retrieve the same output every time we pass the same inputs. Now let's examine the following `GenerateRandom()` function, which we can also find in the `HonestSignature.csproj` project:

```
public partial class Program
{
  public static int GenerateRandom(
    int max)
  {
    Random rnd = new Random(
      Guid.NewGuid()
      .GetHashCode());
    return rnd.Next(max);
  }
}
```

From the preceding code, we can see that we will retrieve different output although we pass the same input continually. Suppose we have the following `RunGenerateRandom()` function:

```
public partial class Program
{
  public static void RunGenerateRandom()
  {
    for (int i = 0; i < 10; i++)
    {
      Console.WriteLine(
        String.Format(
          "Number {0} = {1}",
          i,
          GenerateRandom(100)));
    }
  }
}
```

If we run the preceding `RunGenerateRandom()` function, we will get the following output on the console:

From the preceding code snippet, we invoke the `GenerateRandom()` function 10 times by passing the exact same argument, that is, 100. As you can see in the preceding figure, the function returns a different output for each of the 10 invocations. So, we have to avoid functions such as the `GenerateRandom()` function in order to create a pure function since it is not a mathematical function.

Now let's take a look at the following `Divide()` function, which will divide the first argument by the second argument:

```
public partial class Program
{
  public static int Divide(
    int a, int b)
```

```
    {
      return a / b;
    }
  }
```

The `Divide()` function looks similar to the `SumUp()` function since the signature of the `Divide()` function accepts any two integers and returns another integer. So if we pass the exact same argument, it will return the same output. However, how about if we pass 1 and 0 as input parameters? The `Divide()` function will throw a `DivideByZeroException` error instead of returning an integer value. In this case, we can conclude that the signature of the function does not deliver enough information about the result of the operation. It looks like the function can handle any two parameters of the integer type, but it actually cannot. To solve this problem, we can refactor the preceding `Divide()` function to the following one:

```
public partial class Program
{
  public static int? Divide(
    int a, int b)
  {
    if (b == 0)
    return null;
    return a / b;
  }
}
```

As you can see in the preceding `Divide()` function, we add the `nullable` type by adding a question mark after `int` so that the return of the function can be null. We also add an `if` statement to make sure that `DivideByZeroException` error will never be thrown.

Refactoring a mutable class into an immutable one

Immutability is very important in functional programming, since a mutable operation will make our code dishonest. As we discussed previously, we need to prevent dishonest operations in order to create our pure function approach. Immutability is applied to a data structure – for instance, a class means that the objects of this class cannot be changed during their lifetime. In other words, we can say that a class is mutable if the instances of the class can be changed in some way, while it is immutable if we cannot modify the instance of that class once we create it.

Now, let's take a look at the following code, which can be found in the
`Immutability.csproj` project to continue our discussion:

```
namespace Immutability
{
  public class UserMembership
  {
    private User _user;
    private DateTime _memberSince;
    public void UpdateUser(
      int userId, string name)
    {
      _user = new User(
        userId,
        name);
    }
  }
  public class User
  {
    public int Id { get; }
    public string Name { get; }
    public User(
      int id,
      string name)
    {
      Id = id;
      Name = name;
    }
  }
}
```

As you can see in the preceding code, we have a simple composition. The `UserMembership`
class consists of the `_user` and `_memberSince` properties. We can also see that the `User`
class is immutable since all the properties are defined as read-only. Because of
immutability, the only way for the `UserMembership` method to update the `_user` field is to
create a new `User` instance and replace the old one with it. Note that the `User` class itself
doesn't contain the state here, whereas the `UserMembership` class does. We can say that the
`UpdateUser` method leaves a side-effect by changing the object's state.

Now let's refactor the `UpdateUser` method and make it immutable. The following code is
the result of refactoring the `UpdateUser` method:

```
namespace Immutability
{
  public class UserMembership
  {
```

```
    private readonly User _user;
    private readonly DateTime _memberSince;

    public UserMembership(
       User user,
       DateTime memberSince)
    {
        _user = user;
        _memberSince = memberSince;
    }
    public UserMembership UpdateUser(int userId, string name) {
       var newUser = new User(userId, name);
       return new UserMembership(newUser, _memberSince);
    }
  }

  public class User
  {
    public int Id { get; }
    public string Name { get; }
    public User(
       int id,
       string name)
    {
       Id = id;
       Name = name;
    }
  }
}
```

As you can see, the `UpdateUser()` method no longer updates the structure of the `UserMembership` class. Instead, it creates a new `UserMembership` instance and returns it as a result of the operation. By refactoring the `UpdateUser` method, we have eliminated the side-effect from the method. Now it's clear what the actual output of the operation is. The usage of immutable data makes the code more readable and also helps to provide a good understanding of what is going on right away without too much effort.

Avoiding mutability and temporal coupling

Sometimes, the use of the methods with side-effects will damage readability. The invocation of one method is coupled with the other's method invocation. To make things clear, let's take a look at the following code, which we can find in the `TemporalCoupling.csproj` project:

```
public class MembershipDatabase
```

```
{
  private Address _address;
  private Member _member;
  public void Process(
    string memberName,
    string addressString)
  {
    CreateAddress(
      addressString);

    CreateMember(
      memberName);
    SaveMember();
  }

  private void CreateAddress(
    string addressString)
  {
    _address = new Address(
      addressString);
  }

  private void CreateMember(
    string name)
  {
    _member = new Member(
    name,
    _address);
  }

  private void SaveMember()
  {
    var repository = new Repository();
    repository.Save(_member);
  }
}

public class Address
{
  public string _addressString { get; }
  public Address(
    string addressString)
  {
    _addressString = addressString;
  }
}

public class Member
```

```
  {
    public string _name { get; }
    public Address _address { get; }

    public Member(
      string name,
      Address address)
    {
      _name = name;
      _address = address;
    }
  }

  public class Repository
  {
    public static List<Member> customers { get; }

    public void Save(
      Member customer)
    {
      customers.Add(customer);
    }
  }
```

From the preceding code, you can see that we have a MembershipDatabase class, which processes a new member. It retrieves input parameters named memberName and addressString and uses them to insert a new member in the database. The Process() method in the MembershipDatabase class invokes the CreateAddress method first, which will create the address and then save it to the private field. The CreateMember() method then retrieves the address and uses it to instantiate a new Member parameter, which is saved in another private field named member. The last method, the SaveMember() method, saves the member to the database (in this example, we use list). There is a problem here. The invocations in the Process() method are coupled with temporal coupling. We have to always invoke these three methods in the right order for this code to work properly.

If we don't place the method in the right order – for instance, if we put the CreateAddress() method invocation, after the CreateMember() method invocation the resulting member instance will be invalid since the member will not retrieve the required dependency address. Likewise, if we put the SaveMember() method invocation above others, it will throw NullReferenceException because, when it tries to save a member, the member instance would still be null.

Temporal coupling is a consequence of the method's signature dishonesty. The `CreateAddress()` method has an output, creating an `address` instance, but this output is hidden under a side-effect because we mutate the `Address` field in the `MembershipDatabase` class. The `CreateMember()` method hides the result of the operation as well. It saves `member` to the private field, but it also hides some of its input. From the signature of the `CreateMember()` method, we might think that it needs only the name parameter in order to create `member` while it actually refers to a global state, the `address` field.

This happens to the `SaveMember()` method as well. To remove the temporal coupling, we have to specify all of the input and output in the method's signatures explicitly or, in other words, move all side-effects and dependencies to the signature level. Now, let's refactor the preceding side-effect – containing code to the following code:

```
public class MembershipDatabase
{
  public void Process(
    string memberName,
    string addressString)
  {
    Address address = CreateAddress(
      addressString);
    Member member = CreateMember(
      memberName,
      address);
    SaveMember(member);
  }

  private Address CreateAddress(
    string addressString)
  {
    return new Address(
      addressString);
  }

  private Member CreateMember(
    string name,
    Address address)
  {
    return new Member(
      name,
      address);
  }

  private void SaveMember(
    Member member)
```

```
    {
      var repository = new Repository();
      repository.Save(
        member);
    }
  }

  public class Address
  {
    public string _addressString { get; }
    public Address(
      string addressString)
    {
      _addressString = addressString;
    }
  }

  public class Member
  {
    public string _name { get; }
    public Address _address { get; }
    public Member(
      string name,
      Address address)
    {
      _name = name;
      _address = address;
    }
  }

  public class Repository
  {
    public static List<Member> customers { get; }

    public void Save(
      Member customer)
    {
      customers.Add(customer);
    }
  }
```

From the highlighted code, we can see that we have refactored the CreateAddress(),
CreateMember(), SaveMember(), and Process() methods.

The `CreateAddress()` method now returns `Address` instead of saving it to the private field. In the `CreateMember()` method, we add a new parameter, `address`, and also change the returning type. For the `SaveMember()` method, instead of referring to the customer private field, we now specify it as a dependency in the method's signature. In the `Process()` method, we can now remove the fields, and we have successfully removed the temporal coupling with this change.

Now, it's impossible for us to put the `CreateAddress()` invocation method after the `CreateMember()` invocation method because the code will not be compiled.

Dealing with the side-effects

Although we need to create a pure function in functional programming, we cannot avoid the side-effects completely. As you can see in the preceding `MembershipDatabase` class, we have the `SaveMember()` method, which will save the member field into the database. The following code snippet will explain this clearly:

```
private void SaveMember(
  Member member)
{
  var repository = new Repository();
  repository.Save(
    member);
}
```

To deal with the side-effects, we can use the **command-query separation** (**CQS**) principle to separate methods that generate side-effects and methods that don't. We can call commands for methods that incur side-effects and queries for methods that don't. If the method alters a piece of state, it should be the void type method. Otherwise, it should return something. Using this CQS principle, we can identify the purpose of a method by just looking at its signature. If the method returns a value, it will be a query and it won't mutate anything. If the method returns nothing, it must be a command and will leave some side-effects in the system.

From the preceding `MembershipDatabase` class, we now can identify that the `Process()` and `SaveMember()` methods are commands types and will leave some side-effects since they return nothing. In contrast, the `CreateAddress()` and `CreateMember()` methods are queries and won't mutate anything since they return something.

Separating the code from domain logic and mutable shell

Sometimes, when our code processes a business transaction, it mutates some data several times. In the world of object-oriented programming languages, this is quite a common pattern. We can then separate our code into domain logic and the mutable shell. In domain logic, we simplify the code and write the business logic in a functional way using mathematical functions. As a result, this domain logic will become easy to test. In the mutable shell, we place a mutable expression; we will do this after we finish with the business logic.

Examining the code containing side-effects

Now, let's examine the following code, which contains many side-effects that we are going to refactor, and we can find it in the `DomainLogicAndMutatingState.csproj` project:

```
public class Librarianship
{
  private readonly int _maxEntriesPerFile;
  public Librarianship(
    int maxEntriesPerFile)
  {
    _maxEntriesPerFile =
    maxEntriesPerFile;
  }

  public void AddRecord(
    string currentFile,
    string visitorName,
    string bookTitle,
    DateTime returnDate)
  {
    // The rest of code can be found
    // in the downloaded source code
  }

  private string GetNewFileName(
      string existingFileName)
  {
    // The rest of code can be found
    // in the downloaded source code
  }
```

```
public void RemoveRecord(
    string visitorName,
    string directoryName)
{
  foreach (string fileName in Directory.GetFiles(
        directoryName))
  {
    // The rest of code can be found
    // in the downloaded source code
  }
}
}
```

As you can see in the preceding code, it is written in a straightforward way. We are going to separate its responsibilities into two parts: an immutable core that contains all the domain logic and a mutable shell that contains all the mutable expression.

The `Librarianship` class will keep track of all the borrowers in a library and takes note of the book-returning date. The class uses a log file to store the borrower's name, the title of the borrowed book, and the returning date. The pattern of the log file content is the index number, a semicolon, the borrower name and then the semicolon again, the book title and then the semicolon, and lastly, the returning date. The following is a sample of the log file content:

```
1;Arthur Jackson;Responsive Web Design;9/26/2016
2;Maddox Webb;AngularJS by Example;9/27/2016
3;Mel Fry;Python Machine Learning;9/28/2016
4;Haiden Brown;Practical Data Science Cookbook;9/29/2016
5;Sofia Hamilton;DevOps Automation Cookbook;9/30/2016
```

The class must be able to add a new line in the log file, such as what we can see in the `AddRecord()` method. But before we invoke the method, we have to specify the value for the `_maxEntriesPerFile` field when we construct the class.

The value of the `_maxEntriesPerFile` field will be used when we invoke the `AddRecord()` method. If `_maxEntriesPerFile` is greater than the current total lines of the log file, it will insert the visitor identity into the log file using the following code:

```
if (lines.Length < _maxEntriesPerFile)
{
  int lastIndex = int.Parse(
    lines.Last()
    .Split(';')[0]);

  string newLine =
    String.Format(
```

```
        "{0};{1};{2};{3}",
        (lastIndex + 1),
        visitorName,
        bookTitle,
        returnDate
        .ToString("d")
      );

    File.AppendAllLines(
      currentFile,
      new[] {
      newLine });
  }
```

Otherwise, if the current total number of lines of the log file has reached _maxEntriesPerFile, then AddRecord() method creates a new log file, as shown in the following code:

```
    else
    {
      string newLine =
        String.Format(
        "1;{0};{1};{2}",
        visitorName,
        bookTitle,
        returnDate
        .ToString("d")
        );
      string newFileName =
        GetNewFileName(
        currentFile);
      File.WriteAllLines(
        newFileName,
        new[] {
        newLine });
      currentFile = newFileName;
    }
```

From the preceding code snippet, we find the GetNewFileName() method to generate a new log file name based on the current log file name. The implementation of the GetNewFileName() method is as follows:

```
    private string GetNewFileName(
      string existingFileName)
    {
      string fileName =
        Path.GetFileNameWithoutExtension(
          existingFileName);
```

```
    int index = int.Parse(
      fileName
      .Split('_')[1]);

    return String.Format(
      "LibraryLog_{0:D4}.txt",
      index + 1);
}
```

From the preceding `GetNewFileName()` method's implementation, we can see that the pattern of the log file name is `LibraryLog _0001.txt`, `LibraryLog _0002.txt`, and so on.

The `AddRecord()` method will also create a new log file if the specified log file name is not found. The implementation of this task is as follows:

```
if (!File.Exists(currentFile))
{
  string newLine =
    String.Format(
    "1;{0};{1};{2}",
    visitorName,
    bookTitle,
    returnDate
    .ToString("d")
    );

  File.WriteAllLines(
    currentFile,
    new[] {
    newLine });
}
```

The class also has the `RemoveRecord()` method to remove the visitor identity from the log file. The implementation of the method is as follows:

```
public void RemoveRecord(
    string visitorName,
    string directoryName)
{
    foreach (string fileName in Directory.GetFiles(
        directoryName))
    {
        string tempFile = Path.GetTempFileName();
        List<string> linesToKeep = File
            .ReadLines(fileName)
            .Where(line => !line.Contains(visitorName))
```

```
        .ToList();

    if (linesToKeep.Count == 0)
    {
        File.Delete(
            fileName);
    }
    else
    {
        File.WriteAllLines(
            tempFile,
            linesToKeep);

        File.Delete(
            fileName);

        File.Move(
            tempFile,
            fileName);
    }
  }
}
```

In the `RemoveRecord()` method's implementation, you can see that it removes the selected visitor from the available log file in the selected directory, as shown in the following code snippet:

```
List<string> linesToKeep = File
    .ReadLines(fileName)
    .Where(line => !line.Contains(visitorName))
    .ToList();
```

If `linesToKeep` contains no data, we can securely delete the file using the following code:

```
if (linesToKeep.Count == 0)
{
    File.Delete(
        fileName);
}
```

Otherwise, we just need to remove the visitor identity from the log file using the following code:

```
else
{
    File.WriteAllLines(
        tempFile,
        linesToKeep);
```

[332]

```
            File.Delete(
                fileName);
            File.Move(
                tempFile,
                fileName);
    }
```

Now it's time to try our `Librarianship` class. First, we will prepare a data list that contains the author and the title of the books, as shown in the following code:

```
public partial class Program
{
    public static List<Book> bookList =
        new List<Book>()
        {
            new Book(
                "Arthur Jackson",
                "Responsive Web Design"),
            new Book(
                "Maddox Webb",
                "AngularJS by Example"),
            new Book(
                "Mel Fry",
                "Python Machine Learning"),
            new Book(
                "Haiden Brown",
                "Practical Data Science Cookbook"),
            new Book(
                "Sofia Hamilton",
                "DevOps Automation Cookbook")
        };
}
```

And we have the `Book` structure as follows:

```
public struct Book
{
    public string Borrower { get; }
    public string Title { get; }

    public Book(
        string borrower,
        string title)
    {
        Borrower = borrower;
        Title = title;
    }
}
```

We will invoke the following `LibrarianshipInvocation()` method to consume the `Librarianship` class:

```
public partial class Program
{
    public static void LibrarianshipInvocation()
    {
        Librarianship librarian =
            new Librarianship(5);

        for (int i = 0; i < bookList.Count; i++)
        {
            librarian.AddRecord(
                GetLastLogFile(
                    AppDomain.CurrentDomain.BaseDirectory),
                bookList[i].Borrower,
                bookList[i].Title,
                DateTime.Now.AddDays(i));
        }
    }
}
```

As you can see in the preceding `LibrarianshipInvocation()` method, we call the `GetLastLogFile()` method to find the last available log file. The implementation of the method is as follows:

```
public partial class Program
{
    public static string GetLastLogFile(
        string LogDirectory)
    {
        string[] logFiles = Directory.GetFiles(
            LogDirectory,
            "LibraryLog_????.txt");

        if (logFiles.Length > 0)
        {
            return logFiles[logFiles.Length - 1];
        }
        else
        {
            return "LibraryLog_0001.txt";
        }
    }
}
```

When we call the `GetLastLogFile()` method, it will look for all files that have the `LibraryLog_????.txt` pattern in the directory we specified. It will then return the last member of the string array. If the string array contains no data, it will return `LibraryLog_0001.txt` as the default log file name.

If we run the `LibrarianshipInvocation()` method, we will see nothing, but we will get a new `LibraryLog_0001.txt` file containing the following text:

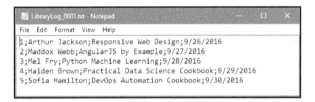

From the preceding output file log, we can see that we have successfully created the `Librarianship` class as expected.

Refactoring the AddRecord() method

Now it's time to refactor the `Librarianship` class for it to become immutable. First, we will make the `AddRecord()` method a mathematical function. To do that, we have to make sure that it doesn't access the disk directly, which we do when we use the `File.Exists()`, `File.ReadAllLines()`, `File.AppendAllLines()`, and `File.WriteAllLines()` methods. We will refactor the `AddRecord()` method as follows:

```
public FileAction AddRecord(
    FileContent currentFile,
    string visitorName,
    string bookTitle,
    DateTime returningDate)
{
    List<DataEntry> entries = Parse(currentFile.Content);

    if (entries.Count < _maxEntriesPerFile)
    {
        entries.Add(
            new DataEntry(
                entries.Count + 1,
                visitorName,
                bookTitle,
                returningDate));
```

```
            string[] newContent =
                Serialize(
                    entries);

            return new FileAction(
                currentFile.FileName,
                ActionType.Update,
                newContent);
        }
        else
        {
            var entry = new DataEntry(
                1,
                visitorName,
                bookTitle,
                returningDate);

            string[] newContent =
                Serialize(
                    new List<DataEntry> { entry });

            string newFileName =
                GetNewFileName(
                    currentFile.FileName);

            return new FileAction(
                newFileName,
                ActionType.Create,
                newContent);
        }
    }
```

As you can see in the preceding code, we modify the `AddRecord()` method signature so that it doesn't pass any filenames now and passes a `FileContent` data type instead, which is structured with the following implementation:

```
public struct FileContent
{
    public readonly string FileName;
    public readonly string[] Content;

    public FileContent(
        string fileName,
        string[] content)
    {
        FileName = fileName;
        Content = content;
    }
```

```
}
```

As you can see, the `FileContent` structure will now handle the filename and its content. And the `AddRecord()` method also returns the `FileAction` data type now. The implementation of the `FileAction` data type is as follows:

```
public struct FileAction
{
    public readonly string FileName;
    public readonly string[] Content;
    public readonly ActionType Type;

    public FileAction(
        string fileName,
        ActionType type,
        string[] content)
    {
        FileName = fileName;
        Type = type;
        Content = content;
    }
}
```

And the `ActionType` enumeration is as follows:

```
public enum ActionType
{
    Create,
    Update,
    Delete
}
```

We also have a new data type, which is `DataEntry`. The implementation of the `DataEntry` structure is as follows:

```
public struct DataEntry
{
    public readonly int Number;
    public readonly string Visitor;
    public readonly string BookTitle;
    public readonly DateTime ReturningDate;

    public DataEntry(
        int number,
        string visitor,
        string bookTitle,
        DateTime returningDate)
    {
```

```
                Number = number;
                Visitor = visitor;
                BookTitle = bookTitle;
                ReturningDate = returningDate;
            }
        }
```

The `DataEntry` structure will handle all the data that we want to write in the log file. And if we examine the `AddRecord()` method again, we don't find the procedure to make sure the log file exists since that will be done in a separate process.

We notice that the `AddRecord()` method invokes two new methods: the `Parse()` and `Serialize()` methods. The `Parse()` method is used to parse all the lines in the log file content and then form the list of `DataEntry` based on the content of the log file. The implementation of the method is as follows:

```
        private List<DataEntry> Parse(
            string[] content)
        {
            var result = new List<DataEntry>();

            foreach (string line in content)
            {
                string[] data = line.Split(';');
                result.Add(
                    new DataEntry(
                        int.Parse(data[0]),
                        data[1],
                        data[2],
                        DateTime.Parse(data[3])));
            }

            return result;
        }
```

On the other hand, the `Serialize()` method is used to serialize the `DataEntry` list into the string array. The implementation of the method is as follows:

```
        private string[] Serialize(
            List<DataEntry> entries)
        {
            return entries
                .Select(entry =>
                    String.Format(
                        "{0};{1};{2};{3}",
                        entry.Number,
                        entry.Visitor,
```

```
                        entry.BookTitle,
                        entry.ReturningDate
                            .ToString("d")))
        .ToArray();
}
```

Refactoring the RemoveRecord() method

Now, we go back to our `Librarianship` class and refactor the `RemoveRecord()` method.
The implementation will be as follows:

```
public IReadOnlyList<FileAction> RemoveRecord(
  string visitorName,
  FileContent[] directoryFiles)
{
  return directoryFiles
    .Select(file =>
    RemoveRecordIn(
        file,
        visitorName))
  .Where(action =>
  action != null)
  .Select(action =>
  action.Value)
  .ToList();
}
```

The `RemoveRecord()` method now has a new signature. It passes an array of `FileContent`
instead of the directory name only. It also returns a read-only list of `FileAction`. The
`RemoveRecord()` method also needs an additional `RemoveRecordIn()` method, which is
used to get the specified filename and file content to target the record that will be removed.
The implementation of the `RemoveRecordIn()` method is as follows:

```
private FileAction? RemoveRecordIn(
    FileContent file,
    string visitorName)
{
    List<DataEntry> entries = Parse(
        file.Content);
    List<DataEntry> newContent = entries
        .Where(x =>
            x.Visitor != visitorName)
        .Select((entry, index) =>
            new DataEntry(
                index + 1,
                entry.Visitor,
```

```
                entry.BookTitle,
                entry.ReturningDate))
        .ToList();
    if (newContent.Count == entries.Count)
        return null;
    if (newContent.Count == 0)
    {
        return new FileAction(
            file.FileName,
            ActionType.Delete,
            new string[0]);
    }
    else
    {
        return new FileAction(
            file.FileName,
            ActionType.Update,
            Serialize(
                newContent));
    }
}
}
```

And now, we have the domain logic code, which is totally immutable and can run this domain logic in a unit testing environment.

Running domain logic in unit testing

Domain logic is an immutable source that is a pure function, so we can run the unit testing over and over again without having to change the testing rules. Here, we are going to test the AddRecord() and RemoveRecord() methods in the LibrarianshipImmutable class. We will have five tests for these two methods. For the AddRecord() method, we will test if the file is overflow. For the RemoveRecord() method, we will test whether the selected record that we want to remove is available. Then, the file becomes empty if the selected record is empty or if the selected record is not available.

Testing the AddRecord() method

Now let's take a look at the following AddRecord_LinesIsLowerThanMaxEntriesPerFileTest() test method, which will add a record to the existing log file:

```
[TestMethod]
// Add record to existing log file
```

```
// but the lines is lower then maxEntriesPerFile
public void AddRecord_LinesIsLowerThanMaxEntriesPerFileTest()
{
    LibrarianshipImmutable librarian =
        new LibrarianshipImmutable(5);

    FileContent file = new FileContent(
        "LibraryLog_0001.txt",
        new[]{
            "1;Arthur Jackson;Responsive Web Design;9/26/2016"
        });

    FileAction action = librarian.AddRecord(
        file,
        "Maddox Webb",
        "AngularJS by Example",
        new DateTime(
            2016, 9, 27, 0, 0, 0));

    Assert.AreEqual(
        ActionType.Update,
        action.Type);
    Assert.AreEqual(
        "LibraryLog_0001.txt",
        action.FileName);
    CollectionAssert.AreEqual(
        new[]{
            "1;Arthur Jackson;Responsive Web Design;9/26/2016",
            "2;Maddox Webb;AngularJS by Example;9/27/2016"
        },
        action.Content);
}
```

In the `AddRecord_LinesIsLowerThanMaxEntriesPerFileTest()` test method, first, we create a `LibraryLog_0001.txt` file containing `1;Arthur Jackson;Responsive Web Design;9/26/2016` and then we add a new record, as shown in the following code:

```
FileAction action = librarian.AddRecord(
    file,
    "Maddox Webb",
    "AngularJS by Example",
    new DateTime(
        2016, 9, 27, 0, 0, 0));
```

From now on, we have to ensure that `action.The type` has to be `ActionType.Update`, `action.FileName` has to be `LibraryLog_0001.txt`, and the `action.Content` has to be two lines, with the first line as `1;Arthur Jackson;Responsive Web Design;9/26/2016` and the second line as `2;Maddox Webb;AngularJS by Example;9/27/2016`.

 The `Assert.AreEqual()` method is used to verify that the specified values are equal. Unfortunately, the use of this method will not override the array data. To compare the array, we need to use the `CollectionAssert.AreEqual()` method, which will verify that two specified collections are equal.

Another unit testing is the `AddRecord_LinesHasReachMaxEntriesPerFileTest()` testing method. The implementation of this testing is as follows:

```
[TestMethod]
// Add record to a new log file
// becausecurrent log file has reached maxEntriesPerFile
public void AddRecord_LinesHasReachMaxEntriesPerFileTest()
{
    LibrarianshipImmutable librarian =
        new LibrarianshipImmutable(3);

    FileContent file = new FileContent(
        "LibraryLog_0001.txt",
        new[]{
            "1;Arthur Jackson;Responsive Web Design;9/26/2016",
            "2;Maddox Webb;AngularJS by Example;9/27/2016",
            "3;Mel Fry;Python Machine Learning;9/28/2016"
        });

    FileAction action = librarian.AddRecord(
        file,
        "Haiden Brown",
        "Practical Data Science",
        new DateTime(2016, 9, 29, 0, 0, 0));

    Assert.AreEqual(
        ActionType.Create,
        action.Type);
    Assert.AreEqual(
        "LibraryLog_0002.txt",
        action.FileName);
    CollectionAssert.AreEqual(
        new[]{
            "1;Haiden Brown;Practical Data Science;9/29/2016"
```

```
        },
        action.Content);
}
```

In this testing method, we want to ensure that a new log file is created if the current log file lines have reached `maxEntriesPerFile`. First, we instantiate `LibrarianshipImmutable` and fill the `maxEntriesPerFile` field with 3 and then we fill the log file with the three visitors, as shown in the following code:

```
LibrarianshipImmutable librarian =
    new LibrarianshipImmutable(3);
FileContent file = new FileContent(
    "LibraryLog_0001.txt",
    new[]{
        "1;Arthur Jackson;Responsive Web Design;9/26/2016",
        "2;Maddox Webb;AngularJS by Example;9/27/2016",
        "3;Mel Fry;Python Machine Learning;9/28/2016"
    });
```

After that, we add a new record using the following code:

```
FileAction action = librarian.AddRecord(
    file,
    "Haiden Brown",
    "Practical Data Science",
    new DateTime(2016, 9, 29, 0, 0, 0));
```

Now, we have to ensure that `action.Type` is `ActionType.Update`, and it creates a new log file named `LibraryLog_0002.txt`. Also, the content of the new log file is `1;Haiden Brown;Practical Data Science;9/29/2016`.

Testing the RemoveRecord() method

As we discussed earlier, we have three tests for the `RemoveRecord()` method. First, we are going to test removing a record from the files in the directory. The code will be as follows:

```
[TestMethod]
// Remove selected record from files in the directory
public void RemoveRecord_FilesIsAvailableInDirectoryTest()
{
    LibrarianshipImmutable librarian =
        new LibrarianshipImmutable(10);

    FileContent file = new FileContent(
        "LibraryLog_0001.txt",
        new[]
```

```
        {
            "1;Arthur Jackson;Responsive Web Design;9/26/2016",
            "2;Maddox Webb;AngularJS by Example;9/27/2016",
            "3;Mel Fry;Python Machine Learning;9/28/2016"
        });

    IReadOnlyList<FileAction> actions =
        librarian.RemoveRecord(
            "Arthur Jackson",
            new[] {
                file });

    Assert.AreEqual(
        1,
        actions.Count);

    Assert.AreEqual(
        "LibraryLog_0001.txt",
        actions[0].FileName);

    Assert.AreEqual(
        ActionType.Update,
        actions[0].Type);

    CollectionAssert.AreEqual(
        new[]{
            "1;Maddox Webb;AngularJS by Example;9/27/2016",
            "2;Mel Fry;Python Machine Learning;9/28/2016"
        },
        actions[0].Content);
}
```

In this `RemoveRecord_FilesIsAvailableInDirectoryTest()` test method, we first create a `LibraryLog_0001.txt` file containing three records. We then remove the first record and make sure that `LibraryLog_0001.txt` will contain only two remaining logs with the proper order number.

The other test is `RemoveRecord_FileBecomeEmptyTest()` with the following implementation:

```
[TestMethod]
// Remove selected record from files in the directory
// If file becomes empty, it will be deleted
public void RemoveRecord_FileBecomeEmptyTest()
{

    LibrarianshipImmutable librarian =
```

```
        new LibrarianshipImmutable(10);

    FileContent file = new FileContent(
        "LibraryLog_0001.txt",
        new[]
        {
            "1;Arthur Jackson;Responsive Web Design;9/26/2016"
        });

    IReadOnlyList<FileAction> actions =
        librarian.RemoveRecord(
            "Arthur Jackson",
            new[] {
                file });

    Assert.AreEqual(
        1,
        actions.Count);

    Assert.AreEqual(
        "LibraryLog_0001.txt",
        actions[0].FileName);

    Assert.AreEqual(
        ActionType.Delete,
        actions[0].Type);
}
```

The `RemoveRecord_FileBecomeEmptyTest()` testing method will make sure that the log file is deleted if it is empty after the record is removed. First, we create a new log file with one record, and then we remove it using the `RemoveRecord()` method.

The last test for the `RemoveRecord()` method is `RemoveRecord_SelectedRecordIsUnavailableTest()`, which will remove nothing if the selected record is unavailable. The implementation of the testing method is as follows:

```
[TestMethod]
// Remove nothing if selected record is unavailable
public void RemoveRecord_SelectedRecordIsUnavailableTest()
{
    LibrarianshipImmutable librarian =
        new LibrarianshipImmutable(10);

    FileContent file = new FileContent(
        "LibraryLog_0001.txt",
        new[]
        {
```

```
                "1;Sofia Hamilton;DevOps Automation;9/30/2016"
        });

    IReadOnlyList<FileAction> actions =
        librarian.RemoveRecord(
            "Arthur Jackson",
            new[] {
                file });

    Assert.AreEqual(
        0,
        actions.Count);
}
```

As you can see, we create the log file containing Sofia Hamilton as the visitor name, but we try to remove the visitor named Arthur Jackson. In this case, the `RemoveRecord()` method will remove nothing.

Executing the test

Now, it's time to run the unit testing for all five testing methods. And here is what we will get after we run the test:

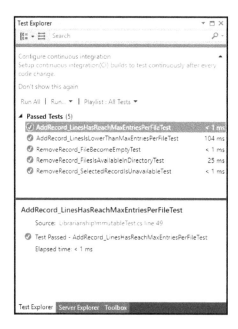

Adding the mutable shell into code

So far, we have successfully created the immutable core and covered unit tests. For now, we are ready to a implement the mutable shell for the rest of the code that is accessing the disk. We will create two classes, `FileProcessor` and `AppService`. The `FileProcessor` class will do all the disk interaction. The `AppService` class will be a bridge between the `LibrarianshipImmutable` class and the `FileProcessor` class.

Now, let's take a look at the following `FileProcessor` class implementation, which we can find in the `FileProcessor.cs` file:

```
namespace DomainLogicAndMutatingState
{
    public class FileProcessor
    {
        public FileContent ReadFile(
            string fileName)
        {
            return new FileContent(
                fileName,
                File.ReadAllLines(
                    fileName));
        }

        public FileContent[] ReadDirectory(
            string directoryName)
        {
            return Directory
                .GetFiles(
                    directoryName)
                .Select(x =>
                    ReadFile(x))
                .ToArray();
        }

        public void ApplyChanges(
            IReadOnlyList<FileAction> actions)
        {
            foreach (FileAction action in actions)
            {
                switch (action.Type)
                {
                    case ActionType.Create:
                    case ActionType.Update:
                        File.WriteAllLines(
                            action.FileName,
                            action.Content);
```

```
                    continue;

            case ActionType.Delete:
                File.Delete(
                    action.FileName);
                continue;

            default:
                throw new InvalidOperationException();
            }
        }
    }

    public void ApplyChange(
        FileAction action)
    {
        ApplyChanges(
            new List<FileAction> {
                action });
    }
    }
}
```

There are four methods in the preceding `FileProcessor` class; they are `ReadFile()`, `ReadDirectory()`, and two `ApplyChanges()` methods with different signatures. The `ReadFile()` method is used to read the selected file and form it into the `FileContent` data type. The `ReadDirectory()` method is used to read all the files in the selected directory and form them into the `FileContent` data array. The `ApplyChanges()` method is used to make an execution to the selected file. If the action is `Create` or `Update`, then the `File.WriteAllLines()` method will be called. If the action is `Delete`, then the `File.Delete()` method will be invoked. Otherwise, the `InvalidOperationException` exception will be thrown.

After we finish with the `FileProcessor` class, it's time to create the `AppService` class. The implementation of the class is as follows, and we can find it in the `AppService.cs` file:

```
namespace DomainLogicAndMutatingState
{
    public class AppService
    {
        private readonly string _directoryName;
        private readonly LibrarianshipImmutable _librarian;
        private readonly FileProcessor _fileProcessor;

        public AppService(
            string directoryName)
```

```
    {
        _directoryName = directoryName;
        _librarian = new LibrarianshipImmutable(10);
        _fileProcessor = new FileProcessor();
    }

    public void AddRecord(
        string visitorName,
        string bookTitle,
        DateTime returningDate)
    {
        FileInfo fileInfo = new DirectoryInfo(
            _directoryName)
                .GetFiles()
                .OrderByDescending(x =>
                    x.LastWriteTime)
                .First();

        FileContent file =
            _fileProcessor.ReadFile(
                fileInfo.Name);

        FileAction action =
            _librarian.AddRecord(
                file,
                visitorName,
                bookTitle,
                returningDate);

        _fileProcessor.ApplyChange(
            action);
    }

    public void RemoveRecord(
        string visitorName)
    {
        FileContent[] files =
            _fileProcessor.ReadDirectory(
                _directoryName);

        IReadOnlyList<FileAction> actions =
            _librarian.RemoveRecord(
                visitorName, files);

        _fileProcessor.ApplyChanges(
            actions);
    }
}
```

}

As we discussed previously, the AppService class is used as the bridge between the LibrarianshipImmutable class and the FileProcessor class. We have the two methods in this AppService class that have completely the same signature with methods in the LibrarianshipImmutable class; they are the AddRecord() and RemoveRecord() methods. And as a bridge, we can see that in the class constructor, the LibrarianshipImmutable and FileProcessor class constructors are invoked to create a new instance. By calling the AddRecord() method in the AppService class, we actually invoke the AddRecord() method in the LibrarianshipImmutable class and then we call the ApplyChange() method in the FileProcessor class. Likewise, the invocation of the RemoveRecord() method in the AppService class will invoke the RemoveRecord() method in the LibrarianshipImmutable class and then the ApplyChange() method in the FileProcessor class.

Summary

The honest signature is important not only in functional approach but also every time we code, since, basically, the signature has to deliver all the information about the possible accepted input values and possible produced output. By implementing honest signature, we will be aware of the value we pass into the method parameter. We have to ensure that we have an immutable class as well in order to get functional because mutable operations will make our code dishonest.

Although we have to avoid side-effects in our pure function, it's nearly impossible to really avoid side-effects in our code. What we can do then is deal with it. We can use the **command-query separation** (**CQS**) principle to separate methods that generate side-effects and methods that don't. If the method returns a value, it will be a query and doesn't mutate anything. If the method returns nothing, it must be a command and will leave some side-effects in the system.

We can also separate our code into domain logic and the mutable shell in order to deal with the side-effects. The domain logic will be our core program, and it must be immutable. All mutable processing will be stored in the mutable shell. By creating the domain logic, we can easily run unit testing on it. We don't need to modify the test scenario or run the mock test for domain logic since it is a pure function.

Index

high-order functions 16
pure functions 19, 20
recursive functions 22
continuation-passing style (CPS) 216
contravariance 78
conversion methods 173
covariance 74, 76, 77, 78
currying
about 12, 13
in C# 33

D

definitions 8
delegate syntax, elements
AccessModifier 56
delegate 56
DelegateName 56
parameters 56
ReturnType 56
delegates
about 55
creating, lambda expressions used 92
multicast delegates 59
simple delegates 57
versus variance 74
direct recursion
versus indirect recursion 218
domain logic, unit testing
AddRecord() method, testing 340
RemoveRecord() method, testing 343
running 340
test, executing 346
domain logic
code, separating from 328

E

element operation 176, 177, 179
EndRead() method
using 188
engine code, creating in functional approach
additional operation, calculating 315
calculation, solving 313
class construction, by clearing properties 309
input, formatting 312
inputted number, appending to text box 310

new properties, adding 307
operation, preparing 311
pattern matching, simplifying 308
properties, assigning 308
engine code, creating in imperative approach
additional operation, calculating 306
calculation, solving 306
class properties, preparing 296
constructor, constructing 297
input, formatting 305
mathematical operation, preparing 303
number, appending to display box 300
properties, clearing 298
event keyword
used, for subscribing event 99, 100, 102
EventHandler
used, for subscribing event 102, 103
events
subscribing, lambda expressions used 97, 99
expensive resources, caching
about 240
initial computation, performing 240, 245
memoization 245, 247, 248, 249
expression trees
and lambda expression 92, 94
expressions
evaluating, substitution used 9
extension methods, calling in other assemblies
about 113
namespace, piggybacking 116, 117
namespace, referencing 114, 115
extension methods, in functional programming
advantages 127, 129, 130
extension methods
about 109
creating 110, 111
in code IntelliSense 112, 113
limitations 130

F

filtering 148, 151
first-class functions 16, 17
fluent syntax
LINQ fluent syntax 143, 146
versus query expression syntax 142

www.ingramcontent.com/pod-product-compliance
Lightning Source LLC
Chambersburg PA
CBHW062050050326
40690CB00016B/3046